Palgrave Studies in Lar
and Sexua

Series Editors
Helen Sauntson
York St John University
York, UK

Allyson Jule
School of Education
Trinity Western University
Langley, BC, Canada

Language, Gender and Sexuality is a new series which highlights the role of language in understanding issues, identities and relationships in relation to genders and sexualities. The series will comprise innovative, high quality research and provides a platform for the best contemporary scholarship in the field of language, gender and sexuality. The series is interdisciplinary but takes language as it central focus. Contributions will be inclusive of both leading and emerging scholars in the field. The series is international in its scope, authorship and readership and aims to draw together theoretical and empirical work from a range of countries and contexts.

More information about this series at
http://www.palgrave.com/gp/series/15402

Natalia Konstantinovskaia

The Language of Feminine Beauty in Russian and Japanese Societies

palgrave
macmillan

Natalia Konstantinovskaia
Busuu, London, UK

Palgrave Studies in Language, Gender and Sexuality
ISBN 978-3-030-41435-1   ISBN 978-3-030-41433-7   (eBook)
https://doi.org/10.1007/978-3-030-41433-7

This Palgrave Macmillan imprint is published by the registered company Springer Nature Switzerland AG.
The registered company address is: Gewerbestrasse 11, 6330 Cham, Switzerland

Acknowledgments

First and foremost, I express gratitude to Dr. Shoichi Iwasaki, who always gave me the support and advice on how to improve and grow as a scholar, guiding me in a way that helped me to develop my ideas. Without his mentorship, this work would not have been possible.

In addition, I also thank Dr. Momoko Nakamura, whose feminist work on Japanese language inspired this book profoundly. Furthermore, I am thankful for Professor Satoshi Kinsui's advising at various points of my career as a researcher. Professor Kinsui kindly welcomed me as an international scholar to Osaka University, supporting me in my doctoral fieldwork. I am grateful to the reviewers and editors of these series, whose insightful comments and suggestions helped me to improve this book.

I also express special thanks to the 44 Japanese and Russian women who shared their thoughts and experiences with me. They helped me to appreciate on a concrete and personal level the nuanced perceptions of gender and language in Japanese and Russian societies.

Finally, I feel blessed to have had the support of my husband Locke Welborn, as well as my family in Khabarovsk, Russia, throughout this journey. They were always willing to discuss my research ideas and read my drafts, making me feel loved and appreciated.

Contents

List of Figures

List of Tables

1

Gender and Language Research and Perceptions in Japanese and Russian Societies

1.1 Motivations, Structure, Scope, and Objectives

In recent years, the concept of 'women's language' has become a focal point of discussion and contention for scholars interested in gender, language, and culture—as well as for the broader public. Discarding traditional assumptions of innate differences in women's and men's language use, contemporary research has begun to elucidate the ways in which gendered language is socially constructed among communities of speakers, and how gendered expectations can subsequently be maintained, transformed, or even subverted. For speakers embedded in a culture in which gender is pervasive and uniquely charged with meanings, licenses, and prohibitions, gendered language is a crucial means of expressing attitudes, affiliations, desires, and other stances connected with gendered roles and identities. These processes are inextricably tied to the changing positions and possibilities of women in different cultures and contexts, and reveal tensions in gender ideologies and in individuals' lived experiences. Thus, far from being innately fixed and harmless, 'women's

© The Author(s) 2020
N. Konstantinovskaia, *The Language of Feminine Beauty in Russian and Japanese Societies*, Palgrave Studies in Language, Gender and Sexuality, https://doi.org/10.1007/978-3-030-41433-7_1

language' (and 'men's language') is a site of struggle, both contested and further contestable.

Despite the increasing awareness that gendered language is constructed through mechanisms that are culturally and historically both heterogeneous and specific, most studies have limited themselves to the investigation of a single language and a single cultural context (usually English). In part, this is reasonable: languages and cultures differ, and it is difficult to examine the encodings and implications of gender with care even for a single language. Yet the emphasis on single-language studies also imposes serious limitations: effects of political, cultural, and economic forces on language use (and vice versa) are conflated and impossible to disentangle. Only through a comparative analysis of 'women's language' in different cultural and linguistic contexts can the relationships between these factors be clarified.

In the present work, I aim to explore the role of 'women's language' related to feminine beauty in two distinct linguistic and cultural contexts: Japanese and Russian. Feminine beauty constitutes an essential aspect of gender-based ideals in both Japanese and Russian societies, and demarcates a field in which conflicts within and between ideologies and identities are visible and significant. As such, it is a fruitful space within which to examine the intersections of traditions and expectations with women's self-concepts, and to observe how these junctions evolve in the face of social change. Of course, 'women's language' pertains to many domains of discourse beyond feminine beauty, and it is my hope that the present focus will encourage readers to engage in comparative analysis and readings of gendered language in these other areas. However, a comprehensive analysis of 'women's language' in other areas of Japanese and Russian language and culture is beyond the scope of this project.

Interestingly, Japanese and Russian contexts have never been explicitly compared and contrasted. Analysis of these two geographically neighboring, yet culturally and linguistically different, societies is fascinating because both of these countries have been undergoing major transformations in their perception of gender and their expectations of men and women's speech. In the 1990s, Japan adopted a series of laws and regulations, which aimed at improving women's work conditions, leading to a pronounced shift in the treatment of women in Japanese society. However, despite decades of reforms aimed at improving women's position in society, in 2018 Japan still occupied 110th place out of 149 countries in the "Global Gender Gap Report" of the Economic World Forum (p. 21). In the same report, Japan and Russia have a similar ranking on the issue of female political empowerment, occupying 125th and 123rd place in the world. In Russia, the concept of gender has also experienced radical changes in recent decades. The collapse of the Soviet Union in 1991 ended the era of communism in Russia, leading to a traditionalist realignment in perceptions of women and femininity in the country. The recent bill decriminalizing domestic violence (2017) in Russia is one extreme example of this resurgence of conservative, patriarchal values. In this book I trace the impact of these societal changes on the perception of gender in Japan and Russia, exploring the media-circulated images of femininity, the agency of Japanese and Russian women in their twenties, and their actual language use. I believe that these types of well-informed cross-cultural comparisons are very productive, as they generate findings that may otherwise escape the attention of the researcher, exposing differences and similarities in how various societies create and maintain gender discourses.

A cross-cultural approach is also essential because it allows for a nuanced understanding that avoids potential pitfalls and over-generalizations. In a single cultural context, correlated aspects of historical change in ideologies regarding gender, femininity, and beauty can make it difficult to disentangle the underlying causal processes. Intercultural, cross-linguistic comparisons can therefore help to (a) reveal underlying similarities in the construction of ideological notions and the ways in which they are processed by women in language, and (b) expose dis-analogies that reveal the importance of cultural idiosyncrasies. In the absence of cultural comparisons, it would be impossible to determine which aspects of gendered representations and language use (if any) are likely to remain invariant and which are most likely to develop in response to historical and social change. Moreover, within a single cultural context, it is difficult to disambiguate the correlated effects of economic, political, and social transformations in order to properly trace the causal relationships underlying changes in language use.

The book consists of five chapters and explores three types of data. In this first (introductory) chapter, I concisely introduce the body of research on gender and language, focusing on the type of theoretical foundations that are at the core of my analysis. I then introduce the scholarship on beauty advertising, femininity, and 'women's place' in Russia and Japan, addressing the main terms and concepts in this area. In the second chapter, I examine televised advertising as the source of circulating gender stereotypes (Goffman, 1979a) in order to investigate the idealized femininity features in Japan and Russia. This chapter focuses on media-circulated depictions of women and feminine beauty, and explores the gender ideologies that underlie these depictions in their cultural and historical context. In the third chapter, I analyze conversations among Japanese and Russian women to elucidate their perceptions of ideal womanhood, examining the modes of behavior and speech revealed in their personal interviews. Thus, in contrast to the second chapter, the third chapter engages directly with women's own language about feminine beauty and their ideals regarding their lives as women. In so doing, this chapter assesses the penetration of gender ideologies (such as those promulgated by the media materials examined in the previous chapter) into the women's non-scripted discourse, as well as their own articulations of gendered self-concepts and identities. Finally, in the fourth chapter, using a Japanese blog database and a Russian spoken corpus, I explore the use of conventionally male language by Japanese and Russian women, and analyze the contexts in which this occurs. This chapter thus considers ways in which women explicitly violate or subvert traditional norms regulating gendered speech and writing. In Chap. 5, I summarize and discuss my findings further, addressing the different mechanisms of gender-construction in Japanese and Russian societies. The three-layered structure of the book engages with feminist linguistic theories in a variety of ways, analyzing the differences between Japanese and Russian women's scripted discourses in advertising, their perceptions of their ideal selves, and their real voices.

Categories such as 'women's language,' 'femininity,' and 'Russian/ Japanese women' vastly oversimplify the complex and diverse attributes of women and their behavior, both as individuals and as groups.

Unfortunately, however, these concepts have been frequently grouped together without sufficient differentiation in some earlier scholarship.

An extensive ideology of 'women's language' has been developed in Japan, associated with essentialist notions that stereotypical lexical choices reflect immutable properties that are innate to the essence of women. In fact, this "women's language" is socially constructed, the fictive product of grammar books and state propaganda (Inoue, 2006; Nakamura, 2014). One of the main goals of the book is to problematize the notion of women's language in Japan by contrasting the uses of language in women's spontaneous conversations with the ideological prescriptions regarding language use implicit in media messages. Similar considerations apply to 'women's language' in Russia, although the precise coordinates of women's language within the ideological space of Russian gender norms are different. Especially in analyzing Russian women's usage of stereotypically 'male' language in spontaneous communication, I critique prevailing notions about the parameters that define 'women's language' and 'women's voices' in Russia.

'Femininity' is also a complex concept both in Russia and in Japan. One of the main reasons for exploring these cultures and linguistic communities together, juxtaposed to one another, is the desire to show how modern national cultures with different social and economic histories encode expectations about gender in alternative ways. In the course of this exposition, I will elucidate the underlying similarities in the way patriarchal systems of power shape conceptions of 'femininity,' but also highlight the culture-specific manifestations of ideological distinctiveness. In addition, for a variety of reasons, women accommodate, resist, and transform 'femininity' in different ways in Russia and Japan, based in part on the self-presentation strategies and stances that are most readily afforded to women by the lexical expectations of Japanese and Russian language communities. In these comparisons, it becomes more evident how the construction of femininity represents a sequence of strategic choices and responses, conditioned on the history and culture in which these femininities are embedded and in which they are confronted.

'Womanhood' can take on different valences and significations in different national and cultural contexts, so that 'Japanese women' and 'Russian women' are not neutral terms that can be employed uncritically.

These concepts are deeply interwoven with nationalistic notions in both societies, as the expectations of women are often positioned vis-à-vis their putative obligations to family and society.

While I will advance my own criticisms of these concepts throughout the book, in some senses the women whose words I analyze already do so more ably than a scholar can, through their own linguistic productions. Theory and interpretation are unquestionably useful in examining the potential for concepts to change and evolve through problematization, but it is the actual speakers of the language who challenge these concepts directly. I do my best to interpret the significance of their linguistic behavior, and to point out underlying tensions and inconsistencies, but I also strive not to distort the meaning of their linguistic acts and the forms of femininity they aim to articulate.

Thus, in this book I aim to investigate how the concepts of 'beauty' and 'femininity' are constructed, disseminated, and challenged. Because the ideology of beauty and femininity in both Japan and Russia is intensely focused on youth, the book correspondingly is oriented toward the effects of ideological messages on the target audience: women in age from their late teens to late thirties. One of the principal objectives is to trace the reciprocal interaction between ideological messages and their recipients. This analytic strategy, unfortunately, does not permit a full consideration of the social construction of beauty and femininity for all women. The normative concepts of beauty and femininity in Japan and Russia exclude and marginalize certain subpopulations of women, under-representing them and seeking to disassociate them from aesthetic value and moral worth. The present work does not attempt to resolve the multitude of complex questions concerning women's language and gender ideologies in Russia and Japan. A comprehensive study of women's language either in Japanese or in Russian could occupy numerous volumes—the present work does not aim for this sort of general ambition. It is also not primarily a work of gender theory in the abstract, but a practical exploration of the interdependence of ideology and language as these are developing in two contemporary cultures with respect to a specific domain of behavior and discourse ('beauty' and 'femininity'). Through this research, I seek specifically to explicate the relationship between ideologies related to feminine beauty and women's actual language practices, and gain insights through intercultural comparison. My principal aim is to bring light to the complex changes in patterns of discourse and ideology about femininity in two dynamic societies. In so doing, I explore especially the interplay between directly ideologized conceptions of gender (as presented in media) and the constructions women deploy in their own uses of language. I do not presume that these represent binary or separated discourse spheres, but rather that they are mutually responsive and interconnected. By doing this, I demonstrate the development of gender construction and performativity in two societies that, while dissimilar in many respects, are united by the existence of strong, historically ingrained expectations toward women.

1.2   Feminist Theories of Gender and Language

Now-classic theories of gender and language, articulated in the late twentieth century, emphasized the differences in language used by men and women, and stressed especially the role of patriarchy in creating an oppressive linguistic environment (Bucholtz, 2014; Lakoff, 1975; Spender, 1980). In this vein, Robin Lakoff argued influentially that women are 'trapped' in their attempt to speak femininely, insofar as gender-appropriate speech constrains women to social roles and modes of self-presentation regarded as inferior. If a woman does not talk like a "lady," she is construed as being unfeminine, but if she *does* speak appropriately for her gender, she is seen as unable to participate in serious discussions (Lakoff, 1975, p. 41). In this way, Lakoff tried to demonstrate that women's social inferiority is encoded in the linguistic norms that regulate the use of gendered speech. This repositioned gender difference in language not as representing innate difference between women and men in personality or character, but rather as manifesting the consequences of gendered socialization practices and patriarchal regulatory mechanisms.

While undoubtedly influential and generative, this perspective also imposed certain explicit and implicit limitations on the analysis and interpretation of women's (and men's) language use. First, it tended to pose the sets of 'men' and 'women' speakers as relatively homogenous groups, constructed and maintained by ideology, norms, and practices. As a result, this view failed to fully acknowledge the great diversity of women's voices, and their intrication in intersectional social identities. Gendered language can expose and promulgate attitudes and expectations about sexuality, class, race, and other social categories and distinctions in complex ways. Second, such perspectives prioritize *exogenous regulation* of language over *endogenous use* of language. By regarding gendered language as a product of structural forces, rather than an activity of speakers, views focusing on dominance and difference concentrated attention on ways in which language is controlled and constrained, but diverted attention away from ways in which language is created and employed.

More contemporary feminist theorists (e.g. Butler, 1990, 2004) have sought to expand beyond these limitations. In particular, they have challenged rigidly defined categories of gender and expectations of gender homogeneity. In "Gender Trouble," Butler (1990) challenges the very categories of "women" and "men" and deconstructs what it means to be "female" or "male," emphasizing that "gender intersects with racial, ethnic, sexual, and regional modalities of discursively constituted identities," which in turn makes gender inseparable "from the political and cultural intersections in which it is invariably produced and maintained" (p. 41). Butler and subsequent theorists have emphasized that gender is performative, accomplished by linguistic and non-linguistics behavior, rather than either innately given 'from the inside' or directly imposed 'from the outside.' This body of theory is indebted to the work of J. L. Austin (1975) and other philosophers of language, who elaborate on ways that language can be used to perform actions, for example promising or apologizing. In performative speech acts, a speaker does not describe her apology or promise by making a true or false claim about it—instead, the speaker *enacts* the promise or the apology through the very words used to articulate it. In the same way, for many contemporary scholars, such as Mary Bucholtz, gender is understood as a performative act, rather than a state or condition.

This conceptual shift has had subtle and far-reaching implications. First, it reverses the traditional relationship between identity and action: gender identity is not a permanent condition that can be expressed or manifested through action; gender identity is rather constituted and achieved through actions, carried out by language and discursive acts as well as non-verbal behavior. For this reason, gender is not universal, fixed, or stable, but rather varies across cultures and time (Schippers, 2007). Second, without denying that gender performance is shaped and regulated by powerful forces external to the individual, it renders the field of gender contestable. While constrained by norms and practices, gender performance can also subvert and transform those very norms and practices. Third, the conception of gender and gendered language as performative is consonant with an interactional analysis of the ways identities are achieved and evolve in concert between individuals. Concepts like 'femininity' and 'masculinity' are not achieved in isolation, but are constructed (and questioned) collaboratively, as gender performances by different persons collide and connect dynamically. Even if the 'collaboration' involved does not involve equality of power, status, or influence, it requires action and reaction between persons in order to function.

In the present study, the linguistic analysis of data in both Russian and Japanese is informed specifically by constructionist gender and language theories (Bucholtz, 2014; Coates, 2004). These approaches further extend feminist theory within the domain of language, considering performative aspects of gender in various forms of speech and discourse. They assert that the performance of "feminine" (and "masculine") linguistic and non-linguistic behavior is a result of complex socialization processes that dictate how men and women should act in accordance with their gender (Coates & Pichler, 2011). These theories are useful in understanding language employed by and about women because they explain how language in particular can be strategically used to 'do gender.'

It will be crucially important to consider the fluidity of gender concepts and performances when analyzing the embeddedness of discourse within patriarchal structures of power, understanding that gender is a moving target. We shall assume that uses of gendered language by women typically involve *both* external constraints imposed by various forms of social power *and* women's own concerns, motivations, and values. Indeed, the distinction between 'internal' and 'external' is not always obvious and sometimes arguably not even meaningful. But it is clear that women's enactments of their gender (and other) identities are often not perfectly congruent with the norms and expectations of the communities of speakers and actors in which they are embedded. And these moments of incongruity, dislocation, and discomfort are frequently of the greatest interest both to scholars and to speakers themselves.

How ought we best to analyze such constrained, inflected performances? The approach taken in this manuscript will aim to be flexible, pragmatic, and data-driven. Rather than beginning with a rigid or universal theory of how performances are constrained by power, or how performances contest power, I will aim to use multi-cultural and multi-linguistic data to shed light on these very issues and processes. In the present study, it will also be essential to consider the different ways in which women 'consume' gendered performances, as presented to them in media and in 'natural' discourse. Women do not merely absorb media representations as passive recipients, but engage with and alter their meaning in a continuous process of construction. Contemporary feminist theories of language do not apply in exactly the same form to Japanese and Russian cultural and linguistic contexts because of the different structures that shape and constrain women's choices in these environments. Nevertheless, these theories are appropriate for considering the culture-specific construction of 'femininity,' albeit through different trajectories, in both Japanese and Russian 'beauty' advertising.

This cross-cultural perspective does, however, in itself reflect a certain basic supposition or commitment—namely, that we cannot perfectly inoculate scholarly interpretation and analysis from the explicit and implicit influence of our own gender concepts, performances, and achieved identities. While it is important to be as clear as possible about our theoretical commitments, our methodological choices, and the limitations of our data, no set of safeguards or protective measures will allow us to achieve a 'true' or objective understanding of the material presented in which our own identities do not emerge as factors. Rather, comparison across cultures, languages, and communities is what promises to disencumber interpretation and analysis, as much as possible, of the pitfalls associated with our particular, personal vantage-points.

1.3 Stance and Indexicality in 'Women's Language'

The present study also draws considerably on theoretical work developing the notions of 'stance' and 'indexicality' in the analysis of gendered language. Stance and indexicality frameworks stem from social constructionist theories of 'discourse' associated with post-structural trends in feminism (see Sect. 1.2 and Butler, 2006). These theories contend that all gendered language is developed in interpersonal interactions, in which speakers sequentially take (and sometimes contrast) stances toward attitude objects, and that such stance-taking constitutes an essential part of the conscious or unconscious performance of gender (Coates, 2004). By means of particular locutions, speakers index aspects of their identities both directly and indirectly.

Feminist sociolinguists in this tradition have thus explored differences in women's and men's discourses in terms of stances adopted and indexed, and explicated how various strategies can be used to construct a gendered social identity. For example, Ochs argued that while many stances, acts, and activities are directly indexed, gender is indexed only indirectly (1992, p. 342). However, over the course of repetitious use, specific stances taken on by female or male speakers begin to be indicative of a gender category. Thus, according to Ochs (1992), there is no direct correlation between gender and linguistic form (p. 337). Rather, the relationship between gender and language can only be understood by considering the interaction between social acts and stances thereby adopted. Instead of arguing that women's language is inherently the language of the oppressed (Lakoff, 1975), Ochs (1992) suggests that society tends to associate certain linguistic elements with female or male speech merely because female and male speakers utilize those linguistic elements with differential frequency as part of their stance-taking. The stances thereby expressed are in turn a consequence of societal norms and expectations associated with preferred concepts of masculinity and femininity (1992, p. 342). In summary, the effects of gender norms on language are to be understood, according to Ochs, not as direct effects of patriarchal control or gendered preferences for specific modes of linguistic expression, but rather as mediated by expectations that women and men will adopt different stances in pursuance of distinct social roles.

This perspective does not deny the impact of systemic or structural factors on women's (and men's) language use, but rather seeks to explain how such factors come to exert their impact on concrete instances of language use through the mediation of processes of stance-taking and indexing. For instance, gendered insults are often based upon differences in the types of behavior regarded as gender-appropriate. Insults highlighting a man's lack of power (e.g. "henpecked," "pussy whipped"), and insults highlighting a women's possession of power (e.g. "shrew," "bitch") reflect the social prejudice against powerful women and men's systematic attempt to suppress them (Lakoff, 2003, p. 162). This dynamic can further be seen in the usage of tag questions as a hedging device in English—a phenomenon frequently associated with female speech even though male speakers use tag questions as well. The link to gender, according to Ochs (1992), lies in the socially accepted images of femininity and masculinity: self-confidence and assertiveness are preferred qualities for a man, while a woman needs to appear less straightforward and forceful to be perceived favorably. Thus, because tag questions may convey hesitation and solicit confirmation, both activities favored by women in American society, usage of tag questions has become linked to the female gender (Ochs, 1992, p. 340).

Kiesling (2009) proposes a further distinction between "interior" and "exterior" indexicalities, defining interior indexicality as the indexical meaning created within a given speech event, while the exterior indexicality refers to "indexical meaning that is transportable from one speech event to another, and connects to the social contexts" that do not change from one speech event to another (p. 177). For instance, the word "dude" externally indexes a level of non-intimate, "cool" solidarity and masculinity—but on the interior level it can index various sentiments depending on the context, from diffusing an argument to expressing amazement and positive evaluation (Kiesling, 2009, p. 178). However, the ability to distinguish between the two meanings of the term in practice proves to be a rather difficult task, leading Kiesling to admit that frequently "exterior and interior indexicalities become almost indistinguishable from one another" (p. 178).

Similarly, Bucholtz (2009) analyzes the various stances conveyed by the Spanish lexical item *güey* 'dude' among Mexican high school students, demonstrating that it can be used as a term of address, an insulting reference and discourse marker, as well as an indirect index of intimacy (p. 158). She argues that the media's highly ideologized spaces tend to simplify and erase diverse indexicalities, linking the word *güey* with a "middle-class form of masculinity," and thereby excluding other categories of *güey*'s users (Bucholtz, 2009).

These frameworks help to explain the causal mechanisms that link language to the construction and performance of gender. Specifically, they highlight the ways in which cultures 'index' gender through lexical items, and thereby use words to express gendered stances or social roles. They also reveal how language can be indicative not only of gender but also of associated features and stances. A proper appreciation of the role of stance and indexicality is essential to my analysis, because it demonstrates that in the dynamic relationship between language and gender, women can utilize 'masculine' language to index (and even to appropriate) various stances of power and autonomy (rather than 'maleness' per se). In these situations, women do not typically attempt to 'appear male', but rather to assert stances traditionally associated with masculinity. In so doing, they often face the challenge of integrating stances and attributes typically associated with masculinity with gender identities that are feminine (or non-masculine). An emphasis on how stance-taking occurs, and how gender concepts and ideologies are indirectly indexed, will be essential to the analysis of women's language in such contexts.

1.4 Ideology, Identity, and Intersectionality

The theory of intersectionality (Block & Corona, 2014; Crenshaw, 1991) is also central to my analysis and understanding of gender construction mechanisms in Russian and Japanese societies. One of the objectives of this study is to explore the dislocation between the ideologized notions of femininity and womanhood in Japan and Russia and the lived, intersectional experiences of various women. This analysis is limited in some respects by the specific samples adduced. While these limitations constrain the ability to address certain critical questions, I attempt to elucidate these issues as much as possible by means of the data acquired.

One of the debilitating limitations is the prospect of a successful study of 'women's language' in Russia, specifically. The political climate in contemporary Russia is rather hostile to the open discussion of issues pertaining to gender and sexuality, with legislation explicitly constraining the ability of LGBTQ+ persons to express themselves and advocate for their interests. As such, it is exceedingly difficult to recruit representative samples that adequately reflect the rich diversity of women's experiences and identities in Russia, though some authors have accomplished admirable work in this area (e.g. Stella, 2015).

The central theme of this book is the reciprocal interaction between ideologized conceptions of youth and beauty in media and women's assimilations, transformations, and rejections of these concepts in their speech and writing. As such, consideration of the intersections between gender and age is essential to the overall undertaking. While the interviewees are all relatively young, there is nevertheless considerable variance in their age and class positions, in ways that impinge interestingly upon their articulation and construction of beauty and femininity. There is less variation in the samples in terms of self-reported sexual orientation and race, and this limits the full potential for a thorough exploration of intersectional identities.

The ideologies of beauty and femininity in the cultural communities examined here are intricately connected to conceptual notions that fuse heteronormative, classist, ageist, and racist suppositions. Exploring the ways in which these categories are blended in media messages, and thus become part of a homogenizing whole, is an important aspect of this book. Just as crucial is the discussion of the ways in which women's spontaneous discourses and writings assimilate, modify, and reject the supposed unities promulgated in advertising. Thus, despite the limits of my sample, there is significant internal diversity in the experiences and thoughts considered within the present study. There is also obvious intragroup and inter-group overlap when the interviewees speak about the societal expectations of women, demonstrating the pressures toward conformity inherent in Russian and Japanese 'idealized femininity' and the distinct forms assumed by that conformity.

Nevertheless, the limitations of the present data are considerable, and should not be ignored. Future research will be needed in order to extend the present work, and to render more visible members of marginalized or underrepresented groups, their voices, and their unique conceptions and enactments of beauty. At the outset, I would like to point the reader toward several areas where further research is especially needed.

First, despite the fact that both Russia and Japan are ethnically and racially heterogeneous countries (including both substantial populations of resident foreigners and domestic variation in racial/ethnic heritage and indigenous populations), depictions of feminine beauty tend to represent the women of these cultures as racially and ethnically homogenous. In Japanese advertising, characters are mostly presented as belonging to the ethically dominant group; in Russian advertising, characters are depicted as being ethnically Russian (or otherwise East Slavic European). In this way, racial and ethnic minorities are erased from commercial representation and excluded from many contemporary constructions of beauty. The ways that non-dominant racial and ethnic groups construct their own conceptions of feminine beauty, and strive to integrate or differentiate these conceptions with reigning ideologies and ideals regarding gender and beauty, are an essential topic for further research.

Second, transgender and non-binary identities are almost entirely absent in commercial depictions of feminine beauty in both Japan and Russia. Moreover, the samples of women recruited for the present study (perhaps, in part, due to limitations in free self-expression noted above) did not include any individuals who self-reported as transgender or non-binary. This imposes a critical lacuna on our understanding and comparison of women's voices regarding beauty in Japan and Russia. The depictions and discourses of feminine beauty discussed in the present text are therefore essentially bounded, limited to cisgender expressions of womanhood and femininity. Future research will need to expand and broaden this perspective.

Third, the complex interactions between gender and sexuality in Japanese and Russian cultures are not well-represented in the present materials. Dominant ideological positions are hostile toward lesbian, gay, and diverse queer identities, and seek to actively impede articulation of conceptions of beauty by members of these communities (Stella, 2015). The heteronormative features of the depictions of beauty discussed in this text will be readily apparent. Despite the limitations of the present study, there is interesting empirical work on LGBTQ+ identities in Japan by Hideko Abe (2010) that is relevant to the construction and problematization of feminine beauty in Japan. Future work along these lines will help to broaden and deepen our understanding of the diverse forms of beauty present in Russian and Japanese societies, and better appreciate how they are expressed in language.

1.5   Femininity, Beauty, and a 'Woman's Place' in Russia

Gender ideology in Russian society has been profoundly influenced by the transition from a communist form of socioeconomic organization to the capitalist oligarchy of the present day. Before 1991, discourse about women in Russia (or the 'women's question') focused mainly on how most efficiently 'to accommodate women's innate differences to the ideal of the New Soviet Man.' By emphasizing equality between genders, Soviet dogma had led to the formation of the "idealized dual worker-mother role of women" (Lyon, 2007, p. 28). This rhetoric presented a tenuous "doublethink": women should be treated as men at work, but as women at home (subject to all the household chores and child-rearing) (Johnson, 2017a, p. 7).

Women's struggles in workplaces were frequently not raised or strategically elided by citing official gender equality. This arrangement meant that women were subject to the same workplace demands and expectations as men, but lacked the same privileges and benefits. Throughout the Soviet era prior to Perestroika, women were commanded to work alongside men 'equally.' In 1932, women younger than 56 years lost access to ration stamps for groceries and basic commodities if they did not work (Kozlova, 2000, p. 24). During the later Perestroika period, however, they were directed to return to the home—but at no point were women's preferences (individually or collectively) given serious consideration (Johnson, 2017a, p. 31). Russian society during the Soviet period remained inherently unequal, with feminism disparaged as a capitalist movement from the West (p. 8). However, the transition to a capitalist political economy did not lead to an adoption of feminist ideals either. Compared to the hardships of the 1990s, the problems articulated by Western feminists seemed farfetched and unreasonable to Russian women (Levinson, 2000, p. 43). Feminism was ideologically linked with hatred toward men and family-making, attitudes that contradicted the cornerstones of neo-traditional Russian womanhood—domesticity and the appearance of subservience (Johnson, 2017a, p. 29).

Subservience, however, has frequently been construed as an exterior ruse or strategic image, necessary for women in order to satisfy the heterosexual male gaze.[1] The crucial significance of the male gaze in Russian culture has been portrayed in literature, and has been the subject of analysis from a variety of different perspectives (Kovarsky, 2008; Reyfman, 2008). To cite one classic example, in Tolstoy's novel "Family Happiness," the marriage of the female protagonist falls apart when she can no longer acquire and maintain her husband's interested gaze, inaugurating a sequence of events highlighting the importance of being "a sight" even in a committed relationship (Reyfman, 2008, p. 32). The overriding significance of the heterosexual male gaze, in turn, prompts women to look at themselves (reflectively and reflexively) through men's eyes, molding themselves in a manner aimed at attracting men's glances. In a 1992 essay competition about women's "ideal selves" (organized by a modeling agency), a medical student (age 21) wrote, "If in the course of a day not a single man has looked at me, then the day was wasted" (Kay, 1997, p. 86). Thus, women tended to view themselves through the eyes of men, pretending to be objects of their desires (Turkina, 2000, p. 80). Toward the end of the 1990s and the beginning of the 2000s, many Russian women started to use international dating websites in the hopes of marrying foreigners, most frequently Americans. These women manipulated their introductory narratives in order to create desirable images of

---

[1] The term "male gaze" in this book reflects the concept first devised by Laura Mulvey (1999).

traditional heterosexual femininity and to distance themselves from "feminist American women" (Johnson, 2017a, p. 158).

In post-Soviet Russia, a neo-traditional gender ideology has become dominant, based in part on traditional labor divisions and affected by the values of both past communism and ongoing globalization. A "real" woman was believed not only to be externally beautiful but also to possess a beauty of soul, patience, and generosity, as well as constant sympathy for others (Volkova & Muzychenko, 1993). Some argue that the Soviet ideas of egalitarian gender roles have been completely erased, with the result that masculinity is associated with breadwinning, while femininity is strongly tied with homemaking (Lyon, 2007, p. 31). This argument, however, appears questionable when the discrepancy between abstract perceptions of gender and the reality of women's conduct is taken into consideration. According to Lyon (2007), the impact of Soviet egalitarian policies and rhetoric has not dissipated with the collapse of the USSR (p. 26). Portrayals of women satisfied exclusively with being homemakers and mothers are misleading and inaccurate, because Russian women, although ideologically constructed as desiring men's protection and strength, in reality aspire to self-realization in professional spheres (Kay, 2006). As survey research has shown, Russian women, in contrast to many Russian men, do not work only for income but also for personal and social reasons (Lyon, 2007, p. 32).

The new post-Soviet ideology has also triggered an extreme sexualization of women, emphasizing women's beauty, youthfulness, and attractiveness above other features (Johnson & Robinson, 2007, p. 10; Lipovskaja, 1994). The notion that women must strive to be visually appealing has been fueled by the rejection of the past image of the strong working Soviet woman (who either lacks distinctively feminine characteristics or suppresses them). Thus, the necessity of appearing beautiful has not been recognized as a limitation of freedom or pressure to conform to male expectations, but rather idealized as a "release from austerity and hardship" of the Soviet era (Kay, 1997, p. 82).

The widespread social restructuring after the fall of the Soviet Union has allowed feminist discourse to emerge and to be acknowledged only to a limited degree. Women's crisis centers were organized in order to 'renegotiate understandings of domestic violence and gender.' Previous discourse had either completely neglected domestic violence or blamed victimized women for provocative behavior and a supposed "inability to perform their domestic duties selflessly," with an emphasis on societal decline in women's morality (Johnson, 2017b, p. 43).

Overall, the unstable economic and political climate, however, led to a dramatic deterioration of the job market, which more profoundly affected the availability of jobs for women than for men. The vast majority of the newly unemployed and individuals living below the poverty line were women, while the amount and availability of social support for females decreased strikingly. Furthermore, women almost disappeared from the political arena after the 1990s. Currently, Russian women are still under-represented within elected bodies, while female politicians do not have considerable influence on the state of affairs (Shevchenko, 2007, p. 128). In light of diminished job opportunities, maintaining a pleasing appearance and demeanor became a practical necessity for women. Job advertisements listed attractiveness as one of the preferred characteristics for female applicants, making beauty a woman's strongest asset (Kay, 1997, p. 82).

In a survey of 120 letters written by Russian women in 1992 as submissions to a competition 'The Perfect You,' women expressed their views on what being an ideal woman entailed. The results of the survey showed that Russian women placed beauty high on the list of priorities for an ideal woman. In their essays, women repeatedly stressed the necessity of remaining fit and good-looking, and advised that one should "never let oneself go," even after marriage (Kay, 1997, p. 82). They also referred to an ideal woman as a 'guardian of the family hearth,' who nevertheless in most cases also aspires to employment and professional self-realization. Communal moral characteristics, such as kindness and fairness, also scored high in these essays, while "independence, self-reliance," and a strong will were mentioned in only half of the entries (Kay, 1997, p. 83). The mixed (and potentially contradictory) nature of these responses may be the consequence of a 70-year-long totalitarian regime, which emphasized both traditional femininity through home-making, *and* mandatory work and annual participation in physically intensive non-paid labor in state-owned agricultural cooperatives for both men and women. The expectation that women *must* work could not be erased from people's minds in post-Soviet Russia, even as a return to traditional gender norms was promulgated through schooling, media, and dominant intellectual discourses. Economic hardship also rendered exclusive domesticity an impossibility for many women, both during and after the transition. For these reasons, the social construction of a woman's place in contemporary Russia has retained the expectation of work outside the home.

1.6   Russian 'Women's Language'

The category of 'women's language' in Russian is not as well established as in Japanese, and research on gendered practices in spoken Russian is also relatively underdeveloped. Similarly to English, the Russian female genderlect contains mostly gender-preferential, as opposed to gender-exclusive, language forms (Bodine, 1975). Russian women are believed to use more diminutive forms, interjections, emphatic and hyperbolic expressions, and expressive adverbs than men (Yokoyama, 1999, p. 408). Unlike men, they tend to provide concrete examples rather than abstract ones, narrate more frequently, and avoid the use of vulgar expressions and swearwords (Zemskaja, Kitajgorodskaja, & Rjazanova, 1993). In addition, women are said to switch from one subject to another more flexibly than men and use technical terminology less often, replacing it with general terms. Furthermore, some scholars claim that Russian women's speech exhibits distinctive phonological patterns such as sound lengthening, sound aspiration, labialization, and nasalization for emphatic purposes (Zemskaja et al., 1993).

Unlike scholarship on Japanese and English, Russian women's language has never been linked to a woman's inferior position as a homemaker, or tied to any specific ideology. Conversely, Russian gender linguists Zemskaja et al. (1993) explicitly avoided connecting women's language with societal statuses, claiming that it would make research less objective (p. 94). Using spoken Russian data, they investigated the major tendencies of female and male speech, using Lakoff's work (1975) as an example. The differences in language between the two genders were attributed to the dissimilar roles that men and women played historically in Russian society, rather than being representative of inequality

(Zemskaja et al., 1993). These Russian linguists' treatment of gendered language can thus be assimilated to the position of the "difference" theory mentioned above (Tannen, 1990).

Zemskaja et al. (1993) acknowledged the existence of certain objectifying terms of address for women such as *rybka moja* "my fish (diminutive)," *ptička* "bird (diminutive)," *kotjonoček* "kitten," *solnyško* "sun (diminutive)," *tsvetik moj* "my flower (diminutive)," *jagodka* "berry (diminutive)," and *detka* "baby." They, however, deemed these terms nonoffensive and argued that these expressions merely "convey supreme tenderness and authentic feelings of love" (p. 96). Zemskaja et al. (1993) claimed that feminist thinking frequently clouded objective linguistic analysis and thus should not be practiced in order to avoid logical leaps and missteps. These researchers frequently resorted to their own nontheoretical intuitions about language, and did not consider the variety of contexts in which the aforementioned terms of address can be used, along with their implications for women. Zemskaja's et al.'s approach (1993) demonstrates the unwillingness of Russian scholars to evaluate sexism in contemporary society and resistance against incorporating feminist thinking in their research on gender. This phenomenon may reflect the impact upon scholarship of the skeptical attitude toward "feminism" in Russian society, which sometimes even convinces women's rights' activists to dissociate themselves from the broader feminist movement (Lipovskaja, 1997, p. 191). The present study will reevaluate some of these prior claims about Russian women's lexicological patterns, such as the use of swearwords, using both qualitative and quantitative methods, and will explore the reasoning behind this phenomenon using spoken corpora of spontaneous conversations in Chap. 4.

1.7 Femininity, Beauty, and 'Woman's Place' in Japan

Historically, women's societal inferiority has frequently been justified and rationalized through ideologies emphasizing that women have different physiological and emotional characteristics from men (Gottfried, 2003).

In the pre-war and wartime periods, Japanese femininity was ideologically perceived in the context of three dimensions—"modesty," "elegance," and "tidiness"—cultivated in women through the process of socialization, or so-called femininity training (Lebra, 1984). These key concepts of femininity in the mid-nineteenth to early twentieth century were dependent upon the Confucian teaching of *ryoosai kenbo* "good wife, wise mother" (Matsumoto, 2004, p. 241). This notion was utilized as an ideological tool to specify a woman's place in the Japanese society, explicating the appropriate ways for female individuals to contribute to the creation of the strong nation (Nakamura, 2014, p. 75).

After ten years of post-war American military occupation, the Japanese government was forced to address the social issue of gender inequality by giving women the right to vote, which encouraged women's liberation movements and related discourses. Although gender discrimination was eventually legally prohibited at all stages of the employment process, these new laws co-existed with a dominant gender ideology that also required women to fulfill their traditional duties as wives and mothers (Tamanoi, 1990, p. 28). The perceptions of an ideal woman as modest, reserved, elegant, and compassionate have remained (Nakamura, 2014, pp. 196, 202).

In contemporary gender ideology, femininity is frequently associated with the notion of *kawaii* or "cuteness" (Kinsella, 1995), which is believed to be a required feature for a young Japanese woman, intimately linked to her natural place in society (McVeigh, 1996). The term *kawaii* is regarded as an important "affect word," connected to femininity (Clancy, 1999). According to Yomota (2006), the fascination of Japanese people with cuteness appeared as early as the eleventh century with Sei Shonagon's *Makura no soushi* 'The Pillow Book,' in which she described what constituted, in her opinion, the 'adorable.' For example, she considered "the face of a child drawn on a melon" and "Not only lotus leaves, but little hollyhock flowers," and other small things to be especially lovable (Burdelski & Mitsuhashi, 2010, p. 67; Morris, 1991, p. 168). Interest in *kawaii* representations can be further observed in the works and theatrical performances of the Edo period, as well as in contemporary literature (Yomota, 2006). In the 1970s, the boom of *kawaii* was especially visible, gradually spreading in Asia and Western countries through Japanese animation and cute-looking commodities, marking an age of "pink glo-balization" (Yano, 2013, p. 6). While Japanese society has long evinced an interest in things cute and adorable, the reigning ideology of *kawaii* cuteness remains in force as an organizing principle.

This boom turned out to be a long-lasting social phenomenon (Burdelski & Mitsuhashi, 2010, p. 67). One cannot escape from the intense cuteness of "acres of wide-eyed little girls, aisles of cuddly animals, screens full of cute little monsters, all in kindergarten colors" surrounding people everywhere in Japan (Richie & Garner, 2003, p. 53). Kinsella (1995) claimed that "cute fashion in Japan was more than just cuddling things; it was all about 'becoming' the cute object itself" (p. 237). But the concept of *kawaii* cannot merely be translated into cuteness; it represents more than just "attractive by reason of daintiness or picturesqueness in manners or appearance, as a child or a small animal," as stated in Webster's dictionary (Richie & Garner, 2003, p. 53). Okazaki and Johnson (2013) suggest that *kawaii* can be translated as "beautiful, lovable, suitable, addictive, cool, funny, ugly but endearing, quirky and gross," describing adorable physical features and anything that provokes feelings of love and motherly instincts to care and to protect (p. 7). It is accorded a high position in the national value system, and is strongly connected with innocence and immaturity (Richie & Garner, 2003, p. 54). Based on interviews with high school girls, "*kawaii* connotes sweetness, dependence and gentleness," which are linked to childhood in the minds of young Japanese women (Allison, 2006). Being *kawaii* is considered desirable in every area of young women's lives, including fashion, manners, and communication (Asano-Cavanagh, 2014); being called "cute" is even preferred over "beautiful," "sexy," or "gorgeous" (Okazaki & Johnson, 2013, p. 8).

Although cuteness can be attributed to anyone, regardless of gender, it is especially young women whose goal is to appear *kawaii*. The ideological gap that separates the Japanese notion of *kawaii* from the Western concept of 'cuteness' is evident in even a cursory online search of the respective terms: a Google image search of the term 'cute' retrieves pictures of cute-looking small animals, while searching for *kawaii* in Japanese writing retrieves primarily images of sexualized young women.

Preschool girls are more likely than preschool boys to view themselves as *kawaii*, as indicated by psycholinguistic interviews (Tomomatsu,

1994). Moreover, this ratio increases drastically from 3:1 among children at three years of age to 9:1 among children age six (Tomomatsu, 1994), suggesting that Japanese people are socialized into the expectation that women must be *kawaii* from early childhood (Burdelski & Mitsuhashi, 2010, p. 68). Feminist linguists have argued that the fascination with cute and immature femininity contributes to the stereotype that women are different from men—fragile, incompetent, and unable to take initiative—and thus impedes women's social opportunities (Asano, 1996). Furthermore, if a woman performs *kawaii* to the extent that it seems insincere, she is labeled *burikko* or "a woman who plays bogus innocence" (Miller, 2004, p. 149). This extreme cuteness is stereotypically characterized by exaggerated displays of childishness, such as nasalized, high-pitch voice, baby talk register, and lifting of the hands to the cheeks when smiling (Miller, 2004). On the other hand, if a woman in her speech or behavior deviates from the prescribed norm of *kawaii* femininity, she then risks being called *ore meshi onna*[2] 'me-food woman.' This term is used to designate a group of women who (putatively) utilize hyper-masculine forms of conduct and expression (Miller, 2004, p. 162). This double standard toward women is reminiscent of Lakoff's deficiency theory, in which she argued that women are blamed regardless of whether they abide by or deviate from the norms of gender-appropriate speech (Lakoff, 1975, p. 41).

Though gender discrimination is officially illegal, Japanese women are nevertheless subject to systematic inequality at the workplace through the two-track employment system (*soogooshoku* 'management track' and *ippan shoku* 'clerical track'). In the management track, workers pursue career promotions and other benefits, but agree to disadvantages such as overwork and the possibility of being transferred to other branches. In the clerical track, however, while one does not have to work long hours and cannot be relocated, one also lacks significant possibilities for wage increases and promotions. Although both men and women in theory may choose either of the two trajectories, there is a social expectation that

---

[2] *Ore* 'I' and *meshi* 'food' are masculine linguistic forms, which parody an autocratic husband's command to his wife to feed him. *Oremeshi onna* 'me-food woman' is a term for a category of women who deliberately choose hyper-masculine language, and refuse to use traditionally feminine speech.

the management track is more suitable for men while the clerical track one is more family-friendly—and thus, more appropriate for women. Overall, even those few women who choose the management track rarely succeed in being promoted through the career ladder, while many women engage in so-called part-time contract jobs. Contract work does not provide the benefits that come with official employment, even though female employees hired under the contract system may work the same hours as full-time employees. Moreover, women are not represented in or supported by worker's unions to the same extent as men; most women are not members of the unions and most unions do not strongly support women's rights (Tamanoi, 1990, p. 25).

Emphasizing the short term of female employment and their decorative, unimportant role at the workplace, female workers are sometimes called *shokuba no hana* "office flowers" (Charlebois, 2014), although this expression has more recently been deemed offensive and officially removed from corporate publications. The justification of male preference in the employment process usually comes from the biologically based reproductive 'duty' of women, who must get married, give birth, and take care of children—and will thus be unable to compete with men in a workplace. The management track is conceptualized as masculine, while quitting one's job and devoting oneself to home is regarded as feminine. A woman is expected to devote her life to family and domestic chores, rather than improving her education and accruing professional achievements (Charlebois, 2014). Japanese femininity is frequently conceptualized as "a form of other-centeredness," in which women are supposed to receive self-fulfillment through supporting the needs and desires of others (Charlebois, 2014, p. 15).

1.8 Japanese 'Women's Language'

'Women's language' (or *onna kotoba/jyosei kotoba*) is a well-defined category in Japanese language encompassing the array of lexical and grammatical characteristics that describe feminine speech. It is commonly believed that *onna kotoba* has had a long history and is rooted in the innate feminine nature that compels women to converse in a beautiful and womanly manner, speaking softly and politely. It has thus been argued to be a precious aspect of Japanese linguistic and cultural heritage (Kindaichi, 1942).

Traditionally, "women's language" in Japan has been linked to the concepts of "refinement," "demeanor," "deference," and "delicacy" (Ide, 1992; Matsumoto, 2004), qualities that are believed to emanate from within a woman's soul. Hyper-polite, "gentle, unassertive, and empathetic speech" is generally considered womanlike (Okamoto & Shibamoto Smith, 2004, p. 3). In particular, it is stereotypically believed that women (1) utilize more honorific expressions, indirect speech acts, interjections, and exclamatory expressions than men, (2) generally employ higher vocal pitch, (3) exclusively use the sentence-final particles *wa*↑ with rising intonation, and (4) avoid the copula *da* and such sentence-final particles as *zo* and *ze* (Okamoto & Shibamoto Smith, 2004, p. 4).

The first Japanese linguist to question the validity of Japanese women's language was Akiko Jugaku, whose book *Nihongo to onna* "The Japanese language and women" (1979) is compared to Lakoff's first publication on gender in its significance (Yukawa & Saito, 2004, p. 26). In her book, Jugaku (1979) analyzed language directed toward female audiences, topics chosen for female readership, and linguistic strategies that indicate that the speaker is female. She concluded that women's language is built on gender ideologies that constrain women's freedom and predetermine their future. Ide (1980, 1990), however, eschewing a feminist critical perspective, suggested that Japanese women's language is characterized by dignity rather than oppression, and contended that women actually possess more power in family matters than their husbands. She was criticized for reinforcing hegemonic gender ideologies by neglecting the systematic oppression of women in Japanese society (Reynolds-Akiba, 1993; Yukawa & Saito, 2004). A series of studies were conducted to question the essential nature of the Japanese women's language. For instance, it was found that Japanese women use a high pitch only when speaking Japanese, but not when speaking English, refuting the notion of the innateness of *onna kotoba* (Ohara, 1992). This finding suggests that women are pressured to speak gender-appropriately to be favorably perceived in Japanese society, while this requirement is no longer relevant in English (Ohara, 1992).

Inoue (2006) calls Japanese women's language an "imagined" construct, which appeared in the process of novel-writing during and after the Meiji period language modernizing reform *gembun'ichi* "unifying speech and writing." When creating reported speech uttered by female characters in their stories, Meiji period writers utilized the speech of *jogakusee* "schoolgirls" as a model and added elaborate honorifics (Inoue, 2006, p. 68). This reported speech of fictional heroines later became the foundation of normative women's language. Thus, Japanese women's language is not a natural outcome of spontaneous women's speech or an endogenous development of Japan's cultural heritage; it is instead a relatively recent imagining of the voices of women by fiction writers that subsequently became associated with ideal femininity, and started to be imitated by actual women (Inoue, 2006).

In a similar vein, Nakamura (2014) has demonstrated that women's language has often been used as a deliberate political instrument of ideological propaganda, aimed at maintaining the social norms of Japan in various periods. For instance, in the war and post-war periods, female language was regarded as a deviation from the norm while male language was classified as standard Japanese, emphasizing masculine superiority. Grammar books written by postwar linguists, who characterized women's language as a speech based on innate femininity, were used as a tool to blunt criticism of gender inequality in society and language (Nakamura, 2014).

Japanese discriminatory expressions, as documented by contemporary and historical dictionaries, also attest to the systematic oppression of women in Japanese society. The terms that describe men tend to emphasize their power, strength, honor, and reliability, such as *shujin* 'master' for husband. Female reference terms, however, venerate passivity, dependence on men, and beauty. For instance, *umazume* (written as 石女) "lit. stone woman" is defined as "a woman without an ability to conceive," although there is no corresponding term for a man (Gottlieb, 2005, p. 109). Another example is the word *miboojin* (written as 未亡人) "lit. not yet dead," "a widow," emphasizing the lost purpose of a woman who has lived on after the death of her husband (Gottlieb, 2005, p. 109).

Female attractiveness and beauty are said to be strongly influenced by a woman's mastery of *onna kotoba* and honorific speech (Okamoto, 2004,

p. 42). Although sociolinguists (e.g. Inoue, 1994, 2006; Nakamura, 1995, 2001) have demonstrated in their diachronic research that Japanese women's language is an ideological construct rather than a reality, the social expectation and pressure for women to speak gently and femininely in order to be favorably perceived are strong. Even nowadays, varieties of speech manuals for women instruct them how to speak in order to appear charming. Such books as *Onna no miryoku wa hanashikata shidai* "Women's attractiveness depends on how they speak," or *Sutekina anata o tsukuru: Josee no utsukushii hanashikata* "To make yourself nice: Women's beautiful ways of speaking" are evidence of remaining unequal gender and language expectations in Japan (Okamoto, 2004, p. 42).

Currently, Japanese society is experiencing significant changes in both the prevailing norms regulating women's speech and women's actual use of language (Okamoto, 2004). On the one hand, *kawaii* (i.e. "cuteness") is regarded as a key element, essential for a woman to possess in both her appearance and language (e.g. Kinsella, 1995; McVeigh, 1996). Such language is different from the traditional women's speech, and presents a set of features utilized by predominantly young women to sound adorable, naïve, and childlike (Miller, 2004). On the other hand, women rarely use in practice elements of traditional women's speech that are characterized by extreme graciousness and linguistic ornamentation. For instance, the sentence-final particle *wa* with rising intonation, auxiliary *kashira, mono* after the copula *desu*, and other features traditionally associated with women's language do not appear frequently in actual use by young Japanese female speakers (Matsumoto, 2004, p. 241; Okamoto, 1995). Instead, they exist mainly in the translations of Western novels, manga, anime, movies, and other forms of virtual language (Kinsui, 2003). Young Japanese women, conversely, sometimes utilize traditionally male speech, such as the sentence-final forms *da yo* and *da* (Okamoto & Shibamoto Smith, 2004). The usage of male language reflects the female speaker's strategic choices, which depend on various social factors not limited to the speaker's gender. The goal of the speaker is to project a certain persona to a specific addressee in a particular context (Okamoto, 1995).

1.9 Gender in Russian and Japanese Advertising

Advertising often produces, engages, and recycles gender ideologies—both normalizing and solidifying them in the minds of viewers (Goffman, 1979a). The primary layer of discourse is constituted by the information (factual and contextual) presented about a specific commercial product; but a second layer supervenes upon the first, comprising the array of social sentiments and cultural ideas implicitly conveyed and reinforced (Yurchak, 2000, p. 65). At a teleological level of analysis, the goal of advertising must be understood not only in terms of concrete effects on the sale of commercial products, but also with respect to the abstract desires related to concerns for social identity that advertising engages and even creates. In the case of "beauty ads," the abstract, libidinal domain of engagement is concerned with visions of femininity and womanhood, and it is idealized portrayals of women that are sold (Turkina, 2000, p. 80). The abundance of visual and auditory advertising material consumed daily is so great that these stimuli act as "socializing agents," influencing attitudes, values, behavior, and thinking (Kang, 1997). Research on consumer behavior has shown that low-involvement learning, based on repeated exposures to gender-stereotypical portrayals, increases the likelihood that people will perceive those portrayals of women as accurate (Hawkins & Hoch, 1992, p. 212). Moreover, when exposed to explicit images of women performing traditional gender roles in advertisements, both men and women show a greater level of acceptance of gender stereotypes (Lanis & Covell, 1995; McKay & Covell, 1997). Thus, by encouraging gender conformity, advertising solidifies in our minds the meanings of "masculinity" and "femininity" and normalizes gender bias (Lindner, 2004, p. 409).

Examination of women's speech and non-linguistic behavior in the commercials thus can unveil the mechanisms by which current gender ideologies permeate society and become normalized. Following Foucault's methodology (1991), Yurchak (2000) studied the discourse strategies that allowed Russian advertisers to introduce and solidify gender norms. He described how, under the influence of Western advertising, Russian post-Soviet commercials started to utilize 'active agents' in their portrayals, attempting to convey strong connectedness to their viewers. Through the use of direct gaze, imperatives, and informal referential forms (e.g. *ty* 'you,'), female characters were presented in the guise of such "active agents" (Yurchak, 2000, p. 71). Even though Russian women thereby seemingly acquired their own voice and gaze, they were being undermined through various "intertextual presuppositions" (Fairclough, 1992a). The meaning of an advertisement frequently must be decoded through the activation of the structured social knowledge in people's minds. By exploiting the presuppositions that were repeatedly associated with specific ideas on gender, advertising normalized various stereotypes and biased perceptions of women (Yurchak, 2000, p. 93). As an example, Yurchak (2000) cites an earlier cigarette-lighter commercial that portrays a smiling female erupting in the flame of the lighter as the background voice says *ne otkažet nikogda* "(it/she) will never refuse." The next scene portrays a partially naked man sitting down relaxed and satisfied. These portrayals, based on the patterns of conservative patriarchal discourse, objectify the women depicted through the activation of gender stereotypes (Yurchak, 2000, p. 75).

In Japanese advertising of the 1980s and 1990s, women were portrayed as pervasively employing stereotypical woman's language, a depiction that consistently stressed their traditional gender roles. For exactly this reason, a widely aired 1983 commercial about instant noodles was perceived to be offensive by Japanese women, and ultimately removed from national broadcasting (Gottlieb, 2005, p. 110). In the commercial a woman says *watashi tsukuru hito* "I am the one who cooks," while the man responds by *boku taberu hito* "I (male) am the one who eats," reinforcing the idea that the woman's function lies in the domestic domain (Gottlieb, 2005, p. 110). Since then, Japan has adopted a Basic Law for a Gender Equal Society (1999) and a Plan for Gender Equality (2000), encouraging media to promote diverse representations of women by highlighting their autonomy and active social roles and avoiding depictions that emphasize women's inferiority (Gottlieb, 2005, p. 121). Because of these reforms aimed at promoting gender equality, and in response to changing social attitudes regarding gender roles, Japanese media have made progress in removing simplistic representations of women as homemakers and have stopped utilizing sexist terminology (Endo, 2004, p. 180).

Despite the attempts to eliminate stereotypical depictions of women, however, gender ideologies still manage to penetrate into the media, revealing ongoing forms of gender discrimination. Women and men continue to be depicted differently in Japanese advertising; women are mostly presented in the roles of "beautiful and wise wives," "young celebrities," and "young ladies attracting people's attention," while men are portrayed as "middle- and old-aged people enjoying private time," and "middle-aged worker bees" (Arima, 2003, p. 87).

The increasing spread of *kawaii* 'cuteness,' a crucial feature of normative femininity in Japan, can also be observed in various forms of mass media alongside traditional gender stereotypes. In commercial media, Japanese women talk politely and gently while appearing *kawaii*. For instance, the initial news coverage of the alleged discovery in stem-cell research made by Haruka Obokata focused profusely on the female scientist's cute appearance, until her fabrication was discovered. In the national broadcast, the reporter stressed that despite being a distinguished scientist, Obokata had *jyosei rashii ichimen* 'a feminine side,' pointing out that she colored the doors and walls of her office in pink, and decorated the working space with numerous drawings of her favorite comic book character Moomin, who 'watched over her.' Her feminine side was further exemplified by the fact that she wore a Japanese-style apron instead of a professional robe, and enjoyed the company of her pet turtle in the research laboratory. Attention to these details demonstrated that femininity remains a necessary attribute even for a potential female Nobel Prize nominee. Furthermore, the features that were described in order to portray the scientist's 'feminine side' are directly linked to the *kawaii* image, emphasizing the woman's childish and cute nature.

Nakamura (2004) observed that media creates gendered communities of consumers by building on existing stereotypes while accommodating new perceptions of idealized femininities. She demonstrated how authors strategically utilize language to depict specific feminine identities and project them on to readers. The existence of an easily recognizable female genderlect in the Japanese language contributes to the ability of media to convey various feminine images, which are based primarily on stereotypical notions about women's verbal behavior. In particular, she found that copious use of exclamation marks, hortative and interrogative constructions, and interactional sentence-final particles construe female magazine readers as inquisitive, emotional, advice-seeking, and helpless (Nakamura, 2004, p. 145). These portrayals reproduce and reinforce both traditional gender stereotypes and more recent images of *kawaii*.

Furthermore, as a response to current societal changes, Japanese and Russian advertising has begun to incorporate postfeminist ideals of 'power femininity' alongside traditional gender stereotypes. Media in various countries began to capitalize on stronger images of women, projecting captions of female power and autonomy in ways that emphasize women's rights to enjoy their beauty, sexuality, and socioeconomic status (Lazar, 2014). Japanese media also attempts to integrate portrayals of women's autonomy, independence, and authority into some commercials by creating strong female characters. However, they are always incorporated into a framework that subverts the projected strength of women.

Furthermore, in the current scholarship on women and media, there is a shift away from viewing media as a negative force re-enforcing female subordination and traditional gender role distribution toward viewing media as an emergent source promoting "girl power" (Gauntlett, 2008) and "power femininity." Some scholars suggest that this can be a salutary process, even if the power of women is initially commodified at a superficial level (Lazar, 2014). A similar trajectory can be traced in Russian and Japanese commercials, but the ways in which 'girl power' is effectuated differs in these cultural contexts.

1.10   Methodology and Data Collection

In this work, I use feminist linguistic theories supplemented by indexicality and stance-taking frameworks in order to analyze how women's voices are exploited in televised commercials to create ideological types of femininities. I will then examine women's real discourses as they engage in discussions of femininity and woman's language, exploring how the gender stereotypes depicted in the advertisements are manifested, evoked, asserted, resisted, and rejected in women's actual speech. Finally, using large corpora of spontaneous conversations and blogs, I will highlight the presence of traditionally 'male language' in women's communication, and investigate the logic underlying this phenomenon.

At a broader level, this book questions the degree to which contemporary theories of gender and indexicality are applicable in cross-cultural contexts, as well as the extent to which these frameworks can inform our understanding of gender in Russian and Japanese societies. By examining the intersection of historico-cultural change and language use, the results of this book contribute to discussions of feminist linguistic theories in particular, and debates about gender and media more generally.

In order for the reader to better follow the arguments presented in each of the subsequent chapters, I wish to briefly summarize the data analyzed in each chapter and the respective methodologies employed. Each of the methods is informed by a distinct theoretical tradition and history of use in empirical work. And sometimes, there are theoretical and conceptual disputes between the proponents of these various methods. I do not aim to resolve these broader issues of methodology and theory within the present study. Here, I wish merely to explain why I find each of the methods suitable for the present research, and the ways in which they contribute to my analyses and interpretations.

Chapter 1 examines the construction and promulgation of ideals regarding feminine beauty in contemporary Japanese and Russian beauty ads, using culturally specific materials rather than translated or subsequently localized versions of international advertisements. Rather than attempting to investigate representations of women in advertising worldwide, I intend to conduct a focused analysis of idealized femininities in two dynamic contemporary societies: Japan and Russia. The reason for this emphasis lies in the culture-specific orientation of the present research toward gender and ideals of femininity: the features that are valued in women are "neither universal, nor fixed," but vary across cultures and time (Schippers, 2007, p. 14). To ensure that the materials included in the present study are relevant to culture-specific representations of feminine beauty, the 'beauty ads' selected for the analysis are recent productions aired on Japanese and Russian television between 2012 and 2017. The products in these advertisements ranged from hygiene items, such as soaps, shampoos, conditioners, and body wash, to beautifying decorative cosmetics such as lipstick, mascara, and eyeliner. The advertisements considered in this book therefore include the major brands of international or local products present in the two countries, but only those international brands that utilized advertising specifically created for the local market are analyzed (translated versions of the same advertisements shown unaltered were excluded). The international brands that were chosen for the study are Dove and Nivea. Despite advertising similar (or even identical) products in both countries, Dove and Nivea advertisements in Russia differ greatly from their advertising in Japan, portraying two different types of ideal femininities. These international brands were included because cross-cultural comparison of their depictions of femininity can be especially illuminating. In addition to international brands like Dove and Nivea that created culture-specific content, the study incorporates the domestic Japanese brands 'Fasio,' 'Tsubaki,' 'Biore,' 'Kate,' 'Clear,' 'Sekkisei,' 'Je l'aime,' and 'Flowfushi' and Russian brands 'Čistaja Linija,' 'Mirra,' 'Krasnaja Linija,' 'Barhatnyje Ručki,' 'Čjornyi Žemčug,' 'Sto Retseptov Krasoty,' and 'Green Mama.' The length of the selected commercials ranged from 15 to 25 seconds. All words uttered in the advertisements were transcribed, unless they appeared as background song lyrics.

In Chap. 2, I use multi-modal analysis, critical discourse analysis, and feminist post-structuralist discourse analysis (FPDA) to examine the use of women's language and visual images in 50 Japanese and 50 Russian televised 'beauty ads.' These methodologies differ in their origins and assumptions, but are united by the fact that they focus on the analysis and critical interpretation of communicative acts, as presented through linguistic and sometimes also through non-linguistic channels.

Multi-modal analysis investigates several modalities of interaction simultaneously, understanding that linguistic communication does not occur in isolation, sealed off from non-linguistic forms of communication and from the larger social context within which communicative acts occur. Multi-modal analysis is especially crucial in examining televised commercials, as in such advertisements both women's language and various extra-linguistic parameters are used to construct potent images of feminine beauty. In particular, in addition to linguistic cues, I will analyze the gestures, movements, and postures of the men and women characters in each commercial.

Goffman (1979a) argued that gender is frequently highlighted in advertisements through several distinct but interacting channels. For example, the (extra-linguistic) use of "feminine touch" can convey feelings of delicacy and fragility, while the simultaneous incorporation of "family" as a (linguistic) theme can emphasize women's traditional roles as homemakers (31). In their study of advertising, Harris and Stobart (1986) analyze such varied categories as gender, ethnicity, credibility, role, place, background, persuasion type, product type, and gender of voice-over. Further supplementing this list, Arima (2003) adds consideration of age, dress, reference to the company and product name and branding, camera work, camera angle, and target audiences (83).

I have drawn upon these studies to define the categories of extra-linguistic elements available for analysis and to code them in the transcripts of the advertisements. These elements fall into four overarching or superordinate categories: location, background, touch, positioning, and role. The first category, location, focuses on the physical and social space in which the advertisement is set (home, workplace, leisure, commute, etc.), and whether this space contained realistic or imaginary elements. The second category, background, focuses on the type of people or non-human characters that were depicted alongside the central figures (men, women, children), as well as their social identities. The third category, touch, examines women's self-touch, as well as any other forms of physical contact (e.g. hugs, handshakes) depicted. Within the 'positioning' category, I investigate the way women and men appeared in physical space, either alone or in relation to one another. Finally, I explore the social 'roles' that women and men played in the commercials (e.g. actors, educators, scientists, company employees, mothers). By applying these categories systematically, and by transcribing not only characters' utterances but also their gestures and other extra-linguistic devices, I am able to more fully examine the constructed images of idealized femininity.

Critical discourse analysis (CDA), the second approach utilized in this chapter, is an interdisciplinary methodology that focuses on investigating the motivation behind various linguistic choices, as well as the effects these choices have on the interlocutor and the overall social environment

(Fairclough, 1992b). CDA is based on the idea that certain types of language are systematically used to activate various ideological constructs (Halliday, 1985). Thus, this approach allows us to examine women's and men's language about beauty not in complete isolation (e.g. as a mere string of words occurring in a social vacuum), but rather as a contextually situated series of actions forming a socially and politically motivated discourse that is aimed at conveying certain ideological positions. From the perspective of CDA, discourse cannot be fully understood or explicated using a perspective that is purely 'internal' to a given text or utterance; instead, language use is understood to constitute social acts that interface with larger structures of power, obligation, and knowledge. As such, historical and cultural factors impinge upon the analysis of language use within CDA methodology, and the informativeness of such factors for cross-cultural and cross-linguistic comparisons cannot be overstated.

In Chap. 2, CDA methodology is especially useful because advertisements frequently aim to convey a certain story about the product through the discourse of the actors. Thus, my goal is to capture not only what various utterances might mean in isolation, but also to understand what type of narrative they construct as a whole. For this reason, I view various linguistic choices as mechanisms to convey stances and project personas associated with 'femininity' and 'masculinity.' For example, when I analyze interrogative structures, I do not merely examine the direct or surface meanings of these structures, but consider the other contextual elements depicted in the commercial as well as the embedded cultural associations induced by those elements. Similarly, when analyzing onomatopoeic expressions or various metaphors in Japanese and Russian commercials, I investigate the types of contexts where these utterances are frequently used and the types of personas with which these phrases are most often connected.

Feminist post-structuralist discourse analysis (FPDA) is an approach that uses feminist principles to analyze the ways in which speakers negotiate their identities, positions, and relationships embedded in institutional, cultural, and social contexts (Baxter, 2008). Advertisements rely on presuppositions that people have about gender identity, romantic relationships, and normative behavior, frequently recycling and reinforcing those perceptions. Thus, it is essential to analyze such discursive interactions within contexts that assess relations of power (or powerless-ness) between discourse participants, and connect these relations to gen-der ideology. FPDA stresses that men are not always positioned as 'powerful,' while women may not always be construed as the 'weaker' category, but these meanings of power shift between different contexts as well as within one context. Such phenomena will be evident in my analy-sis as well; although male desire (and especially the heterosexual male gaze (as defined by Mulvey (1999)) exerts an undeniable impact on ideol-ogy and ideas of feminine beauty, women are not always reduced to help-less passivity, and occasionally power dynamics are even (in limited respects) inverted.

Similarly to CDA, I apply FPDA in my analysis by examining the nar-ratives that are being constructed in the commercials. I look at the mean-ing of words alongside their capacity to induce associations and instantiate power structures, the contexts in which they are uttered, and the gender identity of the characters as depicted in the scene. For example, the word *mottainai* by itself simply means 'what a waste,' and it is employed in a variety of contexts. However, when uttered by an empowered male speaker in relation to a subordinate woman, it can function to foreground the difference in their expertise and to highlight the woman's incompetence.

This book is informed by both CDA and FPDA in a complementary fashion. In discussions of feminine beauty, language cannot be analyzed in isolation, but ought rather to be conceived as a tool that activates and responds to various gender ideologies. Only by combining these meth-ods, alongside multimodal analysis of linguistic and non-linguistic behav-ior, can we decode the narratives that are being created and promulgated through advertising.

In addition to discourse-based analytic techniques, I incorporate cor-pus linguistic methods to identify the predominant gender in these texts by calculating the word distributions in the Japanese and Russian adver-tising databases. Corpus linguistics uses compilations of texts (in this research, compilations of advertisement scripts) to analyze language quantitatively (Biber, Conrad, & Reppen, 1998). It plays a crucial role in research on vocabulary, allowing us to objectively define the words that are utilized in various texts, and to discern the differences (if any) in the type of vocabulary used by female and male speakers (Anthony, 2017).

To incorporate corpus methods into the analysis of beauty advertisements, I have transcribed the selected commercials, coding the depicted
gender of the speakers, and utilized the Antconc software (developed by
Anthony, 2014) as a tool to analyze text and concordances. This program
facilitates the calculation of the number of words utilized by men and
women and the identification of the most frequent vocabulary choices
made by the male and female speakers. I then perform chi-squared tests
to determine whether differences in the use of specific lexical items
between genders are statistically significant. In addition, I utilize Antconc
software concordance tool (2014) in order to identify the contexts in
which various lexical sequences are used and in order to observe use patterns. In this way, quantitative analysis of the compiled corpora of
Japanese and Russian advertisements helps demonstrate how various
scripted linguistic and non-linguistic apparatuses create artificial types of
femininity, and helps to reveal how the comparatively meager influence
of feminist discourse is strategically utilized and subverted.

In the third chapter, I investigate women's discourses on feminine
beauty and their ideal selves, audio- and video-recorded in Khabarovsk,
Russia, and Osaka, Japan, during a series of fieldwork activities in the
Spring and Summer of 2016. Each interview consisted of interactive discussions involving the researcher and two Russian or two Japanese
women, and lasted approximately one hour. To promote honest and
uninhibited discourse, the pair of speakers in each interview were always
established friends or acquaintances. In total, 10 interviews with Russian
female speakers (20 participants) and 12 interviews with Japanese female
speakers (24 participants) were recorded. Russian women were recruited
from the Far Eastern State University of Humanities, as well as through
personal acquaintance. In Osaka, Japan, recruitment was conducted on
the campus of Osaka University. All interviews were conducted in private
spaces. Although the age ranges of the Russian and Japanese participants
were the same (between 20 and 30 years old), there are differences in the
Japanese and Russian women's demographics. The Russian cohort was
slightly older, averaging 24.6 years of age, whereas the Japanese cohort's
average age was 22.2 years. Perhaps as a consequence of this age difference (and slightly different recruitment processes), the Russian women
interviewees exhibited greater diversity in occupation/employment,

whereas the Japanese women were generally undergraduate or graduate students pursuing academic degrees. More detailed descriptions of the participants' demographic parameters will be provided in Chap. 3. These differences, however, are not regarded as impugning the validity of the research, as the goal is not to provide a one-to-one comparison, which is a challenging task that can lead to flawed generalizations (Antal, Dierkes, & Weiler, 1996; Vinken, Soeters, & Ester, 2004). Instead, the research gives agency to both Japanese and Russian women and allows them to engage meaningfully with the categories of gender and language that are particular to their respective cultures.

All the participants interviewed for Chap. 3 signed a release form kindly allowing me to use their interviews in this book. To protect the interviewees' anonymity, their real names have been replaced by pseudonyms. Women's faces have also been blurred in the Figures in order to further safeguard their anonymity and privacy.

The interviews were divided into three main segments: (1) a natural (undirected) speech segment, (2) a television commercial discussion, and (3) a question-and-answer session directed by the researcher. During the first segment, participants were asked to communicate on a self-selected topic for approximately five to ten minutes. During the second segment, participants were shown three 15-second commercials and were asked to discuss the advertising, focusing especially on representations of men and women. The Russian-language video clips included an advertisement for a Dove cream in which a man makes flattering remarks about his girlfriend's skin, a commercial for sausages in which women receive help from men in exchange for cooking, and an advertisement for a cellular network in which a woman personifies an 'inferior' mobile network, while a man represents the 'superior' advertised network. Japanese women viewed an advertisement of 'Fasio' skin foundation in which a man teaches a woman about beauty, an advertisement for 'Biore' powdered sheets in which a group of girlfriends enjoy their perfect 'feminine skin,' and a 'Fasio' mascara advertisement in which a man beautifies a woman by applying 'cat make-up.' These commercials were selected to engage women's awareness about gender and femininity for the subsequent discussion. After viewing the commercials, the pairs conversed for approximately five–ten minutes about their overall impression of the commercials, the commercials' depictions of women, and the depicted women's language usage. The researcher did not participate in the discussions during this segment of the interview.

In the final segment, I interviewed the pairs of Japanese and Russian participants concerning their visions of ideal womanhood, including the ideal woman's personality and speech, and inquired about the proximity of the interviewees to their own ideals. I also asked follow-up questions on women's actual use of language and modes of behavior in different contexts. This part of the data collection lasted for approximately 20 minutes.

The primary methods of analysis employed for the data in the third chapter include multi-modal analysis and critical discourse analysis (as discussed above), as well as conversation analysis (CA).

In employing multi-modal analysis, I focus on the analysis of language alongside accompanying gestures. I have transcribed these gestures using six categories: gaze, hand and arm gestures, facial expressions (including head movements), leg movements, body positioning, and vocal shifts. The category of 'gaze' is useful in examining where the speaker looked (or did not look) at a certain point in a conversation, and the (real or figurative) objects of discourse that were thereby centered. Hand and arm gestures are similarly analyzed with an emphasis on directionality, such as the use of lifting or stretching movements of the arms to symbolically distance objects of discourse from oneself or to approximate them to oneself. The examined facial expressions include smiling, frowning, laughing, expressions of contempt, and other expressions indicative of various affective states. Examples of 'leg movements' (when visible) include such motions as crossing one's legs and lifting the feet from heels to toes. Within the 'body positioning' category I distinguish between the various physical postures that the speaker may adopt toward the interlocutor, such as leaning toward the interlocutor, withdrawing away from the interlocutor, or leaning to the side without changing the overall distance to the interlocutor. Shifts in vocal characteristics include changes in pitch, intonation, speed, and volume. Examination of the constellation of these non-lexical behaviors holistically allows me to build a more comprehensive understanding of the stances articulated by the participants than would be possible on the basis of their words alone.

The analysis of these non-linguistic cues alongside linguistic devices is especially important when the concept of 'footing' is taken into consideration. Introduced by Goffman (1979b), "footing" focuses on alignments between speakers' sequential utterances. Goffman (1979b) sees some similarities between unscripted acts of communication and theatrical performances, in that each participant, or "actor" occupies a position vis-à-vis other individuals and their assertions, figuratively described as the participant's "footing." These positions are understood through shared knowledge or awareness of sociocultural and narrative frames in which the participants are themselves embedded. Through a variety of linguistic and non-linguistic devices, discourse participants aim to project their stances toward various objects from the vantage point of their footing. To fully explain themselves, however, they sometimes need to 'change footing' or to shift the position from which their utterances (and non-verbal behaviors) emanate and the conditions that shape the interpretation of their communicative acts. Often, they may wish to change footing in order to express the perspective of a different person, while clearly marking that the stance thereby expressed is not 'their position.' These changes in alignment can be signaled by alteration in vocal or physical characteristics, and thus allow speakers not merely to represent themselves but also to animate the roles of other individuals in the course of a single conversation. For example, a speaker may first express her feelings regarding a specific situation, and then shift footing in order to narrate from the perspective of 'an ideal woman,' or in order to present the 'typical utterance of a man.' Our complex identity-expression frequently necessitates the use of multiple personas to explicate (or even intentionally destabilize) our positioning. This is especially true in the third chapter, wherein women attempt to articulate their views on very heterogeneous categories such as 'men' and 'women.' Merely utilizing their voice seems insufficient to describe the many properties these categories dynamically encompass and imply. Thus, women frequently change footing to depict the characteristics or behavior of women and men, thereby signaling, for example, which are normative, which are sincere, and which are duplicitous. The concept of footing is thus helpful in tracking these shifts of alignment both between speakers and within a speaker's self-positioning, and the process of locating these shifts is crucial to decoding the meaning of women's utterances and the identities that they aim to negotiate.

In addition to multi-modal analyses informed by the concept of footing, Chap. 3 also involves the use of critical discourse analysis in a fashion similar to Chap. 2, engaging not with language in isolation but with the meaning of various utterances situated in the context of Japanese and Russian societies. For example, when women use various culture-specific expressions to describe women's behavior, it is essential to unpack the implications of these expressions and the structures and relations of power on which these expressions rely.

Conversation analysis (CA), with its rigorous transcription methodology, helpfully supplements the above methods in the analysis of data in Chap. 3. CA is especially useful for close examination of linguistic and non-linguistic cues involved in conversations, and in the concomitant construction of meaning by the participants (Schegloff, 1997). The clear differentiation of turn-taking pauses within and between utterances, utterance of co-constructions, and interruptions are valuable implements for understanding the nuances in speaker's stances toward various categories and each other.

In Chap. 4, I use corpus analysis as my primary tool to investigate women's appropriations of 'male language' (i.e. language traditionally associated with men and masculinity) in spoken, in-person conversations, and in online blogs. In particular, the study uses the sub-corpus of spontaneous conversations in the National Corpus of Spoken Russian in order to examine women's use of "obscene" emphatic markers, which are traditionally linked to the male language domain (e.g. Zemskaja et al., 1993) and understood as antithetical to ideals of feminine beauty. For the Japanese data, the blog corpus "Goo Burogu" was selected in order to analyze women's use of the conventionally male sentence-final particles *zo* and *ze* (e.g. Miura & McGloin, 2008).

I utilize the aforementioned Antconc software (Anthony, 2014) to calculate the number of the sentence-final particles *zo* and *ze* used by Japanese female and male writers in the compiled Japanese corpora of blogs. In case of Russian swearwords, I used the tools available in the National Corpus of Spoken Russian to calculate the number of specific swearwords used by female and male speakers. Subsequently, I use a chi-squared test to determine whether the difference in use of these language features between male and female writers is statistically significant.

As noted above, the Japanese and Russian corpora are not identical in content or modality. However, dissimilarities in the Japanese and Russian corpora do not substantively obstruct the research goals, because the present study does not intend to make exact intercultural comparisons of strictly identical or isomorphic discourses (a task which, when comparing disparate cultures, is never truly feasible in any case). Instead, it aims to observe and explore women's appropriation of traditionally male linguistic resources using the most representative and suitable data available in each language. In Russian, paradigmatically masculine speech is characterized predominantly by the use of profanities. However, the use of profanities in both formal and informal Russian writing is quite rare, as these lexical items are deemed socially inappropriate and especially impolite in written communication. Thus, women's appropriation of male language in Russian can only practically be studied in corpora of spoken language. By contrast, in Japanese gendered expressions (such as various types of 'male language') are encoded through particles that are used in both spoken language and in certain forms of written language. However, because these particles are strongly tied to a specific kind of coarse masculinity, they are very rare in speech (Shibuya, 2004; Sturtz Sreetharan, 2004). Blogs, however, are replete with male sentence-final particles, and can therefore enhance our understanding of the phenomenon by providing a variety of contextual examples.

Before concluding this introductory chapter, I would like to offer a brief note on terminology employed throughout the book. I shall often have recourse to the words 'male' and 'female' as adjectives (e.g. 'female interviewees', 'male interlocutors'). I do not mean, in using these terms, to suggest or to imply a biological or innate sex, as opposed to a socially constructed gender category. I simply use these terms to denote individuals that identify as women or men (or fictional characters that are identified as men or women in ideological depictions). Similarly, I shall use such constructions as 'male language' to indicate language traditionally or ideologically associated with men as opposed to women. When I wish to refer to the construction of categories or concepts related to gender ideology (rather than merely denote individuals, lexical items, etc. associated with a gender), I shall use terms such as 'feminine' and 'masculine.'

1.11 Summary

This book offers an analysis of language use by (and about) women and feminine beauty in two very different contemporary cultures, both of which have undergone considerable socio-economic changes impacting the role of women in the workforce and in the home. Unequal power and asymmetric gender roles shape ideology and language use in both Russian and Japanese societies, but it is the contention of this study that language also shapes, refines, and challenges both ideological conceptions and the material circumstances with which they are linked. The following analysis thus traces one aspect of the co-constitutive relationship linking language to women's subordination and empowerment. In so doing, it is avowedly committed to and informed by feminist and constructionist perspectives on gender, identity, and sexuality. These approaches help the reader to see the extraordinary power of media to shape and condition women's language, values, and self-perceptions related to beauty. However, they also help to uncover heterogeneity in women's responses to these pressures, and various ways in which women subvert and challenge traditional expectations regarding language use. This book thus offers deep immersion into both the ideals and the actual linguistic practices of young women, as they shape their identities through negotiation and conflict with the gender norms prevalent in their language and society.

References

Abe, H. (2010). *Queer Japanese: Gender and sexual identities through linguistic practices*. London: Palgrave Macmillan.

Allison, A. (2006). Cuteness as Japan's millennial product. In T. Joseph (Ed.), *Pikachuu's global adventure: The rise and fall of Pokemon* (pp. 34–49). Durham, NC: Duke University Press.

Antal, A. B., Dierkes, M., & Weiler, H. N. (1996). Cross-national policy research: Traditions, achievements, and challenges. In A. Inkeles & M. Sasaki (Eds.), *Comparing nations and cultures*. Upper Saddle River, NJ: Prentice Hall.

Anthony, L. (2014). AntConc (Version 3.4.4) [Computer Software]. Tokyo: Waseda University. Retrieved from http://www.laurenceanthony.net/software/

Anthony, L. (2017). Corpus linguistics and vocabulary: A commentary on four studies. *Vocabulary Learning and Instruction, 6*(2), 79–87.

Arima, A. (2003). Gender stereotypes in Japanese television advertisements. *Sex Roles, 49*, 81–90.

Asano, C. (1996). *Onna wa naze yaseyoo to suru no ka: Sesshoku shoogai to gendaa* [Why do women try to lose weight? Eating disorders and gender]. Tokyo: Keiso.

Asano-Cavanagh, Y. (2014). Linguistic manifestation of gender reinforcement through the use of the Japanese term *kawaii*. *Gender and Language, 8*(3), 341–359.

Austin, J. L. (1975). *How to do things with words*. Oxford: Oxford University Press.

Baxter, J. (2008). Feminist post-structuralist discourse analysis: A new theoretical and methodological approach? In K. Harrington, L. Litosseliti, H. Sauntson, & J. Sunderland (Eds.), *Gender and language research methodologies*. Basingstoke: Palgrave Macmillan.

Biber, D., Conrad, S., & Reppen, R. (1998). *Corpus linguistics: Investigating language structure and use*. Cambridge: Cambridge University Press.

Block, D., & Corona, V. (2014). Exploring class-based intersectionality. *Language, Culture and Curriculum, 27*(1), 27–42.

Bodine, A. (1975). Sex differentiation in language. In B. Thorne & N. Henley (Eds.), *Language and sex: Difference and dominance* (pp. 130–151). Rowley, MA: Newbury House.

Bucholtz, M. (2009). From stance to style: Gender, interaction, and indexicality in Mexican immigrant youth slang. In A. Jaffe (Ed.), *Stance: Sociolinguistic perspectives* (pp. 147–170). Oxford: Oxford University Press.

Bucholtz, M. (2014). The feminist foundations of language, gender, and sexuality research. In S. Ehrlich, M. Meyerhoff, & J. Holmes (Eds.), *The handbook of language, gender, and sexuality* (pp. 23–48). Chichester, West Sussex: Wiley-Blackwell.

Burdelski, M., & Mitsuhashi, K. (2010). 'She thinks you're *Kawaii*': Socializing affect, gender, and relationships in a Japanese preschool. *Language in Society, 39*(1), 65–93.

Butler, J. (1990). *Gender trouble: Feminism and the subversion of identity*. New York: Routledge.

Butler, J. (2004). *Undoing gender*. New York: Routledge.

Butler, J. (2006). *Gender trouble: Feminism and the subversion of identity*. New York: Routledge.

Charlebois, J. (2014). *Japanese femininities*. New York: Routledge.

Clancy, P. M. (1999). The socialization of affect in Japanese mother-child conversation. *Journal of Pragmatics, 31*, 397–421.

Coates, J. (2004). *Women, men, and language: A sociolinguistic account of gender differences in language*. Harlow: Pearson Longman.

Coates, J., & Pichler, P. (2011). *Language and gender: A reader*. Chichester, West Sussex: Wiley-Blackwell.

Crenshaw, K. (1991). Mapping the margins: Intersectionality, identity politics, and violence against women of color. *Stanford Law Review, 43*(6), 1241–1299.

Endo, O. (2004). Women and words: The status of sexist language in Japan as seen through contemporary dictionary definitions and media discourse. In S. Okamoto & J. S. Shibamoto Smith (Eds.), *Japanese language, gender, and ideology: Cultural models and real people* (pp. 166–186). New York: Oxford University Press.

Fairclough, N. (1992a). *Discourse and social change*. Cambridge: Polity Press.

Fairclough, N. (1992b). Discourse and text: Linguistic and intertextual analysis within discourse analysis. *Discourse and Society, 3*(2), 193–217.

Foucault, M. (1991). Questions of method. In M. Foucault, G. Burchell, C. Gordon, & P. Miller (Eds.), *The Foucault effect: Studies in governmentality: With two lectures by and an interview with Michel Foucault*. Chicago: University of Chicago Press.

Gauntlett, D. (2008). *Media, gender and identity: An introduction* (2nd ed.). London and New York: Routledge.

Global Gender Gap Report of the Economic World Forum. (2018). Retrieved from http://reports.weforum.org/global-gender-gap-report-2018/

Goffman, E. (1979a). *Gender advertisements*. New York: Harper and Row.

Goffman, E. (1979b). Footing. *Semiotica, 5*(1–2), 1–30.

Gottfried, H. (2003). Tempting bodies: Shaping gender at work in Japan. *Sociology, 37*(2), 257–276.

Gottlieb, N. (2005). *Linguistic stereotyping and minority groups in Japan*. New York: Routledge.

Halliday, M. (1985). *An introduction to functional grammar*. London: Edward Arnold.

Harris, P. R., & Stobart, J. (1986). Sex-role stereotyping in British television advertisements at different times of the day: An extension and refinement of Manstead and McCulloch (1981). *British Journal of Social Psychology, 25*, 155–164.

Hawkins, S., & Hoch, S. (1992). Low-involvement learning: Memory without evaluation. *Journal of Consumer Research, 19*(2), 212–225.

Ide, S. (1980). Language of inferiority and luxury: A sociolinguistic interpretation of Japanese women's language. *Studies in English and American Literature, 15*, 215–226.

Ide, S. (1990). How and why do women speak more politely in Japanese? In S. Ide & N. H. McGloin (Eds.), *Aspects of Japanese women's language* (pp. 63–79). Tokyo: Kurosio.

Ide, S. (1992). Gender and function of language use: Quantitative and qualitative evidence from Japanese. *Pragmatics and Language Learning, 3*, 117–129.

Inoue, M. (1994). Gender and linguistic modernization: Historicizing Japanese women's language. In M. Bucholtz, A. C. Liang, L. A. Sutton, & C. Hines (Eds.), *Cultural performances: Proceedings of the third Berkeley women and language conference* (pp. 322–343). Berkeley: Berkeley Women and Language Group.

Inoue, M. (2006). *Vicarious language: Gender and linguistic modernity in Japan.* Berkeley: University of California Press.

Johnson, E. (2017a). *Dreaming of a mail-order husband: Russian-American internet romance.* Durham: Duke University Press.

Johnson, J. E. (2017b). Contesting violence, contesting gender: Crisis centers encountering local governments in Barnaul, Russia. In J. E. Johnson & J. C. Robinson (Eds.), *Living gender after communism* (pp. 40–62). Bloomington: Indiana University Press.

Johnson, J. E., & Robinson, J. C. (2007). Living gender. In J. E. Johnson & J. C. Robinson (Eds.), *Living gender after communism* (pp. 1–24). Bloomington: Indiana University Press.

Jugaku, A. (1979). *Nihongo to onna.* Tokyo: Iwanami Shoten.

Kang, M. E. (1997). The portrayal of women's images in magazine advertisements: Goffman's gender analysis revisited. *Sex Roles, 37*, 979–997.

Kay, R. (1997). Images of an ideal woman: Perceptions of Russian womanhood through the media, education and women's own eyes. In M. Buckley (Ed.), *Post-Soviet women: From the Baltic to Central Asia* (pp. 77–98). Cambridge: Cambridge University Press.

Kay, R. (2006). *Men in contemporary Russia: the fallen heroes of post-Soviet change?* Aldershot, England: Ashgate.

Kiesling, S. F. (2009). Style as stance. In A. Jaffe (Ed.), *Stance: Sociolinguistic perspectives* (pp. 171–194). Oxford: Oxford University Press.

Kindaichi, K. (1942). *Kokugo kenkyuu* [A study of the national language]. Tokyo: Yagumo shorin.

Kinsella, S. (1995). Cuties in Japan. In L. Skov & B. Moeran (Eds.), *Women, media and consumption in Japan* (pp. 220–255). Honolulu: University of Hawai'i Press.

Kinsui, S. (2003). *Wacharu nihongo: yakuwari go no nazo* [Virtual Japanese: Mystery of role language]. Tokyo: Iwanamishoten.

Kovarsky, G. (2008). Learning how to look: Nastasia Filippovna in "The Idiot". In H. Hoogenboom, C. T. Nepomnyashchy, I. Reyfman, & M. Ledkovskaja-Astman (Eds.), *Mapping the feminine: Russian women and cultural difference* (pp. 51–70). Bloomington, Indiana: Slavica.

Kozlova, N. (2000). *Ženskij motiv* [Women's motif]. In A. Al'čuk (Ed.), *Ženščina i vizual'nye znaki* (pp. 19–30). Moscow: Ideja press.

Lakoff, R. T. (1975). *Language and woman's place.* New York: Harper & Row.

Lakoff, R. T. (2003). Language, gender, and politics: Putting 'women' and 'power' in the same sentence. In J. Holmes & M. Meyerhoff (Eds.), *The handbook of language and gender* (pp. 161–179). Malden, MA: Blackwell Publishing.

Lanis, K., & Covell, K. (1995). Images of women in advertisements: Effects on attitudes related to sexual aggression. *Sex Roles, 32,* 639–649.

Lazar, M. M. (2014). feminist critical discourse analysis: Relevance for current gender and language research. In S. Ehrlich, M. Meyerhoff, & J. Holmes (Eds.), *The handbook of language, gender, and sexuality* (pp. 180–199). Hoboken: Wiley-Blackwell.

Lebra, T. (1984). *Japanese women: Constraint and fulfillment.* Honolulu: University of Hawaii Press.

Levinson, A. (2000). Ženščina kak tsel' i kak sredstvo v otečestvennoj reklame [A woman as a goal and a means in Russian advertising]. In A. Al'čuk (Ed.), *Ženščina i vizual'nye znaki* (pp. 43–65). Moscow: Ideja press.

Lindner, K. (2004). Images of women in general interest and fashion magazine advertisements from 1955 to 2002. *Sex Roles, 51,* 409–421.

Lipovskaja, O. (1994). The mythology of womanhood in contemporary 'Soviet' culture. In A. Posadskaja (Ed.), *Women in Russia: A new era in Russian feminism.* New York: Verso.

Lipovskaja, O. (1997). Women's groups in Russia. In M. Buckley (Ed.), *Post-Soviet women: From the Baltic to Central Asia* (pp. 186–200). Cambridge: Cambridge University Press.

Lyon, T. (2007). Housewife fantasies, family realities in the New Russia. In J. Johnson & J. Robinson (Eds.), *Living gender after communism* (pp. 25–39). Bloomington: Indiana University Press.

Matsumoto, Y. (2004). Alternative femininity: Personae of middle-aged mothers. In S. Okamoto & J. S. Shibamoto Smith (Eds.), *Japanese language, gender, and ideology: Cultural models and real people* (pp. 240–256). New York: Oxford University Press.

McKay, N. J., & Covell, K. (1997). The impact of women in advertisements on attitudes toward women. *Sex Roles, 36*, 573–583.

Mcveigh, B. (1996). Cultivating "femininity" and "internationalism": Rituals and routine at a Japanese women's junior college. *Ethos, 24*(2), 314–349.

Miller, L. (2004). You are doing *burikko*! In S. Okamoto & J. S. Shibamoto Smith (Eds.), *Japanese language, gender, and ideology: Cultural models and real people* (pp. 148–165). New York: Oxford University Press.

Miura, A., & McGloin, N. H. (2008). *An integrated approach to intermediate Japanese*. Tokyo: Japan Times.

Morris, I. (1991). *The pillow book of Sei Shônagon*. New York: Columbia University Press.

Mulvey, L. (1999). Visual pleasure and narrative cinema. In L. Braudy & M. Cohen (Eds.), *Film theory and criticism: Introductory readings* (pp. 833–844). New York: Oxford University Press.

Nakamura, M. (1995). *Kotoba to feminizumu* [Language and feminism]. Tokyo: Keiso Shobo.

Nakamura, M. (2001). *Kotoba to jendaa* [Language and gender]. Tokyo: Keiso Shobo.

Nakamura, M. (2004). "Let's dress a little girlishly!" or "Conquer short pants!" Constructing gendered communities in fashion magazine for young people. In S. Okamoto & J. S. Shibamoto Smith (Eds.), *Japanese language, gender, and ideology: Cultural models and real people* (pp. 131–148). New York: Oxford University Press.

Nakamura, M. (2014). *Gender, language and ideology: A genealogy of Japanese women's language*. Amsterdam: John Benjamins Publishing Company.

Ochs, E. (1992). Indexing gender. In A. Duranti & C. Goodwin (Eds.), *Rethinking context: Language as an interactive phenomenon* (pp. 335–358). Cambridge: Cambridge University Press.

Ohara, Y. (1992). Gender-dependent pitch levels: A comparative study in Japanese and English. In K. Hall, M. Bucholtz, & B. Moonwomon (Eds.), *Locating power: Proceedings of the second Berkley women and language conference* (pp. 469–477). Berkley: Berkeley Women and Language Group.

Okamoto, S. (1995). "Tasteless" Japanese: Less "feminine" speech among young Japanese women. In K. Hall & M. Bucholtz (Eds.), *Gender articulated: Language and the socially constructed self* (pp. 297–325). New York: Routledge.

Okamoto, S. (2004). Ideology in linguistic practice and analysis: Gender and politeness in Japanese revisited. In S. Okamoto & J. S. Shibamoto Smith (Eds.), *Japanese language, gender, and ideology: Cultural models and real people* (pp. 38–57). New York: Oxford University Press.

Okamoto, S., & Shibamoto Smith, J. (2004). *Japanese language, gender, and ideology: Cultural models and real people.* New York: Oxford University Press.

Okazaki, M., & Johnson, G. (2013). *Kawaii!: Japan's culture of cute.* Munich: Prestel.

Reyfman, I. (2008). Vision and revision. Female voice and male gaze in Leo Tolstoy's 'Family Happiness'. In H. Hoogenboom, C. T. Nepomnyashchy, I. Reyfman, & M. Ledkovskaja-Astman (Eds.), *Mapping the feminine: Russian women and cultural difference* (pp. 29–50). Bloomington, Indiana: Slavica.

Reynolds-Akiba, K. (1993). Gengo no seesa no kenkyuu [The study of sex differences in language]. *Nihongogaku, 12*(5), 224–234.

Richie, D., & Garner, R. (2003). *The image factory: Fads and fashions in Japan.* London: Reaktion.

Schegloff, E. A. (1997). Whose text? Whose context? *Discourse and Society, 8*(2), 165–187.

Schippers, M. (2007). Recovering the feminine other: Masculinity, femininity, and gender hegemony. *Theory & Society, 36,* 85–102.

Shevchenko, I. (2007). Does the gender of MPs matter in postcommunist politics? The case of the Russian Duma, 1995–2001. In J. Johnson & J. Robinson (Eds.), *Living gender after communism* (pp. 128–148). Bloomington: Indiana University Press.

Shibuya, R. (2004). *A synchronic and diachronic study on sex exclusive differences in modern Japanese language.* Doctoral dissertation, University of California, Los Angeles.

Spender, D. (1980). *Man made language.* London: Routledge & Kegan Paul.

Stella, F. (2015). *Lesbian lives in Soviet and post-Soviet Russia.* London: Palgrave Macmillan.

Sturtz Sreetharan, C. (2004). Japanese men's linguistic stereotypes and realities: Conversations from Kansai and Kanto regions. In S. Okamoto & J. S. Shibamoto Smith (Eds.), *Japanese language, gender, and ideology: Cultural models and real people* (pp. 275–290). New York: Oxford University Press.

Tamanoi, M. (1990). Women's voices: Their critique of the anthropology of Japan. *Annual Review Anthropology, 19,* 17–37.

Tannen, D. (1990). *You just don't understand: Women and men in conversation.* New York: Ballantine.

Tomomatsu, H. (1994). Jidoo no kotoba no jikohyooka: kodomo wa 'kawaii' ka? [Child language and self-evaluation: Are children kawaii?]. *Nihon hoi-*

kugakkai taikai happyooronbun shooroku [Proceedings of the Japan Childcare Conference], *47*, 90–100.

Turkina, O. (2000). Pip-šou (idioadaptatsija obraza ženščiny v rossijskoj reklame) [Peep-show (ideological adaptation of a woman's image in Russian advertisement)]. In A. Al'čuk (Ed.), *Ženščina i vizual'nye znaki* (pp. 78–86). Moscow: Ideja press.

Vinken, H., Soeters, J., & Ester, P. (2004). *Comparing cultures: Dimensions of culture in a comparative perspective*. Leiden: Brill.

Volkova, I., & Muzychenko, V. (1993). Nastojaščaja ženščina [Real woman]. *Sudarushka*, 27.

Yano, C. R. (2013). *Pink globalization: Hello Kitty's trek across the Pacific*. Durham: Duke University Press.

Yokoyama, O. T. (1999). Russian genderlects and referential expressions. *Language in Society, 28*(3), 401–429.

Yomota, I. (2006) *'Kawaii' ron* [Theory of 'Kawaii']. Tokyo: Tikuma Sinsyo.

Yukawa, Y., & Saito, M. (2004). Cultural ideologies in Japanese language and gender studies: A theoretical review. In S. Okamoto & J. S. Shibamoto Smith (Eds.), *Japanese language, gender, and ideology: Cultural models and real people* (pp. 23–37). New York: Oxford University Press.

Yurchak, A. (2000). Po sledam ženskogo obraza [Following a woman's image]. In A. Al'čuk (Ed.), *Ženščina i vizual'nye znaki* (pp. 65–77). Moscow: Ideja press.

Zemskaja, E. A. (1973). *Russkaja razgovornaja reč'*. Moscow: Nauka.

Zemskaja, E. A., Kitajgorodskaja, M. V., & Rjazanova, N. N. (1993). Osobennosti mužskoj i ženskoj reči [Features of feminine and masculine speech']. In E. A. Zemskaja & D. N. Shmelev (Eds.), *Russkij jazyk v ego funktsionirovanii* (pp. 90–136). Moscow: Nauka.

2

Women's Voices in Russian and Japanese 'Beauty Ads'

2.1 Overview

As noted in the introductory chapter (Chap. 1), the present study pursues a tri-partite investigation of feminine beauty in Russian and Japanese language and culture, as encountered in (1) media-circulated messages regarding women and beauty, (2) women's explicit ideals and the language used to articulate them, and (3) women's own linguistic productions in everyday speech and writing. This first chapter engages with images of women and feminine beauty promulgated by commercial media in the process of advertisement, and attempts to explain and critique the gender ideologies that underlie these images in historical and cultural context. Subsequent chapters will then assess the ways that women absorb, question, and reimagine these gender ideologies in their own thought, language, and action.

In this chapter I closely examine the portrayal of women in 50 Japanese and 50 Russian televised commercials for beauty and hygiene products, aired from 2012 to 2017, with the goal of generating comparative insights. The characteristic feature of such advertising is that it targets female consumers specifically, with the aim of cultivating desires and

© The Author(s) 2020
N. Konstantinovskaia, *The Language of Feminine Beauty in Russian and Japanese Societies*, Palgrave Studies in Language, Gender and Sexuality,
https://doi.org/10.1007/978-3-030-41433-7_2

behaviors oriented toward the pursuit of (culturally appropriate conceptions of) beauty. To explore the representations of women and feminine beauty in these materials, I employ corpus linguistics methods, multi-modal analysis, critical discourse analysis, and feminist post-structuralist discourse analysis. In the course of the analysis, I consider linguistic features that are deliberately employed to express certain types of idealized femininities in Japan and Russia, drawing cross-cultural comparisons and contrasts between these depictions. According to Nakamura's dynamic model of language and gender (2004, p. 135), media messages produce and reproduce gender ideologies by recycling traditional stereotypes and contemporary popular images of femininity. I will argue that Japanese and Russian commercials depict women both as incessantly concerned with their femininity and actively seeking to display it to others. These constructions of feminine beauty involve both questioning and reaffirming the authenticity of one's femininity, through processes that must engage with male desire and approval interactively. I contend that media depictions reflect a synthesis of current gender ideologies with more traditional ideals, alongside token inclusion of 'postfeminist' tropes. By using multi-modal analysis, feminist poststructuralist discourse analysis, and critical discourse analysis, this chapter explores the linguistic mechanisms through which beauty and hygiene products receive a gendered representation for targeted female audiences in Russia and Japan.

First, I aim to identify the dominant voice in Russian and Japanese advertisements, in a rough and heuristic sense, by calculating the number of words that are attributed to men and women, as well as determining the number of televised commercials that do not incorporate male voices at all. While it might seem sensible that female voices would predominate, perspectives and opinions of (or attributed to) male speakers are pervasive in the material analyzed. Next, I investigate the linguistic structures that are commonly used in advertising, such as interrogatives, imperatives, and hortatives (Nakamura, 2004), and identify the most typical lexical patterns. These indices will then be used to further an in-depth examination of the types of femininities that are being created and cultivated in the Russian and Japanese advertising.

2.2   Who Says What in Russian and Japanese 'Beauty Ads'?

Frequency of utterance in media messages regarding beauty and hygiene products is only a very rough index of voicing. Speech can be centered and privileged in discourse without necessarily being prolific. Nevertheless, an assessment of the absolute quantity of utterances by male and female speakers is a useful starting-point for subsequent, more nuanced analysis. Moreover, quantitative assessment of the *types* of utterances deployed by female and male speakers can lay the groundwork for qualitative interpretation of differences in content.

In the Russian commercials the dominant voice was universally female. In total, women uttered 1903 words, while men uttered 450 words. In the 23 commercials incorporating male voice, women uttered significantly more words: 711 words (61%) in comparison to 450 words for men (39%), ($\chi^2(1) = 68.95$, $p < 0.001$), as presented in Fig. 2.1.

On average, women uttered 30.9 words per commercial, while men were allotted only 19.6 words. The primary difference in vocabulary between female and male speakers in the Russian advertisements was the use of interrogative words: Russian women asked 22 questions, while Russian men never did. This portrayal—in which women are depicted as

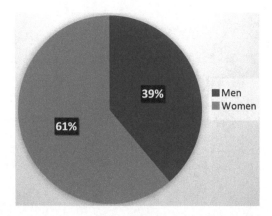

Fig. 2.1   Proportion of words uttered by female and male speakers in Russian televised commercials

questioning, while men are shown providing reliable information in response—relies upon and reinforces the stereotype that women are inquisitive, hesitating, and deficient in knowledge.

In the analyzed Japanese commercials, Japanese women uttered 862 words, while men uttered 709 words. Out of the 50 commercials, 14 commercials did not incorporate male voice in any form. However, in the remaining 36 commercials incorporating male voices, women uttered only 425 words (37 percent) in contrast to 709 words (63 percent) spoken by men, as shown in Fig. 2.2. A chi-squared test confirms that male word-utterances are significantly more frequent than female word-utterances in these mixed-gender advertisements ($\chi^2(1) = 68.95$, $p < 0.001$). In one commercial women did not speak at all, while in many others women uttered only one or two words. On average, Japanese men uttered 19.6 words per mixed-gender commercial, while Japanese women uttered only 11.8 words. Thus, it is not the case that women's voices are systematically excluded from beauty and hygiene ads: as noted above, many ads do not feature the male voice at all. However, when male and female speakers are considered alongside one another, it is male speech that predominates.

This predominance in expression was matched by a complementary priority in content. Japanese men functioned as the primary storytellers, narrating the plot in each mixed-gender advertisement and providing detailed information about the advertised products. Women, in turn, passively

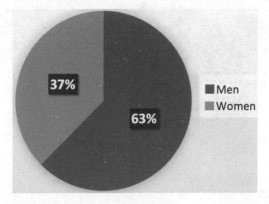

Fig. 2.2 Proportion of words uttered by female and male speakers in Japanese televised commercials

displayed their beauty and their contentment using the product, entrusting male protagonists with the care and cultivation of their appearance. Thus, despite the fact that the advertisements were targeted at female audiences, and promoted products specifically for women, the male voice nevertheless was dominant. The portrayal of women in Japanese advertising thereby conforms to ideals of traditional submissive and subservient femininity, in which women are silenced in public or mixed-gender settings. From the seventeenth century to the modern age, conduct books for Japanese women praised a woman's ability to refrain from "excessive" talkativeness, calling a silent woman "elegant and prudent" (Nakamura, 2014, p. 50).

The type of vocabulary that men and women used in the 50 analyzed commercials also differed considerably. For example, the second most frequent word used by men in the commercials was *kami* 'hair,'—a content word. In contrast, the six most frequently used words by female speakers were function words; only the seventh most frequent word used by female speakers was a content word (also *kami* 'hair'). Among the function words, Japanese women used interactional sentence-final particles more than men. In total, Japanese women uttered 14 particles (ten tokens of *ne*, two tokens of *yo*, one token of *kashira* and one token of *wa*), while men uttered only three sentence-final particles (two tokens of *ne* and one token of *yo*). This difference recapitulates the stereotype that women are more emotional and hesitating than men—inclined to use sentence-final particles aimed at soliciting confirmation, even when talking about themselves—while men are self-confident and thus do not need to use this linguistic strategy. Moreover, Japanese women used politeness suffixes *desu/deshita* and *masu/mashita* much more frequently than men did. Women uttered 23 tokens of the politeness suffixes (or 2.7 percent of all the words uttered by female speakers) in relation to eight tokens uttered by male speakers (or 1.1 percent of all the words pronounced by male speakers). This conforms to the social expectation that women must be more polite than men in order to be perceived as sufficiently polite and respectful as interlocutors (Ide, 1992, p. 119). These findings are summarized in Table 2.1.

Men also function as the primary arbiters of beauty, and thereby of the utility of the advertised products. As seen in the table, men complimented women on their looks using assessment words such as *kirei, utsukushii*, and

Table 2.1 Gender-based distribution of language choices in the Japanese commercials

	Number of tokens (percentage)		
	Women (out of 862)	Men (out of 709)	Proportion test
Sentence-final particles	14 (1.6%)	3 (0.4%)	$\chi^2(1) = 4.18$, $p = 0.040$
Politeness suffixes	23 (2.7%)	8 (1.1%)	$\chi^2(1) = 4.00$, $p = 0.045$
Kirei, utsukushii, byu-tifuru 'beautiful'	0 (0%)	12 (1.7%)	$\chi^2(1) = 12.55$, $p < 0.001$
Tanjyoo 'creation'	1 (0.1%)	11 (1.6%)	$\chi^2(1) = 8.77$, $p = 0.003$

byu-tifuru (all meaning 'beautiful'), while women did not use these terms at all. Thus, men play the role of evaluators of female beauty, explicitly commenting on women's appearance. Lastly, it was predominantly men who announced the *tanjyoo* 'creation' of the new product, reproducing and re-instantiating the stereotype that men are the chief innovators while women do not have intellectual or creative potential. Based upon the corpus analysis, Japanese women are depicted as emotional, polite, docile, and praise-seeking, while men are presented as knowledgeable and dynamic innovators.

The preceding quantitative analysis of Russian and Japanese commercials lays the preliminary foundation for the qualitative analysis to follow, which examines the ways in which linguistic structures and lexical items are manipulated to create various types of idealized femininities. In the remaining sections of the chapter, I will address the linguistic mechanisms that were deliberately used in Russian and Japanese advertisements to project the voice of female consumers.

2.3   Interrogative Structures in Russian Commercials

The majority of the Russian-language commercials commenced with an inquiry regarding the current state of affairs of a female protagonist, highlighting issues that (supposedly) she might be likely to experience as a woman. These portrayals frequently emphasized women's dispositional anxiousness and inability to resolve 'common problems' without the aid of 'an expert' (typically a male figure). The focal issue is thus framed as a 'common problem' that supposedly challenges the fictive audience of female users and the actual population of potential female consumers. The 'problem' is usually posed by a female speaker in voice-over, expressed as a question directed to other female characters in the commercial as well as to female viewers. The speaker inquires in a knowledgeable manner about the 'problem' that women putatively experience, positioning concern for this problem as normative for women generally. Excerpts (1)–(5) demonstrate how the opening questions in the advertisements strategically define the potential gendered audience.

(1)   -*Vy   by   soglasilis' vyiti iz   doma   bez   makijaža?*
       you would agree   leave from house:GEN without makeup:GEN
       'Would you agree to leave your house without makeup?'
       -*Bez   makijaža? Ne   za   što!*
       without makeup   NEG for what
       'Without makeup? Never!'

(2)   *Leto   vysushilo vashi volosy?*
       summer dried   your   hair
       'Summer has made your hair dry?'

(3)   *A   vashe mylo ostavljaet naljot   na kože?*
       and your   soap   leaves   coating on skin:PREP
       'Does your soap leave a coating on your skin?'

(4)   *Hočeš' pritjagivat' vzgljadom?*
       want   attract   look:INST
       'Do you want to attract with your eyes?'

(5)   *Ideal'nye brovi?*
       'Ideal eyebrows?

In context, all the interrogatives above clearly imply that the intended consumer of the products is female. Moreover, as seen from the substance of the questions, it is presumed that all women experience similar problems: inability to go outside without applying makeup, dryness of hair due to summer heat, and dissatisfaction with their soap. The general applicability of such feelings to the majority of women is emphasized through the visual representations of the women characters. For instance, the question presented in (1) above is accompanied by an image of several women congregated together, as if the group represents womanhood as such (or at least a sufficient quorum). The three women are asked if they are willing to go outside of the home without applying makeup, to which the women respond implicitly, 'Without make-up? Never!' Interestingly, however, the spoken response is not articulated by the women themselves but conveyed gesturally: they shrug their shoulders, avert their gaze from the viewer, and smile reservedly. A separate female speaker, through voice-over, interprets their facial expressions and vocalizes the response on behalf of the women.

There are several interesting points to note about this silent response. First, by generalizing women's reactions, the advertisement normalizes women's lack of self-confidence in their appearance as a natural and rea-sonable character trait. The unanimity of the women's non-linguistic cues, alongside the explication of the voice-over, reinforces the perception that the majority of Russian women would and should have similar stances. Having constructed and articulated the problem of female self-doubt, it then provides 'a solution' that would give women the courage to leave the house without make-up. In this way, the importance of beauty and self-monitoring is elevated and standardized through the general-ized use of interrogatives and images of women expressing their emotions non-verbally. Women are portrayed as hesitating, insecure, routinely worried about their appearances, and unable to solve everyday problems. Second, the silence of the women implicates them in such anxious con-cern with the cultivation of beauty, even if they would not explicitly voice their agreement with the framing. The suggestion of this silence is that concern with cultivation of beauty is universal, even if unexpressed, and by extension, this ambition is not something that female viewers can evade. The voice-over speaks not only for the characters but for the puta-tive audience, conveying an understanding of their desire for beauty and the sometimes-hidden barriers to the attainment of this desire. The female viewer is constructed according to a twofold necessity of self-presentation, conveyed by a twofold compact: women agree not to present themselves without make-up, and agree not to verbalize their desire for beauty (and associated anxieties).

A similar generalized use of an interrogative structure is presented in excerpt (2) above ('Summer has made your hair dry?'). This query is framed by a portrayal that emphasizes the importance of collective norms of beauty: a woman is disturbed by her female friend's appearance. The scene presents two women happily greeting each other with an embrace, when suddenly one woman discovers that her friend has dry hair. The woman's dazzling smile is rapidly replaced by an expression of confusion, anxiety, and discomfort, conveyed through both her gaze and accompanying hand gestures. The extent to which her emotional state is transformed by the unsatisfactory condition of her friend's hair demonstrates to viewers the paramount importance of female appearance. Furthermore, the woman's marked shift in stance toward her friend stresses that attributes such as poor hair quality may have consequences for women's interpersonal relationships. Women may be judged by both friends and relatives if they fail to pay sufficient attention to their looks. Having received this helpful admonishment, the friend is presented in the next scene with radiant and smooth hair—after having tried Dove nourishing shampoo. Meanwhile a voice-over encourages female viewers to follow her example in order to avoid social censure for dry hair. The women in contemporary Russian commercials for hygienic products are thus presented as obsessively focused on the value of their physical appearance, monitoring not only their own looks but also the looks of other women, and are constantly concerned with other people's perceptions of their beauty (or lack of it). The necessity of other-centeredness that is reinforced by these commercials will be further discussed in Sect. 2.5.

Even though excerpts (4) and (5) ('Do you want to attract with your eyes?'; 'Ideal eyebrows?') are framed as interrogatives, the queries are rhetorical, presupposing that the answer is apparent to the target audience and universally applicable to all women. Posing rhetorical questions sets the goal and agenda for the advertisement: explicating how a particular product will enhance a woman's appearance and increase her attractiveness, presumably for the opposite gender. The interrogatives are followed by imperatives, urging Russian women to take action to become more beautiful. The portrayal of women as inquisitive and ignorant of crucial information is consistent with the traditional gender stereotype that women are anxious about their looks and deficient in knowledge. In contrast, men in Russian commercials do not appear to be lacking relevant information or lacking confidence about their appearances; instead, advertisements targeted for male audiences merely describe the benefits of the product directly. Russian women, however, are urged to monitor their appearances and strive to be as beautiful as possible, with the suggestion that beauty is imperative in order to maintain successful friendships and relationships, as well as to be confident and emotionally healthy. Through the women's anxious voices and behaviors, female viewers are encouraged to take initiative in their appearances, thus engaging traditional feminine stereotypes and appealing to the female agency at the same time. In this way, Russian commercials offer women autonomy in only a restrictive sense: they are permitted to solve problems that have been constructed for them by advertisers based upon the normative expectations of traditional gender ideology.

Some commercials incorporated the use of 'troubled' self-directed voice that accomplished the same function as the interrogative structures: conveying women's anxiousness and unsettled feelings. For example, in a shampoo commercial for the Russian brand *Čistaja linija* 'Pure line,' a woman looks in the mirror and notices that her hair resembles a bouquet of straw in her room. Alarmed, she approaches the mirror and examines her dry hair. Her internal monologue is presented by voice-over: *moi volosy stali suhimi i lomkimi* 'My hair became dry and breakable.' Her concerned inner voice, the disheveled appearance of her hair, her inquisitive self-touch, and the worried gaze she levels at her reflection, all combine to leave the viewer with no doubt that the woman is dissatisfied with her appearance. She does not speak overtly in the commercial, but conveys her stance implicitly through her internal monologue and non-linguistic cues. After using the advertised product, we see a very different image of the woman. She is no longer looking at herself in the mirror, but gazing directly and confidently at the viewer, projecting radiance and happiness. The endogenous nature of this cycle of problem, desire, and fulfillment is worth noting. It is the inner nature of women, according to Russian beauty advertisements, to be concerned with their external appearance. A short circuit is thus achieved between the expectations of others and satisfaction with the self: the interior space of female desire is characterized as other-centric and externally oriented.

In this way, Russian commercials elevate the importance of physical appearances for women by suggesting that there is a strong correlation between a woman's emotional state and her external attractiveness. Women are portrayed as insecure and unconfident when their appearance falls short of the ideal, and are restored to happiness and fulfillment only when they achieve the desired beauty. In addition, the advertisements stress the necessity for women to engage in constant self-monitoring, looking at the physical and social mirrors in their environment to assess whether they measure up. It is women themselves or their female friends who notice appearance-related issues, while men tend to appear later in the commercials to emphasize a woman's successful transformation. In this way, while the direct role of the heterosexual male gaze (Mulvey, 1999) is subdued, it is nevertheless the end goal toward which women's self-improvement and concomitant economic consumption is oriented.

2.4   Imperative Structures in Russian Commercials

Russian advertisements also depend crucially on the strategic deployment of imperative constructions aimed at viewers. Imperative structures tend to occur at the end of the commercials, often as a closing statement aimed at convincing women to purchase the product.

For instance, at the end of a Dove hair shampoo commercial, a female voice-over says encouragingly, *Ne bojtes' menjatsja. Dove pozabotitsja o vashih volosah* 'Do not be afraid to change. Dove will take care of your hair.' These types of *fear*-derivative words were a common lexical item in the Russian advertisements. In the same commercial, this tactic was used earlier when the narrator insists, *S Dove možno ne bojatsa povreždenij* 'With Dove you do not need to be afraid of damage.' In this way, women are depicted as fearful of novelties and needing confirmation from an expert in order to assure them of the safety of new endeavors—even if the novelty is merely trying a new shampoo or a new soap. The interaction between female viewers of the commercials and a female authority figure thus forms a ranked or status-dependent relationship. The figure of female authority in the commercial frequently directs and supports women in their insecurities, supplements their knowledge with her expertise and provides comfort. However, this fictional, high-status female authority also carries a regulatory force, reminding women of the gender-based expectations to which they must conform.

At times, the direct instructions and explanations given to the female audience can appear condescending. For example, after dramatizing an experiment in which Dove soap is compared to an ordinary glycerin soap, a female authority states, *Esli daže eto ne smoglo vas ubediť, togda ja ne znaju, čto smožet* ('If even that could not convince you, then I don't know what can.') The intensifying adverb *daže* 'even' here is used to emphasize the ridiculous nature of a woman who would not believe the undeniably transparent evidence of the benefits of Dove soap. At the conclusion of the commercial (after the experiment comparing Dove soap to the alternative soap has been completed), the female authority encourages women to try the product themselves and directs women to purchase the soap as soon as possible, as seen in excerpt (6).

(6)   *Počuvstvujte raznitsu   sami.* (…)   *Nu   idite,   idite.*
        Feel   difference selves   well go:IMP go:IMP
        'Feel the difference by yourself. (…) Well, go, go.'

The hierarchical relationship between the female authority-figure in the commercial and the potential consumers is conveyed through the repetitive use of the imperative form *idite* 'go' and the interjection *nu* 'well' aimed at urging women to sample the new Dove product. It is also emphasized through the use of hand gestures paired with a gentle, encouraging smile, which serves to mitigate the potentially rude and offensive nature of her command. When telling women to go to the store and to purchase the product, the authority-figure lifts her arms and gestures with her palms. The content and presentation of the message, combined with the non-linguistic devices deployed, helps the authority-figure to convey a strong epistemic stance of superiority. Her bathrobe outfit (unnecessary for testing a hand soap) and her amiable smile portray her as a friendly and approachable expert. Though the female authority-figure in this commercial possesses some knowledge of the product, she can hardly be described as a scientist or a scholar. Her utilization of imperatives when paired with her appearance and facial gestures lean heavily on her feminine characteristics, conveying her closeness to the female consumers. It is possible for her to give direct imperatives to women and blame them for indecisiveness precisely because she is an in-group member and thereby possesses the same concerns as the audience. In this way, an 'insider' is used to subordinate women's judgment to that of the advertisers, treating the viewers as hesitating, slow to grasp information, and lacking in knowledge and good judgment. Interestingly, there are no commercials in the analyzed Russian corpus in which male actors use imperatives. Having a male authority-figure urge women to purchase the advertised products using imperative constructions might make him appear excessively arrogant and patronizing. Thus, men do not need to utilize strong language to sound persuasive, while women have to put in additional effort (Ide, 1992). If a male authority-figure were to emphasize female insecurity and ignorance, his evaluations and suggestions might be rejected by viewers; however, patriarchal suppositions of female inferiority are successfully inserted into the dialectical structure of the advertisement through the use of a gender-conforming female authority. Viewers are implicitly encouraged to abandon their own deliberative thinking and follow the judgment of the (fictional) female role model provided in the advertisement.

Imperatives presented in excerpts (7)–(9) also overtly encourage female viewers to perform certain actions to improve their looks.

(7)   *Podarite volosam   v   tri   raza bol'she pitanija.*
       give   hair:DAT in three times more   nutrition

       'Give your hair a present of three times more nutrition.'

(8)   *Bud'te prekrasny každyi den' vmeste   s   Dove.*
       be   beautiful every   day   together with Dove

       'Be beautiful each day with Dove.'

(9)   *Podarite sebe   voshititel'nyi uhod s   krem-gelem dlja dusha Dove*
       give   self:DAT entrancing   care with cream-gel   for shower Dove
       Naslajdenie i   Zabota."
       enjoyment   and care

       'Give yourself a present of delightful treatment with shower cream-
       gel Dove
       "Enjoyment and Care."'

Excerpts (7), (8), and (9) show that Russian advertisements explicitly urge women to look beautiful and attractive by treating and pampering their bodies with hygiene products. They stress that beauty is an attribute that is essential for women 'each day,' and that it can easily be bought as a present for oneself. Furthermore, while imperative constructions are quite common in Russian commercials for female hygiene and cosmetic products, they are entirely absent in advertising for male audiences. In the set of 20 commercials of products for men, imperative structures were never used, while almost all of the 50 commercials targeting women used imperatives, often repeatedly. Thus, unlike the commercials for men (which foster a more egalitarian relationship with the viewer), commercials for women display pronounced hierarchy. The assumption in the commercials is that women, in contrast to men, are (1) not averse to receiving direct advice in the form of imperatives, and (2) are perfectly content to subordinate their autonomy to others' judgment if beauty is the end result. This constructs the female audience as cooperative and compliant, yet also hesitating and advice-seeking. Furthermore, the roles that women play in the commercials are limited to the 'suffering women' before the use of the product, the 'rejoicing women' after product use, and the 'expert women' or authority-figures who explain the benefits of the product and persuade other (lesser) women to purchase it. Women rarely, if ever, appear as innovative scholars or professionals, while these empowering depictions are common in commercials for men.

The lack of the imperatives in the commercials for Russian men is consistent with the stereotype that men intensely dislike being told what to do and prefer to make autonomous decisions (Connell, 1995). Thus, it is necessary for the advertisements to construct male consumers as strong and successful individuals who can benefit from the use of the product, while avoiding threatening imperatives. Shampoo commercials for men tend to conclude with phrases specifying the type of men who would prefer the advertised product, such as *Shampun' dlja mužčin, gotovyh pobeždat'* 'a shampoo for the men who are ready to win,' or *Sport Max dlja nastojaščih mužčin* 'Sport Max (shampoo name) for real men.' In this way, the commercials targeting men provide images of success and positivity, highlighting the self-enhancing benefits of the product. A male viewer is never compelled or urged directly to purchase the advertised item, but is granted the freedom to do so, presuming that he will make the right choice. If any negative evaluation is present, it is in the implicit suggestion that a man who does *not* purchase the product is not 'ready to win' or a 'real man.' The failure of the male viewer to live up to the explicitly articulated ideal of true manhood is thereby transferred to his own impotence and his own choice. In this way, advertisements exploit both traditional images of female insecurity and male autonomy in order to manipulate both genders.

2.5 The Heterosexual Male Gaze, Self-Commodification, and Feminine Beauty in Russian Commercials

While Russian commercials for women stress the importance of taking the initiative to be beautiful, the effectiveness of women's action in pursuit of beauty is universally evaluated through positive feedback from others (often men). These others include male partners, husbands, and 'men in the street' as well as women's children and other family members and friends; all are inserted into the commercials to underline women's success at achieving beauty. In this section, I will refer to these people collectively as the third party. They are often not a central component of the fictive dialogue between advertiser and audience, but are selectively recruited as the external context that defines the desire or problem for which the product is advanced as a solution or remedy. In some commercials, female speakers explicitly note the increased level of interest from the third party associated with their use of the product, while in other advertisements the third party expresses admiration verbally, affectively, or through gesture. For instance, in excerpt (10) a Russian woman reflects on her experience using a new Dove soap, conveying the improved attitude of her husband and children.

(10)   *Mne kažetsa, što ja stala   bol'še nravit'sa svojemu mužu   i   detjam.*
I:DAT seem that I became more like   self   husband and children
'It seems to me that my husband and children started to like me more.'

On the one hand, the woman in (10) conveys confidence in her looks. On the other hand, this confidence is achieved through the appreciation of her by others (contingent on her use of the advertised product). Her utterance presupposes that a major concern for Russian women is to find ways to make their kids and husbands love them more. The woman in the commercial provides a suggestion on how to resolve this problem by recommending the use of Dove soap. Thus, women are depicted as caring about their appearances not principally for their own satisfaction, but rather from a desire to appear beautiful for their husbands and to be adored by their children. They monitor themselves for the sake of the third party and his desire, and are also monitored by the third party directly as the final arbiter of whether they succeed or fail in the pursuit of beauty.

This sentiment is especially prominent in the lotion commercial that presents a man describing his girlfriend's skin, utterly convinced that she must have a secret that helps make her skin especially soft. Although he is unable to formulate exactly what that secret is, he stresses that he loves it a lot. The commercial is then followed by a female voice-over appealing to the audience, presented in excerpt (11).

(11)   *Slyšite, emu   nravitsa, čto vy   uhažyvaete za   kožej s los'jonom*
dlja tela Dove.
Listen   he:DAT like   that you care   after skin with
lotion   for body Dove
Uhaživaete za soboj každyj den' i   naslaždajtes' ego vnimaniem.
care   after self   every day   and enjoy   his attention

'Listen, he likes that you pamper your skin with the skin lotion Dove. Take care of yourself every day and enjoy his attention.'

The advertisement concludes with the man saying *Očen' ljublju tselovat' ejo s golovy do nog* 'I really love kissing her from head to toes,' reinforcing the effectiveness of the product. The commercial thus emphasizes both the importance and fragility of female beauty; it is a powerful influence on others but only effective if maintained properly. As a result, women are portrayed as constantly needing to appear physically attractive in order to receive male attention, which is presented as a crucial component of women's happiness. As noted above, by imputing other-centered motivations to women as innate, internal concerns, the ideological positioning of this advertisement creates a direct link between interiority and exteriority. The commercial does offer the woman limited autonomy in the retention of her 'secret,' which gives her control of male desire and leverage over his affection. However, the content of her autonomous feminine power does not stem (as in some traditional gender ideologies) from her character or her purity or her wisdom—in this instance it is reduced to a skin cream.

Through the insertion of the third party, Russian commercials manipulate depictions of feminine confidence, cultivating the illusory image of an accomplished woman capable of attracting and sustaining men's attention. For example, in a commercial for Nivea cream, a woman is shown successfully acquiring (and enjoying) the heterosexual male gaze after application of the advertised cream. Indeed, the man is so impressed with the woman's appearance that he quickly purchases flowers for her as a demonstration of his love. She revels in this attention and the concomitant boost to her self-confidence, playfully winking at the hypothetical viewer in order to share her success.

Interestingly, the woman is shown in the midst of a daily commute to work by car, adding to the impression that she is 'in charge' of both personal and professional outcomes. Nevertheless, the male interruption of her commute to work is both encouraged and appreciated; the solicitation of his desire is prioritized over whatever professional attainments she might be on the way toward. She confidently embraces her feminine self, enjoying her attractiveness—but her confidence is contingent upon the presence and power of the heterosexual male gaze (Mulvey, 1999). Thus, postfeminist ideals are conveniently combined with the traditional representation of beauty, helping to craft a "postfeminist feminine subjectivity" (Lazar, 2014).

As the woman receives the flowers from the handsome male stranger, a voice-over insists, *Ty gotova k novomu dnju i komplimentam* 'You are ready for a new day and for the compliments,' creating the image of a woman ready to be both successful and feminine. Her femininity is indexed through the word 'compliments,' implying that every woman appreciates compliments from acquaintances and strangers. Compliments are not depicted as something that might be bothersome (especially when coming from a stranger) or constitute harassment, but understood merely as desirable praise. In this way, Russian commercials effectively embed a limited postfeminist self-centeredness within a circumscribing framework of traditional feminine other-centeredness. In order to provide evidence of women's beauty, it seems necessary to incorporate a (typically male) third party, in order to add credibility or warrant. Under the guise of a liberated and autonomous woman, the commercial reinforces traditional stereotypes about femininity: beauty is necessary to gain interested heterosexual male gaze. There is a poignant irony in the double-deflections of desire and gaze accomplished by these advertisements: the dictates of patriarchal desire shape commercials that demand and sustain the attentions of women precisely by promising products that will demand and sustain the attentions of men. In addition, women are deflected from their own autonomous pursuits by a cultivated image of a post-feminist role model who cultivates an image appealing to men.

Self- and other-centeredness and self-commodification along with traditional values were also emphasized through direct and indirect evaluations from the family members that made women feel happy and satisfied. For instance, in 'Čistaja linija' hair shampoo commercials, women's daughters and husbands conveyed their appreciative stances toward the women's beauty, as seen in excerpts (12) and (13).

(12)   Daughter: *Ma:močka,   ty   vygljadeš na pjat'.*
                 mother:DIM you look   on five
                 'Mommy, you look on A.'

          Husband: *Na pjat' s   pljusom.*
                  on five   with plus
                  'On A+.'

(13)   Daughter: *Ma:močka, ty   oslepitel'na!*
         mother:DIM you dazzling
         'Mommy, you are dazzling!'

Thus, the commercials stress the importance of family and their approval for a woman. Excerpt (12) presents both the daughter and the husband expressing positive assessment of the woman's appearance. The daughter uses a sound prolongation in the word *Ma:močka* 'Mommy,' extending the initial syllable, thus conveying her affective stance toward the mother. She also uses a diminutive suffix *očk*, softening her speech and emphasizing her love for her mother. The husband then upgrades the daughter's assessment, giving his wife an A+ for her appearance rather than an A. The woman does not respond verbally but merely smiles, happily receiving praise from her husband and daughter, while a female voice-over concludes, *Teper' volosy- eto vaša gordost'* 'Now your hair is your pride,'—reinforcing the perception that beauty is woman's strongest asset (Kay, 1997, p. 82).

Similarly, excerpt (13) presents a woman surrounded by her family, as she receives a compliment from her daughter. The daughter's lexical choice of *oslepitel'na* 'dazzling' as a positive, evaluative term sounds distinctly unnatural in a child's register, exposing the scripted nature of the commercial. In both excerpts, the nuclear family is depicted in intimate closeness, touching and holding one another, demonstrating their overall unity.

Women are portrayed acquiring ultimate happiness from family life as a result of their beauty, as assessed by their husbands and children. They are encouraged to be in charge of their looks and take pride in achieving beauty, but their joy is gained only when they feel appreciated by others. The traditional representation of women as keepers of the family hearth is combined with the portrayals of their feminine achievement, creating another mixture of self-oriented and other-centered subjectivities.

Self-centered subjectivity paired with dramatic sexualization of the female body is also visible in the Russian brand of hygiene products *Krasnaja Linija* 'Red Line.' Women are assured that they need to look gorgeous at all times in order to be successful: female beauty is presented as a cornerstone for good relationships (with men, family members, and female and male friends) to such an extent that a woman's happiness depends primarily on whether or not she is beautiful. Each *Krasnaja Linija* advertisement promises women that the achievement and maintenance of beauty will result in ultimate self-fulfillment. The promised transformation from mundane mediocrity to fulfilling and beautiful happiness is possible, but only once women realize that they must apply effort to maintain their appearances with the help of the advertised products as seen in excerpt (14).

(14)　*Ja vsegda starajus' vygljadet' bezuprečno, a dlja togo,   štoby moi volosy*
　　　 I   always try   look   impeccable but for that:GEN so
　　　 that my hair

　　　 vygljadeli takže, ja vybiraju šampun' Krasnaja Linija.
　　　 look:PAST same I   choose shampoo red   line

　　　 'I always try to look impeccable, and in order for my hair to look the same, I choose the shampoo "Red Line."'

The woman in excerpt (14) accentuates the need to apply effort constantly in order to appear beautiful and desirable, while stressing the importance of shampoo choice. The advertisement projects a highly sexualized image of the woman's body, implying that 'impeccable' looks are necessary to attract heterosexual male gaze.

The integration of self-oriented concerns with normative other-centeredness can also be observed in a *Krasnaja Linija* body wash commercial, as a woman in a soft, whispery voice encourages female viewers to exert their feminine power in their interactions with men, as seen in excerpt (15).

(15)　°*Soblaznjaj v svojo udovol'stvije.*°
　　　 seduce in your pleasure
　　　 'Seduce as much as you please.'

Women are encouraged to enjoy a seductive influence over men that can only be achieved through truly flawless beauty. The emphasis here is on female pleasure and power in seduction, adding a (post)feminist overtone to the advertisement's framing. The woman pronounces her liberating imperative in a hushed tone, suggesting that the art of seduction is a secret shared between women and should not be overheard by the outsiders (men). On a broader scale, however, women are again encouraged to beautify themselves in order to attract and please male partners, even in a commercial for body wash.

In Russian commercials, male figures frequently evaluate the effectiveness of the product through non-verbal expressions of interest in the female protagonist that indicate her attractiveness. Advertisements summarize the usefulness of cosmetics by such slogans as *Inogda dostatočno odnogo vzgljada* 'Sometimes one glance is enough,' implying that even one glance toward a man is sufficient for seduction if a woman is wearing the right makeup. Interestingly, however, the men in Russian commercials, unlike in Japanese advertisements, rarely explicitly state their perceptions of women's beauty. They tend not to compliment women or comment directly on their attractiveness, but are used to dramatize the efficacy of the product.

Furthermore, Russian women's autonomy and power are centered through epithets such as *roskošnyje ženščiny* 'gorgeous women,' and *rokovaja krasavitsa* 'fatal beauty,' as well as catch phrases such as *privykay byt' v tsentre vnimanija* 'get used to being the center of attention,' and *pokori vzgljadom* 'conquer by one glance.' Thus, Russian advertisements are infused with postfeminist representations of self-centered female power, in which women are encouraged to be strong and self-sustaining even when the goal is appealing to male affections. These types of commercials, nevertheless, exploit liberated images of women as a "feminism commodity," in which femininity and feminism are entangled together as a common project (Goldman, 1992). Russian women are urged to take initiative *to become more beautiful and feminine*, thus combining both the feminist value of 'self-confidence' and the imperatives of traditional gender norms, which dictate that women must be pretty and desirable.

2.6   Interrogative Structures
in Japanese Commercials

While interrogatives were also frequently utilized in Japanese advertisements for beauty and hygiene products, the function of these lexical items differed from their use in Russian-language advertisements. Instead of serving to problematize the situation (and provide a pretext for the introduction of a product that would purportedly resolve the consequent dilemma), interrogatives in Japanese advertisements were often utilized by female actors to express surprise and astonishment in response to new information, or to make (usually erroneous) guesses as to the 'magic' behind the product's efficacy.

For example, in the commercial below three women are trying out a new Dove soap bar while they shower and listen attentively to edifying information about the product. Excerpt (16) presents the off-screen informant's explanation that Dove's soap has a secret, followed by a woman's partial repeat, which emphasizes her bewilderment, hesitation, and interest.

(16)   - *Dabu   no   awa   ni   wa   himitsu ga   arimasu.*
        Dove GEN foam DAT TOP secret NOM exist
        'There is a secret in Dove's foam.'

        - Kono awa ni?
        this foam DAT
        In this foam?'

By repeating a part of the statement, the woman conveys her surprise and lack of understanding, projecting a childish persona. This representation of childishness is further emphasized by the woman's delighted remark about the Dove soap after having tried it, *konna no hajimete!* 'It's the first time that I see such!' The intense type of childish naivety she exudes, absent in the depictions of women in Russian commercials, is a prime example of the cute femininity of *kawaii*.

Interrogatives communicating surprise were frequently employed in order to highlight characters' feminine cuteness. In another Dove commercial, Japanese women were video-recorded before and after they had tried a new body wash, in order to demonstrate the increased frequency and pleasure of self-touch. The advertisement begins with a background female voice-over inquiring, *dabu de hada ni fureru kaisuu wa doo kawaru?* 'How has the number of times you touch your skin changed with the help of Dove?' At the end of the commercial, a woman uses an interrogative structure to convey her surprise, transcribed in excerpt (17).

(17)   *Watashi, konna ni   sawatteta   n   desu ka.*
       I   this   DAT touch:AUX:NONPAST SE COP Q
       'Did I really touch (my skin) this much?'

The advertisement shows the woman's exuberant non-verbal expression of surprise and modesty. While observing the video recording of her self-touch after using Dove, she covers her mouth in order to conceal a smile, a canonical gesture of *kawaii* cuteness (Miller, 2004, p. 149). With the help of the interrogative structure, combined with the woman's expression of astonishment, the advertisement conveys an image of natural naivety, child-like cuteness, and modest femininity.

Unlike Russian commercials, in which women were frequently portrayed as sad and anxious, Japanese commercials depicted women as highly sentimental, cute, and slightly childish—thereby satisfying the requirement of being *kawaii*. Desire manifests itself in Russia beauty ads as a lack or a need, stemming from a potential failure in the eyes of men, family members, and friends. In Japanese beauty ads, the desire to achieve a beautiful, *kawaii* femininity is instead constructed as an effervescent outpouring of innate sentimentality.

Interrogatives were also deployed in order to reveal women's inexpert assumptions about the products, which could then be corrected and further refined through the advertisement. In this maneuver, the dialectical emphasis is again placed on women's naivety and lack of knowledge. For instance, excerpt (18) begins with a woman asking if the soap will make her skin dry. She is subsequently corrected by an informed Dove specialist, who explains to her the beneficial (and non-desiccating) properties of Dove soap.

(18)   -*Sengan   ga   uruoi   o   ubau tte honto?*
facial soap NOM moisture ACC steal   Q   real
'Is it true that facial soap deprives you of moisture?'

-*Iie, chigaimasu.*
no differ
'No, that's wrong.'

The woman is thus portrayed as unsure, excessively anxious about her skin, and ill-informed about soaps, needing help from the experts in order to make an educated decision. Similarly, in a shampoo commercial for the brand 'Clear,' a female narrator uses an interrogative form to suggest that women have erroneous beliefs and perceptions regarding hair damage. Her utterance is presented in excerpt (19).

(19)   *Kami no   dame-ji, mada kesaki   no   kea dake? Jitsu   wa   anata ga*
hair   GEN damge   still   hair end GEN care only   actually
TOP you NOM
miotoshite ita   no   wa toohi no   oku.
neglect:TE-AUX:PAST NML TOP sculp GEN depth

'Hair damage, do you still only take care of the ends? Actually, you neglected the scalp.'

Using an interrogative form, the female informant in excerpt (19) suggests that women have a general misconception about their hair treatment, the nature of which she then identifies explicitly. By using the adverbial expression *jitsu wa* 'actually,' she signals her superior epistemic stance vis-à-vis the following information. Thus, women (this time, the viewers themselves) are portrayed as naïve, lacking correct information, and in need of an expert's advice and support. Just as a child plaintively seeks help from his or her parents, Japanese women in commercial advertisements are shown calling for help in taking care of their own appearances.

Intriguingly, the same advertisement attempts to accomplish a limited infusion of (post)feminist ideas into the female persona. In the commercial, the actress (Miyazaki Aoi) strides powerfully across a bridge in high heels and a short black dress; her gaze is direct, and her overall posture radiates confidence. This image, however, is detached from real women's lives and resembles a scene from a futuristic movie. Rather than showing a woman empowered by the achievement of success in the concrete relationships of her actual, lived experience, it presents an illusory, superficial abstraction conveying only a pretense of empowerment. In fact, when the female voice-over utters an interrogative (*Kami no dame-ji, mada kesaki no kea dake?* 'Hair damage, do you still only take care of the ends?), the woman's confidence seems shattered, and she looks at her hair ends in a naïve and confused way.

This commercial repeatedly incorporates key words tied to post-feminist self-construal (*utsukushii* 'beautiful' and *tsuyoi* 'strong'), but immediately undermines their agentic potential. Thus, the commercial splices together a distorted image in which the female protagonist is both a confident, beautiful woman and a cute, confused girl, assimilating post-feminist ideals while simultaneously dissolving their challenge in *kawaii* femininity.

The image of a strong woman is also engaged in another 'Clear' shampoo commercial that subverts the potential strength and autonomy of its central female character. The protagonist is introduced as a strong female executive with a fearsome slogan: *watashi wa dakyoo o shinai* 'I do not compromise.' A male voice then asks her about various hair settings, such as *kayumi* 'itchiness' and *sawayakasa* 'freshness,' to which she gives one-word directions: 'On' or 'off.' Apart from these terse commands, however, the woman does not speak, while the male voice-over voluminously explains the benefits of the product. She has agency to make uncompromising choices, but only from the predefined categories stipulated by the male expert. Affectively, she is depicted as robotic, stripped of any human emotion or feeling, with the implicit suggestion that a woman must curtail her natural sentimentality in order to be authoritative.

Interrogatives were also used to present women in stances of anxiety, hesitance, and uncertainty. For example, in excerpt (20), a woman sits closely beside a man in an automobile, looking directly into his eyes; the overall atmosphere is romantic. After a male voice-over describes the laudable properties of her mascara, a female voice, putatively representing the internal monologue of the woman in the car, asks a final question, with which the advertisement concludes:

(20)   *Honki de   aishiteru?*
         really INST love:TE-AUX:NONPAST
         'Do you really love me?'

In excerpt (20) the protagonist, seeking the man's evaluation of her attractiveness, plays on the homophony of *ai* 'love (Japanese),' and 'eye (English).' Ultimately, the value and effectiveness of the mascara are judged solely by the man whose approval she implores. Although the woman does not receive a direct verbal confirmation of love, the man's kiss in response to her query is taken as indicative of his affection and approval. Thus, the advertisement reiterates women's constant need to be reassured of a romantic partner's love—a positioning which is consistent with the ideological construction of women as perpetually anxious, nervous, suspicious, and doubtful. The effectiveness and power of this depiction is apparent in the fact that the narrative of the advertisement does not even need to involve direct speech. The woman's need for affection can be presupposed, her judicious selection of mascara is an attempt to solicit this affection, and his response does not need a verbal explanation. The viewer is taken to understand that the need for affection is universal and transparent, with male and female figures knowingly and wordlessly playing their respective parts in the evocation and resolution of female insecurity.

Furthermore, interrogatives were used to reinforce stereotypes regarding female emotionality. For example, in another mascara advertisement, a beautiful woman is portrayed crying and rubbing her eyes for approximately eight seconds, trying to wipe the tears off her face. The scene is then followed by a question in female voice-over, in excerpt (21).

(21)   *Anata no   masukara shokku furii desu ka*
         you   GEN mascara shock free COP Q
         'Is your mascara shock-free?'

The question in (21) invokes the stereotype that women are emotional and irrational creatures, whose moods change rapidly and unpredictably.

For this reason, they require cosmetics that can adjust to their behavior by being 'shock-free,' and remaining intact even in extreme emotional distress. Crying and inability to control oneself are seen as children's attributes, and are often favored in Japanese culture as manifestations of *kawaii* (Okazaki & Johnson, 2013). The commercial does not need to depict the circumstances that elicited the emotional response; it is understood by the viewer that women cry over a variety of trivial circumstances. Both interrogative constructions in (20) and (21) suggest that women possess deleterious temperamental characteristics—such as insecurity, lack of confidence, and vulnerability—leading to constant distresses that conform to the pattern of traditional gender and the ideology of *kawaii*.

Even fantastic female creatures conform to the *kawaii* ideals by expressing naivety through their use of interrogative structures. For example, a shampoo commercial 'Je l'aime' features a mermaid surrounded by two men. They touch her hair and convey a critical stance toward her appearance, suggesting that she should eat kelp in order to have stronger hair. The mermaid produces only a single-word response, *Hontou* 'Really?' communicating her surprise, disbelief, and state of despair.

This exchange is followed by the appearance of two better-informed, 'real' experts who intervene in the discussion, shouting *Uso da*! 'That's a lie!' and give the mermaid a bottle of 'Je l'aime' shampoo. Throughout the rest of the advertisement, the mermaid does not speak, but displays the beauty of her recently washed and purified hair alongside her much improved emotional state. At the end of the commercial, she looks gratefully toward the two male figures who introduced her to 'Je l'aime' shampoo, leaning seductively on one man's shoulder. Thus, throughout the whole duration of the commercial, the female speaker utters only a single word of surprise, while the male characters collectively utter 35 words. Men also dominated the images in sheer number—four male critics appear to judge the physical appearance of the mermaid, and subsequently to save her from the state of misery their disapprobation has induced. The mermaid, however, does not appear to have any agency over her fate, merely following the advice of the men and seeking male protection and approval. This portrayal corresponds to the traditional stereotype of incompetent femininity, while also engaging the powerless but adorable femininity of *kawaii*.

As seen from excerpts (16)–(21), Japanese female consumers, much as their Russian female counterparts, are confronted with depictions that frame them as inquisitive and lacking knowledge, often with the help of interrogative structures. The difference, however, is that women in the Russian commercials are urged to take initiative and control over their appearances by realizing imperfections of their own accord, or with the help of female friends. In this way, Russian advertising creates the illusion that women are active agents in the creation of their distinctive beauty. In Japanese commercials, however, the agency of a woman is significantly undermined, while men are depicted as the chief decision-makers—even when it comes to a woman's appearance, they seem to possess innate and superior knowledge. Japanese women are portrayed as easily surprised, naïve and passive, thereby satisfying the requirements of the *kawaii* persona. Even in advertising that aims to convey a postfeminist representation of a powerful woman, the confidence depicted appears counterfeit and unnatural when combined with the highly unrealistic settings and male-dominated narrations.

2.7   Use of Hortative Structures in Japanese Commercials

Both hortatives and imperatives are grammatical structures that invite the interlocutor to perform an action, but imperatives place the responsibility for carrying out an action on the addressee of the message; hortatives, on the other hand, convey the sentiment that the action will be performed by both the addressee and the speaker (Haspelmath, Dryer, Gil, & Comrie, 2005). While imperatives are frequently used in Russian commercials for female audiences, they are avoided in Japanese advertising for women. Imperatives in Japanese are considered a natural feature of the men's language, and (in contrast to Russian advertisements for men) are commonly incorporated in advertisements targeted at male consumers (Nakamura, 2004). In Japanese, hortatives can be formed using a verbal volitional form, or a negative invitational verbal form— *masenka*. In advertising for men, however, the hortative forms are not utilized, confirming that this is a female-oriented approach.

Excerpts (22)–(24) present the typical usage of these hortatives in Japanese televised commercials.

(22)   *Odoroku   hodo danryoku no   aru   awa o   tameshite miyoo.*
        Be surprised level elasticity GEN foam ACC try:TE-ASP:VOL
        'Let's try out the foam that is so resilient that you will be amazed.'

(23)   *Atarashii Dabu o tameshite mimasen   ka.*
        New   Dove ACC try:TE-ASP:NEG Q
        'Why not try out new Dove?'

(24)   *Tokihanatou*
        release:VOL
        'Let's liberate (something)!'

These hortatives appear in the concluding segments of the advertisements, urging women to make a purchase. By incorporating invitational types of hortatives, these commercials seek to assimilate female viewers within a (fictional) 'inside circle,' creating a sentiment of collectiveness in having to tackle similar issues. For that reason, such hortative structures were always uttered by a female speaker, even when men pronounced every other utterance in the advertisement. For instance, in excerpt 19, the seemingly progressive utterance *tokihanatou* 'Let's liberate (something)!' is the only phrase spoken by a woman in the commercial, while a male speaker utters 22 words, thoroughly dominating the narrative. Female viewers are thus not simply encouraged to try a particular hygiene or beauty product, but invited to participate in the enactment of femininity with a prototypical female counterpart. The rejection of this offer is thereby constructed as a rejection of feminine solidarity, and, in the case of example (25), a refusal of collective freedom.

2.8   Mimetic Expressions, Personifications, and Metaphors in Japanese Commercials

In the materials analyzed, Japanese women utilized a high volume of *gitaigo* 'phenomenon mimetic,' which is one of the cardinal features of hyperbolically cute women's speech (Miller, 2004: 153). This category of words is distinct from that of sound-based onomatopoeic words and is uncommon for European languages, including Russian. In Japanese, however, although skin cannot generate a sound on its own, certain sensations associated with it can be described with the use of mimetic vocabulary. In excerpts (25) and (26) from two Dove commercials, *gitaigo* is utilized to convey the way women's skin feels as they apply soap in the shower.

(25)   A: *Subesube!*
              'Smooth!'
        B: *Yawarakai!*
              'Soft.'

(26)   A: *Aaa tsurutsuru.*
              'Aah, so silky'
        B: *Kimochi yokute, sawacchau ne.*
              'It feels so good. I can't help but touch it.'
        C: *Sugoi mochimochi.*
              'It's really supple.'

The use of mimetic expressions *subesube* 'smooth,' *tsurutsuru* 'silky,' and *mochimochi* 'supple' by women appeals to stereotypes regarding women's emotionality and cuteness. It is further exemplified by Japanese women's use of various metaphors that compare their sensations to sweets and silky clothing items, as seen in excerpts (27)–(30).

(27)   *Shooto keeki no   ichigo   no   kimochi ga   wakaru.*
        short cake GEN strawberry GEN feeling NOM understand
        'I understand how the strawberry feels sitting on the top of shortcake.'

(28)   *Shiruku o   matotteru   mitaina kanji.*
        silk   ACC wrap:TE-AUX:NONPAST like   feeling
        'It's like I am wrapped in silk.'

(29)   *Sofuto kuriimu mitai!*
        soft   cream   like
        'It's like a soft cream!'

(30)   *hoippu kuri-mu mitaina!*
        whipped cream like
        'It's like a whipped cream!'

Women's use of sweet foods, such as an ice cream, whipped cream, and a cake, as well as smooth clothing fabrics, conforms to stereotypes of femininity and cuteness. The implicit suggestion is simple: women enjoy child-like pleasures such as eating cakes and dressing up, and therefore will enjoy body care products that resemble sweets and silky clothes. The image of cuteness is further magnified through the depiction of women talking to their (personified) body parts using sentence-final particles that are commonly used for interactional purposes and are restricted to dialogic speech (Iwasaki, 2013, p. 4). For instance, in excerpt 31 the Japanese woman addresses her personified hair.

(31)   *Moo sunao   ni   iu   koto   o   kiite kureru.*   *Zutto kono*
already obedient DAT say matter ACC listen:TE-give:NONPAST
always this
jyootai de   ite   ne.
state   ACC be:TE PP
'(My hair) already listens obediently to what I say. Stay like this forever, okay?'

As seen from excerpt 31, the woman encourages her hair to remain the same after the use of Dove shampoo for a long time. By doing so, she projects a cute and childish persona conforming to the stereotype that it is essential for a woman to be *kawaii* in all aspects of her being (Asano-Cavanagh, 2014, p. 342).

2.9   Men as Creators of Women's Beauty in Japanese Commercials

While in the Russian commercials analyzed above male figures were used to highlight the effectiveness of achieved female beauty and the enduring value of charming feminine power, in Japanese commercials, conversely, men frequently appeared as explicit innovators and creators of female beauty. Japanese advertising predominantly utilized other-centered subjectivity, in which a woman is deprived of a strong sense of agency though constantly considering other people's views and judgments. The effectiveness of advertised cosmetics is measured and demonstrated through male appraisals (frequently patronizing), such as *o-niai desu* 'it suits you,' with resulting joy and satisfaction for the Japanese women depicted.

The recurrent theme of male creation and control over women's looks can be observed explicitly in the advertising of *Fasio* eye cosmetic products. A series of commercials create an imaginary 'Eyelashes Salon,' whose director is male, and to which various women come in pursuit of beautiful eyelashes. A typical interaction between the eyelashes master and a female customer is presented in excerpt (32).

(32)   Woman: *Itsumo no   onegai.*
                  always GEN request
                  'The usual, please.'

        Man: *Neko meiku   desu ne.*
                  cat makeup COP PP
                  'Cat make-up, right?

        Woman: *Meow*
                  [Cat sound]

        Man: *Mata no   o-   koshi o.*
                  Again GEN HON visit   ACC
                  'I am looking forward to your next visit.'

In the commercial, the eyelashes master uses the politeness suffix *desu* and the honorific structures *irasshaimase* 'welcome' and *mata no o-koshi o* 'I am looking forward to your next visit' when speaking with his female customer, thus outwardly conveying a subservient stance. In reality, however, he is presented as a successful businessperson, while the woman is portrayed as both lacking independence (even when it comes to her own appearance) and relying on a man to make her attractive. In addition, her words are limited to a single phrase in which she asks for 'the usual,' and by the end of the commercial she is stripped of her humanity completely, mimicking a cat's 'meow' as she transforms into a cute kitten. This depiction is representative of the current gender stereotype, which links femininity to the pet-like appeal of subservient *kawaii* cuteness.

Male power over female beauty is further seen in another Fasio powder commercial that again incorporates the *matsugeya san* 'eyelash master.' This time, he travels by train and gives advice to a female traveler who happens to be in the same car. He offers to show her a compact powder, to which she responds with the interrogative *kore nani kashira* 'What is it, I wonder?' The question particle *kashira* 'I wonder,' is traditionally considered a feature of women's language, and serves both to index her femininity and to highlight her proper upbringing and gentle nature. The man then applies cosmetics to the woman's face, while explaining the product's properties.

On the one hand, the man is again portrayed in a nominally subordinate position, serving a woman in order to enhance her beauty. On the other hand, the woman is merely a recipient of the benefits of his expertise, lacking in knowledge and unable to take care even of her own appearance. Rather than a servant, the man is presented as an expert teacher, helping and educating the female population about beauty. The woman is so caught up in admiration for her new, beautiful look that she almost forgets to get off the train. The man once again has to educate her, saying *Shuuten desu* 'It's the final stop,' in order to bring the woman back to her senses. She is thus portrayed as lacking knowledge throughout the commercial, while the male eyelashes—and apparently also powder—master is presented as more rational and better informed in several respects. The lack of agency and understanding, elegance of style, and absorption in her looks present a combination of traditionally feminine traits alongside the characteristic features of contemporary *kawaii*.

The incorporation of a male figure as an innovator of female beauty is not limited to the products of the Fasio brand. Another popular Japanese hair product, *Tsubaki*, utilizes a similar trope. A male master holds a shampoo salon that is frequented by various women. In the commercial, he greets a customer silently, looks at the arrangement of her hair in a ponytail, and gives a positive assessment *anata ga nani yori mo utsukushii kara* 'you are more beautiful than anything.' While the woman is seated, the man swiftly and patronizingly pulls off her hairband.

Elevation of men over women in advertising is considered one form of the "ritualization of subordination"—a man's higher physical place symbolizes his social superiority (Goffman, 1979, p. 43). After removing the hair band, the master and his female customer sit facing one another. The man's overall posture is relaxed, his legs are crossed and his back is leaning against the armchair. In contrast, the woman projects nervousness and formality—sitting on the edge of her chair with her back straightened and her hands folded neatly on her lap. Finally, after a three-second pause, the man utters a negative assessment—*mottainai* 'what a waste,' suggesting that the woman is not realizing the full potential of her hair.

The master then shampoos the woman's hair, making it softer and healthier and thereby improving the woman's mood. She leaves the salon happily proclaiming *kimochi ii ne* 'It feels good.' In this way, the man not only grants the woman beautiful, lustrous hair, but emboldens her with confidence so that her stress evaporates. These portrayals recycle and reinforce the stereotype that men are women's saviors and benefactors, while women are helpless and cute. In this example, her beauty is wasted until it becomes subject to his control and improvement, and meets his final approval. The result of subordinating her body and her beauty to male control is happiness for the otherwise-helpless woman.

Strict assessment and monitoring of women's beauty is also seen in a shampoo commercial for the brand 'Je l'aime.' In it, a male shampoo-master is responsible for taking care of and critically evaluating women's hair. He goes through a long line of women like a connoisseur—touching their hair with expert discernment and rendering his judgments—while the women inform him of which shampoo that they use (Je l'aime).

While the male expert's face is visible throughout the advertisement, the women are always facing away, wearing identical white dresses and devoid any signs of uniqueness or individuality. By depicting women as faceless, passive objects of male judgment, standing obediently for inspection, the advertisement reinforces stereotypes of female subservience and male superiority. The male expert is pleased with the quality of the female hair and says, *Kono uruoi, kono kaori* 'This moisture, this scent.' His admiring stance is also conveyed through his happy smile and his satisfied gaze. He is portrayed as a knowledgeable teacher and a hair professional, while the women are portrayed as his inferior apprentices or tutees, working hard to keep up the high quality of their hair. Importantly, there are no comparable advertisements for male hair products; women are never depicted as experts or connoisseur evaluators of men's beauty or competence.

Some commercials employed more subtle allusions to male superiority, but the idea that men are creators and innovators while women are consumers and beneficiaries was persistent. For instance, in a lotion commercial for the 'Sekkisei' brand, a woman murmurs the following prayer in front of her mirror, presented in excerpt 33.

(33) *Onegai! Kyou no   watashi no   hada ga   ichi nichi jyuu   shittori*
 request today GEN I   GEN skin NOM one day during damp
 uruottete,   nikkuki shigaisen   ni   semerarete   mo zenzen
 moisturize:TE-AUX:TE accurse ultra-violet ray DAT attack:PSS:TE
 but at all
 hiyake nanka   shinakute,   eetto sorekara, meiku   wa   mochiron
 norinori no
 suntan EMPH do-NEG:TE HES also   make-up TOP certainly
 perfect GEN
 mama de, toumeikan   ga   zutto, zutto, zutto,
 zutto, tsuzuki   masu
 as is LK feeling of transparency NOM always always always
 always continue POL
 you ni.
 for DAT

 'I am asking you. I wish for my skin to be well moisturized throughout the day, and even under the attack of the ultra-violet rays, not to tan, and also, (I wish) for my make-up to stay perfect as it is now, and (I wish) for the feeling of transparency to stay always and always and always and always.'

The woman starts her prayer with the emphatic expression *onegai!* (lit. 'request!') 'I am asking you!' calling upon the power of her lotion, as though it has some supernatural efficacy. She describes in detail the properties of her desired skin, repeating the lexical item *zutto* 'always' four times, emphasizing the importance of skin transparency to her in a highly emotional, childlike manner. Even though she is not addressing another person, but merely looking at herself in the mirror, she still utilizes the politeness suffix *masu* to end her wish, personifying the lotion as her benefactor. Immediately upon completion of her prayer, a male voiceover assures the viewer that the new lotion from Sekkisei responds perfectly to her wish by providing transparently beautiful skin that will not tan. In his utterance, he does not use affective markers, such as repetition and mimetic expressions, or polite register, but presents the information in a concise and direct manner. The male voice is portrayed as concerned with realizing the woman's dreams and knowledgeable about the beauty and happiness Sekkisei lotion can provide for her. In contrast, the woman is depicted as an emotive, innocent, naïve, and powerless being, unable to obtain the beauty she desires on her own, and therefore having to resort to the supernatural power of a lotion (and ultimately to the male intellect that is presented as its creative source).

In these ways, Japanese advertising frequently positions a woman as devoid of agency even when it comes to her own appearance. She is depicted as lacking competence, knowledge, and ability to improve her appearance on her own, and is instead dependent upon men's support and expertise. Men are portrayed as the ultimate creators of female beauty in the roles of various salon masters and connoisseurs whose goal is to enhance women's looks. In addition to positively changing women's physical appearance, men also craft women's emotional states as they increase their confidence and happiness through the beautifying process. They are also the final judges and arbiters of the beauty they themselves create, and their positive evaluations of their own handiwork evince a certain hollowness. In Japanese advertisement, the feminine is a product of the male imagination imposed upon passive recipients for male consumption and admiration.

2.10   Summary

Overall, the analysis of Russian and Japanese televised commercials has demonstrated that products designed for women are marketed in a manner that reinforces existing gender stereotypes while accommodating (in limited ways) new perceptions of femininity in contemporary societies. Both Japanese and Russian women are portrayed as inquisitive and deficient of information on how to tackle issues pertaining to their beauty, attractiveness, and sexuality.

Russian commercials frequently commence with the portrayal of a miserable woman, besieged by various beauty-related problems with which she cannot cope on her own, followed by the explanation of how a certain product will help and save her. A positive judgment regarding the efficacy of the product is often connected to or justified by a man's evaluation. A woman may explicitly state her husband's increased appreciation, or it might be conveyed implicitly by a change in his non-verbal behavior such as smiling, winking, or laughing. Russian commercials for female audiences portray a double-image of idealized femininity, a novel, evolving synthesis that fuses traditional gender ideologies with more recent (post)feminist perspectives. On the one hand, Russian women are urged to be consciously aware of others (especially men and children). Indeed, others' views and behaviors determine women's usage of even basic products such as a soap or a shampoo. On the other hand, women are also encouraged to take the lead in constructing and expressing their feminine attractiveness, and to be confident in their success as architects of their own beauty. This meager influence of feminist discourse is ironically subverted, as it is strategically utilized to center the heterosexual male gaze (Mulvey, 1999) under the guise of liberation and women's personal choice.

In Japanese commercials, women are portrayed as cute, innocent, slightly naïve, and perpetually seeking advice. Men are fictionally postulated as the creators and *explicit* evaluators of female beauty. The scripted speech of female characters contains lexical and grammatical choices that emphasize woman's cuteness and naivety, such as abundant usage of mimetic vocabulary, interactional sentence-final particles, endearing metaphors, and other subtle linguistic elements. The traditional stereotypes of women's elegance and emotionality are reproduced, while the childlike and highly incompetent depictions of women promote further the idealized powerless femininity of *kawaii*. Some Japanese commercials (more similar to Russian advertising) tactically utilized (post)feminist representations, attempting to project a strong, confident, and non-*kawaii* woman. In fact, in one of the analyzed commercials, a Japanese woman even claims *watashi wa kawaii kara sotsugyou suru* 'I graduate from *kawaii*.' The implacable dominance of the male voice and the absence of female characters who would possess real power, however, make portrayals of strength in Japanese advertisements farfetched and implausible. As long as women are constrained to stances of confusion and naivety, meaningful departure from the disseminated representation of *kawaii* vulnerability will remain impossible.

In the next chapter (Chap. 3), I examine the ways that women interviewees consume, interpret, question, and sometimes reject the ideological depictions of women and feminine beauty promulgated by commercial media. While the power of advertising to reinforce traditional gender norms and stereotypes is considerable, women are not merely passive recipients of the messages and concepts that seek to capture and develop their desires vis-à-vis beauty. As we shall see, the women interviewed in the present study construct their own ideals of womanhood and beauty, influenced by, but distinct from those presented to them by, advertisements and other ideological sources.

References

Asano-Cavanagh, Y. (2014). Linguistic manifestation of gender reinforcement through the use of the Japanese term *kawaii*. *Gender and Language, 8*(3), 341–359.

Connell, R. (1995). *Masculinities*. Berkeley: University of California Press.

Goffman, E. (1979). *Gender advertisements*. New York: Harper and Row.

Goldman, R. (1992). *Reading ads socially*. London: Routledge.

Haspelmath, M., Dryer, M. S., Gil, D., & Comrie, B. (2005). *The world atlas of language structures*. Oxford: Oxford University Press.

Ide, S. (1992). Gender and function of language use: Quantitative and qualitative evidence from Japanese. *Pragmatics and Language Learning, 3*, 117–129.

Iwasaki, S. (2013). *Japanese*. Amsterdam: Johns Benjamins Publishing Company.

Kay, R. (1997). Images of an ideal woman: Perceptions of Russian womanhood through the media, education and women's own eyes. In M. Buckley (Ed.), *Post-Soviet women: From the Baltic to Central Asia* (pp. 77–98). Cambridge: Cambridge University Press.

Lazar, M. M. (2014). Feminist critical discourse analysis: Relevance for current gender and language research. In S. ssEhrlich, M. Meyerhoff, & J. Holmes (Eds.), *The handbook of language, gender, and sexuality* (pp. 180–199). Hoboken: Wiley-Blackwell.

Miller, L. (2004). You are doing *burikko*! In S. Okamoto & J. S. Shibamoto Smith (Eds.), *Japanese language, gender, and ideology: Cultural models and real people* (pp. 148–165). New York: Oxford University Press.

Mulvey, L. (1999). Visual pleasure and narrative cinema. In L. Braudy & M. Cohen (Eds.), *Film theory and criticism: Introductory readings* (pp. 833–844). New York: Oxford University Press.

Nakamura, M. (2004). "Let's dress a little girlishly!" or "Conquer short pants!" Constructing gendered communities in fashion magazine for young people. In S. Okamoto & J. S. Shibamoto Smith (Eds.), *Japanese language, gender, and ideology: Cultural models and real people* (pp. 131–148). New York: Oxford University Press.

Nakamura, M. (2014). *Gender, language and ideology: A genealogy of Japanese women's language.* Amsterdam: John Benjamins Publishing Company.

Okazaki, M., & Johnson, G. (2013). *Kawaii!: Japan's culture of cute.* Munich: Prestel.

3

Russian and Japanese Women's Perceptions of Feminine Beauty

The previous chapter (Chap. 2) examined the role of beauty advertisements in constructing ideologies of gender and beauty in both Japanese and Russian culture. However, these depictions (and the ideological content at their core) are efficacious only to the extent that they capture and cultivate women's ideals and desires. In the present chapter, I analyze the discourse of women interviewees as they speak about their ideals regarding womanhood and beauty. In so doing, I assess the ways in which they negotiate the space between their own autonomy and the gendered expectations prevalent in Japanese and Russian societies. We shall observe both the enduring impact of media-circulated messages on women's ideals and aims, and instances in which women reject or transform the meaning of traditional concepts of gender and beauty. It is important to ground this analysis in an understanding of social and economic changes in Japan and in Russia. After situating readers with respect to such crucial features of Russian and Japanese societies, I proceed to use multi-modal discourse analysis, critical discourse analysis, and conversation analysis to explore women's struggle to form and transform their ideals of feminine beauty.

© The Author(s) 2020
N. Konstantinovskaia, *The Language of Feminine Beauty in Russian and Japanese Societies*, Palgrave Studies in Language, Gender and Sexuality, https://doi.org/10.1007/978-3-030-41433-7_3

3.1   Overview and Sample Characteristics

Conflicting images of ideal womanhood in contemporary Russian culture have been attributed to the tension between lingering Soviet rhetoric (which valorized the role of the dual mother-worker) and rapid changes in Russian society calling for the restoration of traditionally feminine ideals (Kay, 1997; Lyon, 2007). In the preceding chapter, I have argued that sexist media depictions of gender dynamics also shape women's often-contradictory self-representations. Indeed, Russian society is replete with triggers urging women to conform to traditional gender norms and stereotypes. These messages are not limited to the televised commercials discussed above, but also permeate other social spaces: street advertisements, online social network services, and even airplane safety manuals contain a range of gender-biased representations and images. As I will show below, disempowering depictions of women as incompetent in the workplace and emotionally unstable at home contribute to the formation and solidification of gender stereotypes in the minds of both men and women.

When asked about their personal images of the ideal woman, all 20 interviewees articulated the tensions and contradictions implicit in contemporary Russian femininity. On the one hand, interviewees discussed the crucial importance of independence, self-reliance, and autonomy; on the other hand, they emphasized that it was indispensable to cultivate a pose of weakness in front of men, reiterating men's authority and positioning men as 'winners' in social engagements.

Below, I have summarized the demographic parameters (age, educational background, and current occupation) of the 20 female Russian respondents whose utterances I will quote and analyze in this chapter. When necessary, I will also include additional information regarding the respondent's family upbringing, social identifications, and other personal details.

3.2 Russian Women's Discourses on Feminine Beauty

3.2.1 Heterosexual Male Gaze and the Duality of Female Personas

As will become apparent in the following sections, the desire to solicit and sustain the positive attention of the heterosexual male gaze (Mulvey, 1999) is one of the principal reasons why female interviewees in the present analysis frequently brought up the necessity of maintaining appearance (e.g. emphasizing the application of well-chosen makeup, recommending daily exercise and dietary habits to help stay slim and fit, and insisting that a woman must never "let herself go" after having married). In these instances, women encounter and react to a heterosexual male gaze that is both direct and encompassing.

The predominant influence of male gender-perceptions is encountered in a still deeper sense when interviewees described their attempts to conform to men's expectations regarding gender roles. In attempting to validate men's expectations of female dependency and weakness, women felt the need to conceal their virtues and deprecate their strengths, enforcing a kind of double-consciousness. The practical and existential necessity of independence, autonomy, and self-confidence co-existed in female respondents' minds with a marked preference to conceal these very attributes from men. They claimed that the tremendous, innate emotional (and sometimes physical) reserves of women had to be hidden from the heterosexual male gaze—as though they were somehow repugnant. This finding resonates with Kay's results (1997) on the importance of modesty as a social value for Russian women, who felt the need to underestimate their real abilities in communication with men (p. 83). Kay (1997), however, did not conceptualize this type of response as representative of a larger phenomenon, or locate its ultimate origin in the centrality of the heterosexual male gaze in Russian society.

The importance of wearing a 'mask'—one that would present a woman in an attractive and compliant light in front of men—runs through the dialogs of all 20 women. In discussing their ideals of femininity, women used the token *mužčina* ('man') 243 times, and *paren'* ('young man') 28 times, while the word *ženščina* ('woman') was used only 146 times, and *devuška* ('young woman') appeared 325 times. Given the fact that the conversations were supposed to focus exclusively on women and femininity, the frequency with which 'men' both as concrete and abstract entities appeared in the discourse is remarkable. Of course, discussion of ideal femininity might prompt women to discuss their relationships with men, but it is notable that they speak about men more often than work, hobbies, home life, or children—all potentially relevant to their ideals of femininity. For comparison, the token 'work' and its derivatives occur 85 times, 'family' 32 times, 'happiness' 4 times, and 'career' 2 times, demonstrating that women speak about men more frequently than about any other area of their lives when elaborating on their ideals. In addition, the term 'young woman' seems to be more preferred when talking about 20- to 30-year-old women, while the token 'young man' is rarely used for the same age group (with preference given to the lexical item *mužčina* 'man'). Calling an older woman *devuška* "young woman" is actually regarded as a compliment, while the straightforward *ženščina* "woman" can be perceived as offensive (Johnson, 2007, p. 125). The emphasis on youth may connote positive attributes such as beauty, health, and vigor, but it can also be deployed to construe women as juvenile and inferior.

Thus, despite the fact that the interviewees were not explicitly asked about men, but merely about their ideas concerning the ideal woman, they were not able to distance themselves from hypothetical men's perceptions, viewing themselves through the prism of male consciousness. The centering of male desire in the discourse of the interviewees also highlights the essentially heteronormative nature of gender ideologies in contemporary Russian society. The presumption is that ideal womanhood is (largely) a response to male sexual-romantic partners and their needs. Other ideals for female (or non-binary) sexuality are excluded, or at least regarded as deficient.

The interviewees provided positive and negative features of women's personalities primarily based on their estimations of men's tastes and likes. For instance, Maria (21) provides reasoning for her selection of an ideal woman's traits, citing men's preferences explicitly in excerpt 34.

(34)   *Ona dolžna byt'miloj, koketlivoj, potomu čto mužčinam vsjo-taki nravjatsja, kogda devuška milaja, živaja, a ne sidit tam dumaet kak vot o smysle žizni, formuly tam kakie-to vyvodit.*
'She must be sweet, coquettish, because men still like it when a woman is sweet, lively, and doesn't just sit there and think about like meaning of life, deducing some (mathematical) formulas.'

Maria's response in (34) indicates that docile personality features are considered mandatory for a woman, and supplements her reasoning by noting that such features correspond to men's preferences. Interestingly, Maria seems to consider a pensive woman, immersed in her thoughts, as especially unattractive to men. When describing such an undesirable woman, Maria lifted her arms and stretched them away from her body, as if to distance herself symbolically from the taboo of the female intellectual. On the contrary, a pleasing woman, in her opinion, is lively, sweet, coquettish, and charming. She needs to constantly play along with an implicit set of rules that subordinates intelligence to affability.

Repeatedly, the ideal woman was depicted from the vantage point of the heterosexual male gaze in women's discourses, while adopting 'dual personalities' in the presence and absence of men was normalized and considered essential. In addition to presenting the personality features noted above in excerpt (34), almost all the interviewed women expressed (in one form or another) the opinion that women need to be or appear to be emotionally weaker than men. At the same time, women stressed that they must be wiser than men and apply this wisdom to make men feel secure in their masculine strength and power. In elaborating this notion, women frequently utilized a Russian proverb: *mužčina golova, a ženščina-šeja* 'The man is the head, and the woman is the neck.' This idiom is used to describe a woman's seemingly inferior, yet ultimately directive position—one that allows her to control the man's vision, behaviors, and attitudes (i.e. the superior male 'head' must follow where the inferior female 'neck' directs it). In excerpt (35) Angelina (age 20) uses this saying to explain how women ought to behave with men, emphasizing the importance of guiding men, while maintaining the pose of inferiority.

(35)   *Devuška dolžna kak by pokazat', što vot ja ne mogu, vot pomogi mne, pomogi. To, što on ej pomogaet, to on kak by sebja vyše stavit, nu grubo govorja, ja vot molodets, ja vot pomogaju, vsjo takoje, a na samom dele, nu devuški oni umnee i oni kak by ljubjat i umejut mužčinami krutit', tak skazat' napravljat ih tuda, kuda nado. Mužčina golova, a ženščina-šeja. Devuška kak by napravljaet.*

'A woman must sort of show that 'look I can't, help me, help.' When he is helping her, he sort of puts himself higher, roughly speaking, 'I am so great, I am helping here' and such, but in fact young women are smarter and they like and can have a string on men to, let's say, guide them into the right direction. A man is a head, but a woman is a neck. A woman sort of directs a man.'

Angelina frames her speech in a way that emphasizes that a woman must inhabit two personas: her 'true' self and an artificial, inferior persona that she employs in order to make men feel valued. This duality is emphasized in the shift of her vocal pitch and volume when she says, *vot ja ne mogu, vot pomogi mne, pomogi* 'look I can't, help me, help.' The slightly higher pitch, quieter volume, and the repetition of the word 'help' enable Angelina to serve as an animator of the category 'ideal women,' depicting the feigned helplessness the ideal woman must display. As seen in Fig. 3.1, when portraying a hypothesized 'ideal woman' Angelina changes her body position by leaning forward to emphasize her solicitation. She places her hands on her knees with her palms open invitingly, withdrawing her gaze from the interviewer and looking down in deference.

These non-linguistic devices combine with her utterance to paint a vivid portrait of a modest, reserved, and helpless woman. From her other comments, we know that this is the dual self, the constructed persona she maintains to elicit male approval and affirm male expectations. By adopting the role of animator, Angelina is able to portray this complex category

Fig. 3.1 Portrayal of a helpless woman. Left to right: Angelina, Natasha

(an ideal woman displaying a partial or feigned persona to a man). As she explicitly states later in the interview, she does not self-identify with this category (ideal women); however, she clearly displays the behavior she deems appropriate. Linguistically, she produces a twofold utterance, shifting her footing through the change of vocal contours and body positioning, in order to create a depiction emblematic of the twofold personality of the feminine ideal.

To illustrate the effectiveness of the ideal woman's strategy for manipulating men's behavior, Angelina changes footing again, taking on the role of animator for a typical man. She starts with the adverbial preface, *grubo govorja* 'roughly speaking,' initiating a hypothetical man's reported thought in response to a woman's plea for help. In this shift of footing, she adopts a lower pitch—signaling that the forthcoming message is from a male speaker. Simultaneously, she lifts her hands, saying *ja vot molodets*

Fig. 3.2   Portrayal of a superior man. Left to right: Angelina, Natasha

'I am so great,' graphically demonstrating the feeling of the man's superiority over a woman (see Fig. 3.2).

Angelina ends her animated utterance with the hedge *i vsjo takoe* 'and all such things,' which is used to express the exhaustive nature of lists and to signal the difference between the footing of the animator and author of the utterance. She thus is able to return to her real position and continue articulating her own views on the subject. In actuality, she believes that women are more intelligent than men, and it is for this reason that she is able to employ dual personas to fool a man (sometimes even for his own benefit). In her view, the ability to convincingly feign incompetence is important in making a man feel cognizant of his 'higher' societal position. The speaker seems not to mind the implied patriarchal relationship, perhaps because she views this relationship merely as a play or contrivance, behind which the woman is situated in the key position (i.e. as a man's directing 'neck').

The necessity for Russian women to sustain dual personas can be most clearly observed in Aria's discourse, in which she describes the swift change, or pivot in behavior a woman must employ before and after engaging in a traditionally male domain such as martial arts. Aria (27) stresses that when a woman is in the gym practicing karate, she is free to be equal with her male partner. In fact, equality is a precondition of respectful engagement with the martial art and productive training for the woman and her partner. Once the session is over, however, it is imperative that she return, quickly and gracefully, to her feminine self. For instance, on the way home from such physical exercises, Aria insists that it must be the man who opens the door for a woman. In excerpt (36), Aria declares that she would not open the door to a building herself when she is with her male partner, even in extreme cases.

(36)   *Ja daze, kogda Danja s millionami paketov, ja vsjo ravno stoju i ždu, daze kogda dožd idjot na ulitse, liven', ja stoju i ždu.*

'I, even when Danja (i.e. name of the speaker's fiancé) is with millions of bags, I stand still and wait even when it rains outside, when it showers, I stand and wait.'

As seen from excerpt (36), Aria insists that even in the cases when her partner carries 'a million bags' and the rain is pouring heavily, she would not open the door by herself but rather wait for the man to do it. She later explains in excerpt (37) that encouraging chivalrous behavior in men is necessary, as it is a woman's duty and responsibility to mold a man.

(37)   *Kak by mužčinu sozdajom my. Vsegda mužčinu sozdajot ženščina, kotoraja rjadom nahoditsa. (…) Esli ty hočeš sil'nogo mužčinu, krepkogo, kotoryj uveren v sebe, uveren v tom, čto on zaščitnik i opora sem'i, to ty slabaja i ty dlja nego podderžka vo vseh ego načinanijah.*

'We are the ones who sort of create men. Always a woman creates her man. If you want a strong vigorous man, who is self-confident, confident that he is the protector and the supporter of the family, then you must be weak and you support him in all of his endeavors.'

Aria claims that it is essential to mask the woman's true self with an alternative persona that enables the male partner to enjoy and develop his masculinity. Aria does not state explicitly that women are smarter than men (as Angelina did), but she expresses a similar idea: according to her, it is women who are in fact *spiritually* superior to men, and thus can afford the pretense of appearing weaker. Aria then explains that men prefer for the boundaries between male and female domains to be clearly demarcated, simultaneously reinforcing this statement by gesturing toward two different spaces with her arms. While Aria does not overtly examine the reason why women would need to appear weak in order to validate male strength, it is likely that it reflects the presumption of spiritual weakness. Because men cannot always be affirmed in their strength and confidence in professional and public endeavors, it may be even more important to buoy up their vulnerable masculinity in the domestic sphere. Interestingly, Aria is a founder and a director of a tourist company, while her husband works as a hairdresser. Despite this seemingly non-traditional (and even counter-stereotypical) distribution of occupations in the family, Aria retains traditional views on femininity and a woman's role in interactions with her husband. This substantiates Lyon's claim (2007) that Russian women's gender beliefs and real practices frequently do not correspond. Although Russian women often have clear and traditional beliefs regarding what women should do in a household, they nevertheless do not always put these ideas into practice in their own homes. Even, as in Aria's case, when the occupational roles diverge profoundly from normative expectations, the framework of male-superiority and male-centric decision-making is retained and reiterated symbolically.

Another example of dual personas is found in the discourse of Alla (27), who after talking at length about women's need for independence and autonomy, later states that women must pretend to be weaker than men. In excerpt (38) below, she expresses the opinion that women should perform a kind of balancing-act in the precarious middle ground between a compromise and self-deprecation.

(38)   *Ženščina dolžna delat' tak, čto by mužčina byl sil'nee ejo, ne fizičeski,*
       net, moral'no. Prosto sozdaj uslovija, čto by on čuvstvoval sebja glavoj,
       čuvstvoval sebja sil'nej. Ona možet byt' ne to, čto ona možet byt' i
       sil'nee, no ona mudree.

'A woman must behave in a way that would make a man feel stronger than her, not physically, no, but emotionally. Just create conditions in which he feels as a head (of the family), feels stronger. She can be, it doesn't mean-, she might not be stronger, but she is wiser.'

Alla emphasizes that a woman exercises a special wisdom in allowing the man to feel comfortable and strong. She then continues her discourse by stating that even if a woman is stronger, she must maneuver in her relationship carefully, by avoiding direct confrontation and resorting to compromise. Alla does not utter the word 'maneuver,' but moves her hand in a serpentine curve (shown in Fig. 3.3), suggesting that a woman must flexibly adapt to changing circumstances and re-negotiate terms when necessary. The fact that she lowers her voice during this utterance suggests that the maneuvering must be covert, or at least hidden from male attention.

Fig. 3.3   Female maneuvering. Left to right: Alla, Dina

In excerpt 39, Alexandra (26) also concurs that women must pretend to be weaker in order for men to feel comfortable in their masculinity. She argues that a woman has both the ability and the responsibility to make her partner feel manly, and to this end, she must provide him with opportunities for masculine agency.

(39)   *Ona možet byť siľnaja. Ona možet delať vsjo, čto nado. (…) No s mužčinoj ona dolžna byť slaboj, mužčine ona dolžna davať prosto vozmožnosť byť mužčinoj.*

'She (a woman) can be strong. She can do anything that is needed. But with a man, she must be weak. She must just give a chance to a man to be a man.'

These twofold claims (of both subordination to and directive influence over men) diverge substantially from traditional gender ideologies, and present a more complex picture of women's ideals and self-construal . Whenever interviewees reiterated the necessity of prioritizing male leadership in decision-making, they immediately qualified these assertions by means of an additional clause in which they reestablished their worthiness (e.g. "in reality women are smarter," "she is wiser"). The interviewed women aimed to clarify that they did not actually believe in the woman's weakness. Rather, they merely acknowledged the necessity of appearing weak in the cultural context of contemporary Russian gender relations, both in order to bring satisfaction to their male partners and to achieve their own goals. These objectives range from molding an ideal man to achieving a happy and balanced relationship. It is noteworthy that (as seen in Table 3.1) only two women (Alla and Katya) did not work outside the house (both were on maternity leave). None of the women interviewed expressed a desire to stay at home and devote themselves exclusively to homemaking, even though they resorted to the traditional gender frameworks of women as homemakers and subordinates in order to explicate the ideal feminine personality. This is yet another instance in which Russian women's perception of ideal womanhood differed from their actual practices.

Table 3.1 Russian female respondents' demographic data

Pair number	Pseudonym	Age	Educational background	Current occupation
1	Ekaterina	22	BA in Japanese	English instructor
	Maria	21	BA in engineering (4th year)	Student
2	Olga	20	High school diploma	Part-time worker
	Aria	27	BA in tourism	Tourist company director
3	Darina	25	BA in Japanese	English instructor
	Marusya	25	BA in Japanese	English instructor
4	Alexandra	26	Certificate in design	Dance instructor
	Rosa	30	Certificate in accounting	Manicurist
5	Diana	22	BA in Japanese	Tour guide
	Olga	20	BA in Japanese (3rd year)	Student
6	Natasha	20	Certificate in communication	Part-time worker
	Angelina	20	Certificate in hairdressing	Hairdresser intern
7	Alla	27	BA in Japanese	Housewife (1 newborn)
	Dina	20	BA in stomatology (3rd year)	Student
8	Barbara	26	BA in Japanese	Salesperson
	Marina	26	BA in economics	Marketing specialist
9	Katya	28	Certificate in hairdressing	Housewife (3 children)
	Nelly	30	MA in Japanese pedagogy	Japanese instructor
10	Elina	27	BS in programming	Programmer
	Mila	30	Certificate in art design	Painter, designer

In these ways, the interviewees conceptualized the ideal woman as one who pretends to be weaker in order to be in charge, exerting wiser or more effective autonomy. Behind the veil of feigned weakness, women professed that, far from suppressing their independence, male authority instead functions as its most effective vehicle. This thinking could be a strong source of female emotional empowerment, implicitly relying upon the supposition of women's spiritual superiority. On the other hand, it may reflect a symbolic form of compensation, in which, deprived of some measure of actual power by patriarchal norms, women valorize a limited autonomy that must operate only derivatively, effectuated through the influence they exert on their partners.

Perhaps because the (covert) directive role of women over their male partners was legitimized by putative female moral superiority, all the interviewed women suggested in some way that the purpose of women's directive action was a beneficent attempt to bring light and kindness to the whole of society. These moralistic ideas about the role of women in society, frequent in textbooks on ethics and the psychology of family life, link women's elevated spiritual values with their nurturing qualities and their motherly instincts (Kay, 1997, p. 84). For instance, Marina (age 26) in excerpt 40 suggests the following mission for a young woman:

(40)   *Devuška, smysl jejo nesti etot svet v mir, ona dolžna byt', dolžna ukrašat'*
         soboj i zabotit'sja obo vseh, kto jejo okružaet nevažno skol'ko ej let.

'A young woman's mission is to bring her light to the world; she must beautify (the environment) by herself and take care of everyone around her no matter how old she is.'

The generality of Marina's statement is emphasized by such lexical choices as 'her mission,' and 'no matter how old,'—creating an impression that this is every woman's great task in life. This sentiment echoes the findings of "The Perfect You" competition held in 1992, in which women often affirmed that their central task was to bring kindness and joy to the world (Kay, 1997, p. 84). Marina also connects the decorative function of women to such lofty ideals by stating *dolžna ukrašat' soboj* 'must beautify by herself'. The obligatory nature of the modal verb 'must' in Marina's discourse emphasizes her conviction that women's beauty needs to be exercised at all times. Her statement even suggests that it is the woman's moral responsibility to appear visually pleasing, in order to share her loveliness with society and thereby make it a brighter place.

Another common thread in the interviewees' discourse is the awareness of self-worth, both in relationships and at work. While some women stressed that this awareness is self-derived and intrinsically important for maintaining self-esteem, others seemed to cultivate perceptions of self-worth primarily through (and for) the heterosexual male gaze. In other words, by cultivating greater self-worth, in their opinions, they would become more attractive for men. For instance, Rosa (age 30), who works as a manicurist, explicitly states in excerpt 41 that she aspires to look luxurious, and has taken her friend as a role model *precisely because* she is able to demonstrate her worthiness through her (constant) ability to attract men.

(41) *Ona možet prepodnesi sebja nastol'ko dorogo, ja u nejo etomu učus'.*

'She can present herself so luxuriously, that I am learning this from her.'

Even when Rosa describes the necessity for women to be engaged in activities unrelated to concerns of fashion and appearance, her reasoning returns to the centrality of the heterosexual male gaze. In excerpt 42, she explains how women's knowledge can be appropriately applied in conversations with men.

(42) ROS: *Nužno dumat' devuške, nužno byt' vsestoronne razvitoj. Ja ne govorju, čto ona dolžna byt' načitannoj i zaučennoj, prosto real'no-*

'A woman needs to think, she needs to be comprehensively developed. I am not saying that she must be well-read and all-studied, but just really be-'

ALE: *interesovat'sa*

'Have interests.'

ROS: *da, interesovat'sa ne tol'ko šmotkami i trjapkami, no i skazat' oj da ja včera-*

'Yes, have interests not only in clothes and rags, but say, "Oh yesterday I"-'

While Rosa here stresses the necessity for a woman to have casual knowledge in a variety of different spheres, she also suggests that a woman need not be deeply informed or excessively erudite, as this risks placing her into the 'undesirable' category. Her learning, it seems, succeeds to the extent that it makes her interesting, but goes too far if it challenges the epistemic authority of men or dangerously highlights her intelligence. Her negative stance toward scholarly endeavors is indexed through Rosa's usage of the adjectival form *zaučennaja*, which comes from the verb *zaučivat'* 'memorize' and the offensive term *zaučka* 'grind.' Rosa underlines that women do not need to reach the level of a 'know-it-all' and starts a word search by using fillers. Alexandra immediately provides the filler candidate 'have interests,' which Rosa willingly accepts and continues in her utterance. She then specifies that the 'interests' should not be solely centered upon choices of clothing but extend beyond traditional women's hobbies and preferences. She argues that in this case women should be able to boast about their lives, changing footing to a hypothetical exemplary woman who has diverse interests and capabilities. While saying, "Oh yesterday you know I-" she produces rising and falling motions with her palm, as seen in the first and second panels of Fig. 3.4.

Through the shift in footing accompanied by hand gestures and high vocal pitch, Rosa stresses the need for women to respect prevailing social conventions when they contribute to conversations, sustaining a feminine demeanor throughout. The fact that Rosa predominantly describes conversations with male speakers is seen from a personal anecdote presented in (43) below.

(43)   *Ja tam sižu s takimi stiletami i govorju parnju* (0.1) *ja korovy umeju doit'*. (0.1) *Per-pervoje takoje, "hy:"*

'I am sitting there with such long stylish nails, and say to a guy, I can milk <u>a cow</u>. Fir-first he was like, "Huh?"'

Fig. 3.4 Feminine way of storytelling: left to right: Rosa, Alexandra

This story plays off the tensions between traditional concepts of masculinity and femininity in order to illustrate Rosa's thoughts concerning ideal womanhood. She relates her experience with milking cows as an example of the diversity of her interests (the necessity of which she had previously attested). She changes the footing twice: first performing as animator to dramatize her own role in the story, and then subsequently to vocalize the man's reaction. To situate her story, Rosa first explains that the conversation took place when she was looking especially attractive with her long nails stylishly polished. When talking about her nails, she holds them up for inspection, as seen in the first panel of Fig. 3.5 below.

After a brief pause, Rosa returns to direct speech in a steady, unaffected voice, 'I can milk a cow.' After pausing again briefly to let the interlocutor appreciate the comical nature of her story, she turns her gaze to Alexandra to describe the astonished reaction of the male listener. The ridiculousness of the situation is conveyed through Rosa's touch of her temple, followed by spreading of her arms. The lexical item *takoje* 'like' serves as a quotation marker signaling the shift of footing. Instead of providing a verbal reaction from her male interlocutor, she utilizes a mimetic expression *hy* 'huh' (with a prolonged vowel [y]) to emphasize his extreme surprise. She also lifts her arms and head, and widens her eyes to animate her male interlocutor's disbelief upon hearing that Rosa is capable of cow milking. The animated man's reaction is seen in the second panel of Fig. 3.5.

Fig. 3.5 Male reaction to Rosa's milking a cow. Left to right: Rosa, Alexandra

Rosa's performance in enthusiastically animating this anecdote actively expresses the significance for her of soliciting acceptance and approval by men. She does not merely *state* that diverse interests (i.e. in areas not limited to fashion) are necessary for a woman, but tells a story that serves as a validation of diverse knowledge and pursuits. The climax of her story is the reaction of her male interlocutor's impressed amazement and bewilderment, emphasizing that the final justification of these interests is to be found in male approval. Crucially, Rosa does not go on to explain why and under what circumstance she has experience with milking cows, or what this activity means to her. The actual content of her interests and knowledge seems comparatively unimportant; the important point is that she is interesting to her male conversation partner and provides him variety in discourse.

In describing their own conceptions of ideal womanhood, the interviewees rarely evoked explicit epistemic stances, avoiding the use of such expressions as 'I think' or 'in my opinion.' Instead, they frequently generalized their knowledge, a maneuver suggesting that other reasonable women would share their opinions. Despite the fact that the interviewer explicitly asked women to give their *own*, idiosyncratic definitions of the ideal woman, linguistically, the speakers tended to create homogeneous normative categories of women and men, without epistemic reservations. This too serves as evidence that Russian women have internalized and rigidified ideals about femininity and the role of women in society, making it difficult to delineate separately their 'real' individual preferences. In fact, the majority of interviewees responded negatively when asked whether they resemble the ideal woman that they had described, while only four women stated that they were describing themselves. The importance of physical attractiveness and heterosexual male gaze considerations were evoked in almost all female speakers' narratives, suggesting that these notions are still strongly tied with femininity and women's roles in Russia.

Intriguingly, the explicit consciousness of the dual persona as a performance did not seem to prompt the interviewees to consider the performative nature of gender roles more generally. Women and men were held to have intrinsic, innate needs and aptitudes that justified their respective behaviors, obligations, and attitudes. The ideal woman is the one who navigates the given needs of men and the broader obligations to beautify society most effectively. That these needs and obligations are themselves constructed and reproduced and did not emerge prominently in the interviewees' discourse.

3.2.2 Egalitarianism and (Im)Balanced Autonomy

All interviewees in some sense claimed that an ideal young woman of 20–30 years of age should be confident and self-sufficient, and should carefully avoid appearing infantile and immature. Through the use of idiomatic expressions, proverbs, and sayings, the speakers engaged in Russian structured cultural knowledge. Three women produced a well-known Russian proverb *"Russkaja ženščina i v gorjaščjuju izbu vojdjot, i konja na skaku ostanovit"* "A Russian woman can both enter a burning hut, and stop a galloping horse," thereby implying that Russian women are capable of any task, no matter how hard and challenging it may appear. This saying is a paraphrase of two lines of Nikolay Nekrasov's poem (1864) "Frost the Red Nose" about Russian women in the suburbs. At present, this expression has been absorbed into the lexical inventory of Russian proverbs, without reference to its origin, as a way to vividly characterize the resilient and adaptable nature of Russian women. All interviewees' discourses incorporated discussions of women's strength, stamina, and independence as desirable characteristics to some extent. For example, in excerpt 44 Alla (age 27) described her conception of an ideal woman as both confident and autonomous:

(44)   *(…) ženščina dolžna byt' uverennaja, znat' čego hočet, stremitsa k nezavisimosti, (…) dolžna ponjat', čto ej nado.*

'A woman must be confident, know what she wants, seek independence, (…) must understand what she needs.'

Thus, Alla acknowledges that a woman of the 20–30 year age range should start behaving maturely, setting clear goals for herself and outlining the mechanisms for achieving them. In her view, this applies equally to both the professional and personal domains. None of the women, however, self-identified as feminists, a possible consequence of the belief that feminism is a Western European and American notion and the resulting stigmatized pragmatics of the word in the Russian language (Lipovskaja, 1997, p. 191). These connotations have led to frequent misinterpretations and misapplications of the term 'feminist' as a 'man-hater,' or an 'unfeminine, unattractive woman'—and as such, the term can be used as an insult. Upon learning that the researcher considered herself a feminist, the interviewees deployed change-of-state tokens and shifted the topic of conversation after a short pause. As seen in the National Corpus of Spoken Russian, the word 'feminist' frequently collocates with such adjectives as *voinstvujuščaja* 'militant,' *svihnuvšajasja* 'insane,' and *ogoltelaja* 'unbridled' that give the noun phrases in which it is employed negative connotations. This further confirms that the pragmatics of this term in Russian are linked to undesirable characteristics, while the semantics are frequently misunderstood.

The perception that Western European and American influences may corrupt Russian attitudes toward gender and sexuality is likely a significant barrier to the advancement of human rights and social justice. However, to my knowledge, there are no studies that have explicitly addressed putative associations between antipathy toward LGBTQ people and opposition to feminism in Russia. However, research on prejudices toward LGBTQ people in Russia suggests that individuals exhibiting such prejudices are more likely to perceive LGBTQ identities as mere social phenomena rather than to view these identities as deeply rooted in the nature of LGBTQ individuals (Gulevich, Osin, Isaenko, & Brainis, 2016, p. 79). Moreover, survey research has demonstrated associations between prejudice toward LGBTQ people in Russia and religiosity, authoritarianism, and social identification with traditional masculinity (Gulevich, Osin, Isaenko, & Brainis, 2018). While these correlational measures cannot suffice to establish a causal connection between antifeminism and intolerance of LGBTQ individuals in Russia, they are nevertheless suggestive. In the same way that many Russian people perceive feminism as an outside (Western) influence, many also view LGBTQ identities as a corrupting social phenomenon not native to Russian culture (Gulevich et al., 2018). To the extent that they value traditional 'authentically Russian' sources of authority, religion, and masculinity, they may see both advocacy for feminism and LGBTQ rights as exogenous threats.

Perhaps as a result of these dynamics, women are unlikely to self-identify as feminists or conceive of themselves in terms of active struggle for gender equality, even when they construe autonomy and self-sufficiency as indispensable virtues for women. Equality, insofar as it is valued in the discourses analyzed, emerges as an equality of competence and spirit; it is definitely not an equality or equivalence of roles, obligations, and expectations.

3.2.3 Ideal Russian 'Women's Language'

In addition to characterizing the ideal woman's personality and behavior, interviewees were also asked to describe the ways that the ideal woman would employ (or not employ) language. Much of the resulting discourse focused on the use or avoidance of 'strong' language or swear words. The interviewees had somewhat divergent opinions on swearing and its appropriateness for female speakers, but all 20 women emphasized that (in theory) such vocabulary should be avoided by both men and women. In practice, however, interviewees claimed that emphatic swearwords would generally be more permissible if used by a male speaker. Nevertheless, women admitted that they also use this type of vocabulary. Moreover, while the majority blamed themselves for 'foul' language, others admitted that in some circumstances swearing might be appropriate and even necessary. These responses portray both the multiplicity of opinions about swearing and the gap between women's social ideologies and their real language practices.

Nineteen out of the twenty women refuted the notion that most people who swear are male. When asked if men swear more frequently, Rosa responded with a sarcastic *Ja tebja umoljaju* 'I am begging you,' implying that such a belief is counterfactual. Mila elaborated that because of women's strong emotionality, they tend to become agitated and swear more than their more stoic male counterparts. In excerpt 45, Mila expresses her opinion on the underlying difference between the female and male psyche, and construes divergent socially acceptable behavior as a consequence of this dissimilarity.

(45)   *Ja sčitaju, čto mužčina dolžen bol'še sebja v rukah deržat'. Mužčiny vse-taki ne takie impul'sivnye kak ženščiny. Oni dolžny byt' normal'nymi lud'mi takimi, uravnovešennymi.*

'I think that a man must hold himself together. Men still are not as impulsive [lifts her arms] as women. [Waves her arms above the head]. They must be normal people, so, even-tempered.'

When describing the way men must behave, Mila uses the expression *deržat's sebja v rukah*, which literally means 'to hold oneself in one's arms,' implying that men should not lose their temper or act irrationally based on their feelings. The metaphor of arms is later indexed through Mila's non-verbal behavior. She does not state that women do not 'hold themselves in their arms,' but rather shows it by lifting her arms and waving them from side to side to dramatize the instability of women's emotions. She lifts her arms at the word *impulsivnye* 'impulsive' and starts waving them side to side when pronouncing *kak ženščiny* 'as women,' implying that women are very impulsive and cannot control themselves. Iconicity is also noticeable in Mila's vocal shifts. She raises and lowers the volume and pitch of her voice to convey the fickle and unstable nature of women, while when speaking of men, she selects a flatter tone without fluctuation to emphasize their stability. The dynamics of her hand movement can be seen in the Fig. 3.6 below.

After these gestures, Mila continues to elaborate on the type of character men must demonstrate, saying that they should be 'normal' and 'even-tempered.' This description contrasts with the previous demonstration of women's impulsivity. The notion that men constitute the default "normal" form and that women are a deviation or "a departure from the norm" has been quite common in early scholarship on language and gender (Jespersen, 1922). The stereotype of women's changing emotionality and irrationality is frequently utilized in Russian televised commercials, solidifying gender ideology in the mind of the audience by naturalizing and normalizing it.

Fig. 3.6   Impulsive nature of women. Left to right: Elina, Mila

Similarly to Mila, Alla also expressed her doubts about the received notion that women swear less frequently than men, claiming that women and men use swearwords in similar proportions, while Katya protested this idea, using sarcastic *Da, konečno eto ženščiny bol'še, po krainej mere v Rossii* 'Yeah, right, it is women (who use it) more, at least in Russia.' Katya suggests that peculiarities of the social environment in Russia encourage women to use vulgar expressions more frequently. She then clarifies that this happens primarily because 'Russian mentality' forces people to resort to emotionally charged vocabulary. She does not elaborate further on the topic of 'mentality' or cultural peculiarity, but admits that it is still more acceptable to hear a man swear, while a swearing woman triggers concern in passers-by, as presented in excerpt (46).

(46)   *Konečno, na ulitse budet diko slyšat' kogda ženščina materitsa, da i, kogda mužčina   materitsa, ty osobo prohodiš i ne obraščaeš na eto vnimanie, a kogda devuška, to ty uže kak-to smotriš, dumaeš, čto to ne to s nej, °čto kakie-to kosjaki v nej est'°.*

'Of course, in the street it would be wildly strange to hear a woman swear. Well, when a man swears, you pass by and don't pay much attention, but when a woman does that, you then look and think, something must be wrong with her, some issues (*kosjaki*) with her.'

Katya lowers her voice when describing people's reaction to a woman who swears, indicating the inappropriateness of that situation. She uses the lexical item *diko* 'wild' to convey how atypical and abnormal it would be to hear a woman swear in public (in contrast with men). Given that Katya herself admits to swearing, it might seem inconsistent that she cannot tolerate hearing this vocabulary coming from another woman. The difference lies in the acceptable zone of usage. If utilized inside the house, swearing seems to be less disturbing and more acceptable; in the public domain, it is only men who can enjoy this privilege without receiving a strict social judgment. In the speaker's view, a woman who swears 'in the street' must have some *kosjaki* 'issues, problems.' This slang expression originally referred merely to a door or window jamb, but has since developed the novel colloquial meaning of something unpleasant and problematic. Thus, a woman who swears outside the house, in a place where she can be heard by passers-by, risks being labeled as a problematic or disruptive individual suffering from emotional or psychological disorder. Despite the fact that women are held to be more emotional than men (and thus more apt to wish to express themselves in emphatic language), women are also imputed a great obligation to regulate their public behavior.

Another factor constraining the use of swearing vocabulary by women is the identity and nature of the addressee. Many interviewed women claimed that it is a taboo for a woman to swear in the presence of men. Aria, for instance, admits that she sometimes swears, but emphasizes that she avoids doing it in her partner's presence. Despite the fact that women use swearwords privately, she places swearing vocabulary firmly into the male domain, calling this type of jargon *grubaja sostabljajuščaja žizni* 'the rude component of life.' She then reasons that it is inappropriate for a woman's use because a woman is a 'natural carrier of femininity, tenderness, kindness' and a 'keeper of a pure origin.' When describing the innate femininity and kindness of women, she brings her palms to her

Fig. 3.7   Natural carrier of femininity. Left to right: Olga, Aria

chest as seen in Fig. 3.7, indicating symbolically that the sincere qualities of women come directly from their hearts. Aria then elaborates further on her logic, claiming that by swearing a woman loses a portion of her femininity in the eyes of a man and is reduced to his level.

Aria thus suggests that women's appearance and personality are not the only objects of men's meticulous scrutiny: women's language is also observed and regulated by male judgment. Because of this constant monitoring, when a woman swears, according to Aria, she 'loses a part of herself in men's eyes.' Aria then encourages women to realize this difference between the lexical prerogatives of men and women, and thus maintain their place in relation to men, as presented in excerpt 47.

(47)   *Što by mužčina sebja čuvstvoval mužčinoj, >i ty kak ženščina<. esli ty hočeš uvidet' rezul'tatov ot mužčiny, to ty i vedi sebja podobajuščim obrazom.*

'So that a man feels as a man, and you- as a woman, if you want to see the results from a man, then behave yourself appropriately.'

Fig. 3.8   Men's and women's places. Left to right: Olga, Aria

When articulating the necessity of making a man feel manly, Aria lifts up her left hand to indicate a high level. She then adds a lower level gesture with her right hand when she rather rapidly pronounces, 'you – like a woman,' as shown in Fig. 3.8. Finally, she again expresses the opinion that women need to possess dual personalities, behaving 'appropriately' with a man in order to achieve their goals.

The iconic usage of hand gestures emphasizes the woman's subordinate status to the man, while the gap between the hands suggests the degree of this subordination. There is a tension in the spatial metaphor employed here, insofar as a woman must not be 'reduced' to the level of a coarse man, but must appropriately maintain their feminine position (i.e. subordinate to men). This tension is derivative of the emphasis, in traditional Russian gender ideology, on women's purity and kindness of spirit. Incapable of direct agency, women complement male activity with spiritual and material supportiveness. If this nurturing nature is abandoned, their unique mode of feminine elevation is lost. Yet the supposition of this 'loss' is that women cannot hope to achieve men's direct agency, but must exert influence indirectly.

This logic of subordination, and its rather transparent physical demonstration, is common among the interviewees' discourses, but reflects the mainstream mentality rather than diverse individual practices. In fact, like most other respondents, Aria confesses to swearing often. Some women even gleefully demonstrated the extensive usage of this type of vocabulary by building whole sentences out of various obscene words. Nevertheless, the interviewed women had internalized the proscriptions of Russian society so thoroughly that they criticized other women for using these lexical items.

Maria, who acknowledged sporadic usage of obscene vocabulary, suggests that women should control themselves more, as shown in excerpt (48).

(48) 1 MAR: *Ja vsjo-taki sčitaju, čto da, devuške prinjato sebja bol'še kontrolirovat'.*
'I still think that yes, a young woman is supposed to control herself more.'

2 *nu ne krasovo iz ust takoj miloj devočki. [Animates a swearing woman]*
'Well, it's just not beautiful from the lips of such a cute girl.'

3 *[hhh*

4 EKA: *[hhh*
(0.1)

5 MAR: *Nu kak-to (0.1) Ponjatno, čto možno,*
'Well, like, (0.1). Of course, you can,'

6 EKA: [nodding]

7 MAR: *nu, eto delo každogo,*
'well, it's everyone's own business,'

8 *no ja sčitaju, čto lučše kak by,*
'but I think that it's better like'

9 EKA: [nodding]

10 MAR: *po krajnej mere, starat'sja.*
'at least try.'

Maria foregrounds the concern that vulgar language is incongruent with female beauty, reasoning in line 2, *nu ne krasovo iz ust takoj miloj devočki* 'Well, it's just not beautiful from the lips of such a cute girl.' To emphasize the incompatibility of women's appearance with the emphatic swearing, she selects language that emphasizes the cute and innocent nature of a young woman. The expression of *iz ust* 'from the lips' consists of the archaism *usta* 'mouth,' which is almost absent in spoken language, except when it is a part of an idiomatic expression such as the one that Maria employs. Because of its archaic nature, expressions containing this lexical item tend to carry a distinct literary flavor and a beautifying effect. To further demonstrate the despicable nature of a swearing woman, she shifts footing in order to act out a beautiful young woman who uses a swearword. As Maria pronounces the noun phrase 'cute girl' in the first panel of Fig. 3.9, she simultaneously enacts that image by performing a hand waving motion that stresses female naivete, purity, and beauty. Then, in dramatizing the use of emphatic swearing language, she lowers her head deviously, turning it to the side, as seen in the second panel below. Her facial expressions also undergo a visible transformation, turning unpleasantly angry, while she opens her lips as though to utter a harsh swearword. Even though Maria did not actually pronounce the implied swearword, by adopting the role of an animator she demonstrates the inappropriateness of a beautiful young woman's use of swearing.

Fig. 3.9 A beautiful young woman in an act of swearing. Left to right: Maria, Ekaterina

Maria's utterance is followed by shared laughter, but Ekaterina does not take the floor and Maria continues elaborating further on her position. In lines 5–10, she summarizes her position with an epistemic downgrade, stressing the necessity for women to at least try to avoid swearwords in their speech.

3.2.4   Interim Summary

Through the extensive use of gestures and footing, Russian women conveyed their stances toward various categories of women and men. They effortlessly and straightforwardly defined the key notions of femininity, predominantly emphasizing women's roles in relation to men. The interviewees had clear perceptions of the ways a woman must behave toward and converse with a man. They were able to identify the phrases a woman should use, the expressions she should avoid, as well as the topics she should and should not touch upon in the men's presence. All 20 women mentioned the necessity having an 'onsite' and an 'offsite' persona in the presence and absence of a man and the skill to swiftly and flexibly shift between them by adapting to the changing contexts. Thus, the interviewees tended to perceive themselves (and evaluate their self-worth) through the eyes of men, and yet also to emphasize the importance of independence and self-reliance. The female respondents claimed that these qualities must remain hidden from men, as they may appear threatening to male autonomy and agency.

Despite ease and fluency with which the interviewees reproduced ideological tropes related to contemporary Russian femininity, it is not clear to what extent Russian women actually follow the rules that are being imposed by media, advertising, and other "socializing agents" (Kang, 1997). Most of the women admitted that they were far from the ideals they described and needed to work harder to be more successful. Furthermore, the majority of the interviewees confessed that they indeed use swearwords frequently in interactions to express strong emotions. In Chap. 4 of the book, I will further assess the gap between women's real practices and societal perceptions of femininity by examining women's speech from the corpus of spontaneous conversations.

Despite acknowledging divergences between behavior and ideals, the interviewees did not question the constructed nature of gender categories, challenge the binary distinction between men and women, or acknowledge that feminine beauty can flourish outside heterosexual romantic relationships. The ideologically distinct traits, needs, and obligations of women and men, and their mutual constituency vis-à-vis one another, were repeatedly stressed. Unprompted, the interviewees articulated notions of ideal womanhood that were inextricably bound to and defined by relations with men and manhood. These tendencies may reflect, in part, the intensive socialization of women in the age range (20–30 years) examine, as well as the ubiquity of media messages promoting gender ideology (as discussed in Chap. 2). Future research should consider especially how differences in age, class, ethnicity, and sexual identity may disrupt the relatively homogeneous views expressed by the interviewees in the current sample.

3.3   Japanese Women's Discourses on Feminine Beauty

In the next several sections, analysis of Japanese women interviewees' discourse will be presented, with comparisons and contrasts offered to the analysis of the material from the Russian interviewees above. Table 3.2 below summarizes demographic data for the 24 participants, including their age, educational background, current occupation, and region of origin within Japan. Some interviewees indicated the city of their origin, while others only indicated the prefecture. Interviews were conducted in pairs according to the ordinal sequence presented in the table.

As noted in the introduction, the Japanese cohort is slightly younger than the Russian cohort: mean age 22.2 years, whereas Russian cohort's average age was 24.6. Perhaps due to this age disparity, the Russian women exhibited more diversity in occupation/employment, whereas Japanese women were generally undergraduate or graduate students pursuing academic degrees. These differences, however, do not diminish the significance and validity of the current analysis, the goal of which is to

Table 3.2 Japanese female respondents' demographic data

Pair	Pseudonym	Age	Educational background	Current occupation	Origin in Japan
1	Rika	21	BA in literature (3rd year)	Student	Gifu
	Natsu	22	BA in literature (4th year)	Student	Osaka
2	Mana	26	BA in law	Office worker	Tokyo
	Saya	21	BA in dentistry (4th year)	Student	Tokyo
3	Ayaka	20	BA in French (2nd year)	Student	Osaka
	Sari	20	BA in French (2nd year)	Student	Aichi prefecture
4	Aki	20	BA in engineering (3rd year)	Student	Ishikawa prefecture
	Momo	20	BA in nursing (2nd year)	Student	Osaka
5	Yume	23	BA in economics (4th year)	Student	Osaka
	Sako	23	BA in economics (4th year)	Student	Osaka
6	Shoko	21	BA in literature (3rd year)	Student	Akashi, Hyogo
	Eri	22	BA in literature (4th year)	Student	Kumamoto
7	Mari	25	MA in Japanese linguistics	PhD student	Osaka
	Mina	26	MA in Japanese linguistics	PhD student	Okayama
8	Haru	21	BA in literature (3rd year)	Student	Hyogo prefecture
	Yuri	20	BA in literature (3rd year)	Student	Kochi prefecture
9	Hana	26	MA in Japanese literature	PhD student	Toyama prefecture
	Tomoko	26	MA in Japanese literature	Researcher	Tottori prefecture
10	Aika	20	BA in literature (3rd year)	Student	Osaka
	Chika	21	BA in literature (3rd year)	Student	Fukui prefecture
11	Satoko	20	BA in history (2nd year)	Student	Okayama
	Ana	20	BA in linguistics (2nd year)	Student	Kyoto
12	Hanami	21	BA in linguistics (3rd year)	Student	Fukui prefecture
	Kari	20	BA in linguistics (3rd year)	Student	Okayama

explore Japanese and Russian women's opinions and stances on concepts of gender and language within these cultures. Intercultural comparisons, while not entirely unambiguous in all cases, will be examined on a case-by-case basis.

3.3.1 The Value of *kawaii*, and Constant Awareness of Others

Kawaii has been considered an indispensable component of Japanese femininity, required in each of the diverse spheres of a woman's life (Kinsella, 1995). Its meaning and significance extend far beyond a woman's external appearance, and encompass her speech, her habits of economic consumption, and her overall ability to express feelings of feminine gratitude and happiness (Richie & Garner, 2003). As discussed in Chap. 1 (Introduction), scholars have translated the conceptual content of *kawaii* in a variety of different (and sometimes potentially incompatible) ways, including characterizations such as "beautiful, lovable, suitable, addictive, cool, funny, ugly but endearing, quirky and gross" (Okazaki and Johnson, 2013, p. 7). At the same time, the literature has stressed the intimate interconnection between *kawaii* and femininity (Burdelski & Mitsuhashi, 2010, p. 67). In Chap. 2's analysis of Japanese televised commercials, I have shown that many advertisers aim to create a *kawaii* persona in their persuasive appeals by utilizing specific linguistic devices. In this section, I will investigate Japanese women's own ideas on the definitive qualities of the *kawaii* persona, its relationship to their conception of the ideal woman, and its perceived value to them. In the exploration of women's own voices on femininity and *kawaii*, points of consonance and dissonance with the prevailing culture will become more apparent.

As a preliminary metric, and to provide a starting point for subsequent discussion, I asked 24 young female respondents to indicate their visions of a *kawaii* woman in an open-ended, written form (see complete questionnaire in Appendix). The prompt question (presented in Japanese) was 'What kind of woman is *kawaii*, in your opinion?' and participants could indicate up to four characteristics in their responses. Participants were also asked to rate the personal importance of *kawaii* to them, on a scale of 1–5 (with higher values indicating greater personal importance). The results reveal a consistent pattern with respect to the core content of *kawaii*, and show that Japanese women have a clear understanding of its importance in society. However, there are also interesting divergences in the respondents' characterizations of *kawaii*, suggesting that modern Japanese women have a complex relationship with the concept.

Seventeen out of 24 women (71 percent) emphasized that a *kawaii* woman frequently smiles and is always in good spirits (($\chi^2(1) = 4.167$, $p = 0.04$). Five respondents indicated that *amae* 'the skill of relying on other people' makes a woman *kawaii*, while having a slender build, daintiness (*kyasha*), and 'acceptingness' (*sunaosa*) were each mentioned in four entries. Other responses concerning the components of *kawaii* included naivety, cheerfulness, friendliness, sensitivity to other people, a preference to avoid talking behind another person's back, good fashion sense, the ability to enjoy anything, and a tendency to get shy easily. Some respondents went even further, adding that a *kawaii* woman eats a lot, has flawless white skin and large, captivating eyes, wears skirts, particularly favors pink colors, and sports a type of a haircut referred to as *pattsun* (short bob haircut with bangs). Two participants intimated that a *kawaii* persona is selfish (*wagamama*), exhibiting childish behavior and using an annoyingly high pitch when speaking.

Japanese women thus seem to have a detailed understanding of what *kawaii* entails, although some of the features are contradictory, or at least in obvious tension. While most women adhered mainly to positive characteristics such as 'cuteness,' several respondents pointed out the negative side of *kawaii* by linking it to immaturity and infantilism. On average, participants rated the importance of *kawaii* as 3.9 out of a 5-point scale— making it more vital than intelligence (3.6) in the minds of Japanese women, yet less crucial than psychological stamina (4.0) and kindness (4.4). This data implies that despite the ubiquitous presence of *kawaii* in Japanese popular culture and the repetitive images of *kawaii* personas in televised commercials, Japanese women have a complex relationship with the set of characteristics that define *kawaii*.

This multifaceted relationship with *kawaii* was further investigated through interviews in which female participants were asked to elaborate on the importance of *kawaii* in their lives, as well as to describe their aspirations and tactics for becoming (or for avoiding becoming) *kawaii*. In these interviews, the ambivalent nature of *kawaii* became readily apparent, as interviewees expressed mixed attitudes toward different aspects of the concept. The interviewees also treated *kawaii* differentially based upon the modality in which it was expressed, distinguishing between cuteness of appearance, cuteness of speaking, cuteness of behavior, and overall cuteness of personality. This perception of cuteness supports Asano-Cavanagh's claim (2014) that the definition of *kawaii* encompasses not only looks, but also a woman's manner of communication and conduct, and extends even further to include a woman's holistic persona. Women agreed with the notion that *kawaii* has to appear natural and sincere—while created or counterfeit cuteness is undesirable and should be avoided. In excerpt (49), Sari and Ayaka express their stance toward *kawaii*. Previously, Ayaka had claimed that her ideal woman is *kawairashii* 'lovely.' The researcher then asked the interviewees if their ideal woman also possessed other aspects of cuteness. In response, both women raised a broader concern about what it means to be *kawaii*, questioning whether it is possible to deliberately make oneself cuter through effort or practice:

(49)   1 SAR: *Meccha muri ni kawaiku suru hitsuyoo wa nai to omou.* hh
        (nods twice). (0.1)
        'I think there is no point in trying extra hard to be cute'

2   *Nanka shizenna kanji de* (nodes once)
        'Like it (should) be natural'

3 AYA: *Sore ga kawa- shizenna no ga kawaii tte iu no kana.*
        Tsukutteru no- tsukutte

4   *kawaii no wa hontou no kawaii jyanai.* [hh
        'That is cu-. The natural is cute, I should say. The made-
        up, made-up cuteness
        is not a real cuteness.'

5 SAR: [hhhh

Fig. 3.10 True *kawaii* comes from heart. Left to right: Ayaka and Sari

In line 1 of this excerpt, Sari uses the colloquial adverbial intensifier *meccha* 'extremely,' stressing the absence of any strong effort to appear cuter than one actually is. She then nods emphatically, and after a brief pause adds that natural qualities, in particular, are important for an ideal woman. To emphasize that being *kawaii* should come 'from the heart,' Sari brings her palms up to her chest illustratively, as shown in Fig. 3.10. Ayaka then expresses agreement with Sari's stance and claims that a woman can only be truly *kawaii* if she is not pretending; otherwise, the term *kawaii* can no longer appropriately be applied.

Thus, through their speech and associated gestures, Sari and Ayaka explicated that *kawaii* is not an achievement or accomplishment of an ideal woman, that is, something one can become, but rather an innate quality or characteristic of personality, that is, something one is or is not. If a woman tried to deliberately bring herself into closer correspondence with the ideals of *kawaii* cuteness, without being *kawaii* at heart, she would risk being considered *burikko* "fake-*kawaii*" or "a woman who plays bogus innocence" (Miller, 2004, p. 149). While simultaneously stressing that *kawaii* cannot be achieved through effortful action, both Sari and Ayaka said that their ideal woman is *kawaii* and that they strive to approach that ideal as much as possible. These Japanese women appear to be in a kind of ideological double bind: they must approach their ideal but cannot do so consciously or explicitly. Thus, for *kawaii* to be achieved, they must bring themselves in line with the normative ideal in a manner that appears effortless and unforced. Anything else will qualify as insincere and untrue.

Similarly, Chika and Aika argue that *kawaii* is a very desirable quality for a woman, and explain that it consists of a holistic integration of components including cuteness of appearance, cuteness of speech, and cuteness of motion or gesture. Aika emphasized that accumulating all these characteristics is a tremendous challenge for a woman—but stressed that if a woman succeeds, she can be considered truly *kawaii*. The crucial feature of the *kawaii* self-presentation is that it must appear supremely natural so that people will have no cause to doubt the sincerity of a woman's cuteness. Make-up, Chika and Aika emphasized, must also be applied in a way that would make a woman look naturally and effortlessly cute. When Aika was asked if she personally valued being and maintaining *kawaii* in her everyday life, she utilized a hypothetical positive third-party assessment to convey her stance, as shown in excerpt (50).

(50)   *Wazawaza soo shiyoo to wa, so iu soburi o wazato shitari wa shinai n desu kedo, nanka a sonna iikata kawaii yo ne toka, iwareru to a, ureshii na to omoimasu.*

'I don't do, behave in this way on purpose, but if someone tells me, 'Oh your
way of talking is *kawaii*,' I am happy to hear that.'

Thus, Aika views the value of *kawaii* from the perspective of a third person whose positive evaluation of her she genuinely appreciates, but cannot solicit or control. After using the lexical item *nanka* 'like,' which in this context has the function of introducing an example, Aika changes footing in order to give a positive assessment of her own way of talking from the perspective of the hypothetical third party. She then employs the change-of-state token *a* 'oh', which signals surprise—and is regarded as an important component of a polite response to a compliment (because it underlines that the compliment has not been expected (Baba, 1999)). Even though Aika reflects on a hypothetical compliment from an interlocutor that she herself has created, she still uses a linguistic item that suggests unexpectedness. By doing so, she emphasizes that one should not have self-awareness of being *kawaii*, yet merely hope to appear naturally cute. When articulating the hypothetical compliment, Aika stretches her arms in front of herself, projecting the presence of the third party who produces the positive assessment. When changing the footing to show her appreciation of the compliment, Aika brings her arms closer to her chest, saying that she would feel happy. In addition, Aika uses a self-reflexive sentence-ending particle *na*, prolonging the final vowel in order to emphasize the sincere happiness she receives from being (hypothetically) called *kawaii*.

The desire evinced by the female interviewees to be seen as *kawaii* and to be complimented accordingly, together with the previous findings regarding *kawaii*-promoting televised commercials, shows that this concept has a well-established niche in the Japanese societal value system. Two essential facets of the *kawaii* concept that were repeatedly stressed in the interviewees' discourse are its purity and its lack of intentionality or purposiveness. Just as children do not realize their cuteness or cultivate it intentionally, women can only be regarded as *kawaii* if they are not conscious of their cuteness and are not trying hard to appear cute. In this way, it is similar to the concept *muku* 'innocence' with its focus on complete purity. Hana argues that this kind of natural sincerity is an essential component of cuteness (excerpt 51), while purposeful infantilism does not suit women after a certain age.

(51)   *Honnin ga ishikiteki ni kawaiku shiyoo to omotte, itteru tte iu no wa ma, anoo, amari yoku mieru mono de wa nai to omotte imasu.*

'If (the woman) herself consciously speaks trying to be cute, it is, well, it does not look good, I think.'

For precisely this reason, Hana criticized the female scientist Haruka Obokota, who used high pitch and lengthened word endings in a transparent attempt to appear cute. She then acknowledged that cuteness is multi-layered and asserted that a woman should not be faulted if she speaks overly cutely without intending to do so. Hana also added that every woman has her own, distinctive cuteness, which is revealed in various ways and in diverse contexts. Though she had previously suggested that cuteness could not be self-claimed or self-assessed, Hana later commented on the type of *kawaii* that she would aspire to become, as shown in excerpt 52 below.

(52)   *Fudan ni kuuru ni furumatte itemo nanka sono futoshita shunkan ga kawaii toka, nanka*
kooiu kuse ga kawaii toka.

'Even though she acts cool usually, in sudden moments she turns cute, or she has some
cute habits.'

In making this utterance, Hana implicitly acknowledges that there are a variety of ways to appear and behave cute, and that cuteness does not have to be evident in every action a woman undertakes. While she suggests that constantly radiating cuteness would not fit her persona, she does appreciate less overt or frequent forms of cuteness. The emphasis here is again placed on the spontaneity and sincerity of *kawaii* behaviors, conveyed through the use of the noun phrase *futoshita shunkan* 'sudden moments' and the lexical item *kuse* 'habit.' Because a woman may be faulted for faking cuteness, Hana aims to ensure that her ideal cuteness is realized naturally—one cannot forge her unconscious habits or strategically reveal spontaneous and unexpected cuteness. This kind of pure cuteness, absolutely free of pretense or affectation, is something that Hana admires in her ideal woman and hopes to achieve.

Japanese society thus pressures women to conform, without deliberate intention, to standards of cuteness that render them inferior to men in social relationships (Asano, 1996). The gender ideologies upon which the dogma of *kawaii* are based posit that feminine childishness, innocence, and cuteness are natural and innate features, and reject the claim that they are imposed by socialization pressures and gender norms. For this reason, it is unappealing to men to see the underside of their own desire reflected back by the woman who deliberately attempts to pose as *kawaii*. Women are expected to participate in their own assimilation to gender stereotypes without being so rude as to point out to men that they are doing so. By feigning naturalness, women reinforce the male illusion that the social domination of *kawaii* norms is spontaneous and natural, and thereby flatter the male desire for power and privilege.

Hana's friend Tomoko, who also shared the opinion that *kawaii* cannot be feigned, nevertheless suggested that at times a woman may need to lie in order to sound cute—and thereby please her male superiors. An excerpt from her discourse is presented in (53):

(53)   *Tada meue no dansee to hanashi o suru toki nanka ni, ma "shiri-masendeshita" to yutta hoo ga kawaiirashii toki ga jyosei toshite wa aru kana to omoimasu. (0.1) Taboeba, kiita koto ga aru mitaina toki ni mo, "Shirimasendeshita. Hajimete desu" to itta hou ga kono hito ga yorokobu no de areba, watashi wa soo shite imasu.*

'It is just when talking to a male superior, I think there are times when it is cuter for a woman to say, "I didn't know that." For example, at times, even though I have heard about it before, if I say, "I didn't know. It's the first time" it makes a man happy. If that's the case, I do that.'

Thus, according to Tomoko, there are circumstances in which acting cute by concealing one's actual knowledge or experiences is a desirable mode of behavior. In her discourse, she suggests that her behavior can be determined by the male superior's preferences, rather than her own. If something as easy as stating 'I didn't know' would bring him happiness, Tomoko would gladly take this opportunity in order to build a better relationship. This double standard toward *kawaii* and women who use it strategically comes from its high value in the Japanese society and the benefits that appearing *kawaii* may bring, thus making it highly attractive if practiced skillfully. In order to be a skilled practitioner, however, Tomoko must sabotage her attempts to appear knowledgeable or well informed in order to maintain the fictive superiority of the men who hold professional sway over her.

Cuteness is not the sole or even the most important criterion by which a woman's conduct is evaluated, and should be exercised only in a limited set of contexts such as the one presented in excerpt (53). In addition to cuteness, Tomoko also suggested that a woman must always demonstrate a high level of education and culture. She emphasized in the following excerpt (54) that even such simple actions as taking an object should be done gracefully and femininely.

(54)   *Tatoeba mono o toru toki ni gaato torazu ni, koo chanto yubi o soroete toru toka, oto o tatenai toka, soo iu nichijyoo tekina   koto ni, ma soitta koto ni kuwaete kyooyoo ga aru to iu koto daiji kana to omoimasu.*

'For example, when taking things you don't take it roughly, but put your fingers together when taking, and not make noise, in these kinds of daily activities it is important to show your culture.'

Thus, through the example of the care with which one must execute even mundane actions, Tomoko conveys the idea that cultural upbringing and education should shine through in every aspect of a woman's behavior. A woman must always demonstrate a high level of culture, whether conveyed through words, through actions, or through gestures that are beautiful and refined. Such graceful gestures both bring an aesthetic pleasure to others and serve as a visible proof of a woman's worth. Tomoko's views correspond to a traditional understanding of Japanese femininity rooted in visual sophistication and refinement (Ide, 1990). Thus, in her opinion, both the traditional values and *kawaii* properties are essential for women.

Interestingly, even though the interviewees criticized women who merely pretend to be cute in order to gain the appreciation of men or receive other benefits, they still enjoyed watching televised commercials in which women overtly portrayed stereotypical images of feminine cuteness. The female interviewees responded positively to these artificial images of cuteness in spite of the scripted nature of the advertisements. Some women even expressed a desire to attain that kind of idealized cuteness for themselves, and to be able to smile and act adorable like the women in the commercials. For instance, transcribed below in (55) is an exchange between Ayaka and Sari, in which they discuss the way a Japanese actress and model Tsubasa Honda smiles in a commercial for deodorant. Born and raised in Osaka, Ayaka is a speaker of Kansai dialect; her friend Sari, from Aichi prefecture, speaks Nagoya dialect. Prior to this exchange, in excerpt (55), Ayaka and Sari had been discussing the way the actress in the commercial smiles, speculating on whether they would be able to appear as cute if they started using the advertised deodorant. The fact that they would thus be overtly creating or enhancing their cuteness, rather than simply and spontaneously revealing their innate *kawaii* qualities, does not seem to pose a problem.

(55)   1 AYA: *Warattetara kawaii na. Anna waraikata shitai na.*
                  'It's cute when she laughs, right? I want to laugh like that.'

        2 SAR: *Nanka ne-*
                  'Like-'

        3 AYA: *Nanka na, nanka kitanai waraikata jyanakute na. Niko tte na, onna no ko ppoi.*
                  'Like you know, not a rude laugh, but a cute laugh, girl-like.'

        4 SAR: *Soo, risoo tekina waraikata yo.*
                  'Yeah, it is an ideal way of laughing.'

Overall, they used the word *kawaii* seven times in reference to the women in the commercial, supporting the notion that even artificial or fictional cuteness can be appealing. In line 1, Ayaka conveys a positive stance toward the cute nature of the actress's laugh and uses the sentence-final particle *na*, a Kansai dialectal form that corresponds to the particle *ne* in Standard Japanese. By doing so, she elicits confirmation from Sari, who in line 2 starts her utterance (*nanka ne* 'like'), but is interrupted by Ayaka in line 3. Ayaka elaborates further on the type of laugh that she finds especially suitable for girls, using the mimetic *niko* 'smiley.' Finally in line 4, Sari summarizes her stance toward the cute laugh by saying that this is the ideal way to laugh. Thus, Ayaka and Sari have a very clear-cut notion of what constitutes *kawaii* and are able to recognize it easily in cultural representations such as televised commercials. As long as the representation of *kawaii* does not appear overly exaggerated, they are not repulsed by its artificiality and aspire to reproduce it in their personal lives as well. Thus, based on the analysis of the Japanese interviewees' conversations, it seems that a woman must either be innately *kawaii* (if that is in fact possible), or be skilled enough at acting to create a realistic and credibly cute persona. Because *kawaii* is so highly regarded in Japanese society, it is understandable that some women would aspire to explicitly enhance *kawaii* attributes in an attempt to fit in and be positively evaluated.

Rika and Natsu developed this idea further in their conversation, suggesting that women may employ a variety of techniques to become cute—even though they felt unskilled at these tactics personally. They claimed that cuteness can be helpful in a number of different social contexts and that *kawaii* women get better treatment overall. An excerpt from their conversation is presented in (56) below.

(56)   1 NAT: *Gendo ga kawaii hito wa nanka sokosoko atsukai ga chigau to omoimasu.*
'I think that people who speak and act cutely receive a moderately different treatment.'

2 RIK: *Nanka shuudan no naka de ikite iku ue de aru teido kawaikatta hoo ga hhh nan tte iu ka raku desu ne.*
'Like, when living in a group of people, it is, how should I put it? It is easier if you are *kawaii*.'

Both Natsu and Rika agree that being *kawaii* is a beneficial quality and that it can alleviate difficulties by securing positive feedback from society. Natsu uses the adverb *sokosoko* 'moderately' to characterize the difference in treatment that a *kawaii* and a non-*kawaii* woman would receive. Despite the fact that being *kawaii* is understood as a quality that must come spontaneously from within (rather than being cultivated or attained), it is primarily applied and evaluated in interactions with others. Whether or not a woman is *kawaii* can only be assessed from the standpoint of another party, and the ultimate reward of being *kawaii* is a better treatment by others. Thus, while *kawaii* is ideologically articulated as a construct that is innate and dispositional, it is in fact interactional and relational. For this reason, it is unsurprising that Japanese women often aspire to be *kawaii* not because they intrinsically value the associated personal qualities, but in order to 'fit in' to the broader fabric of society and enjoy the benefits of cuteness. Some women explicitly stated that in contemporary Japan, *kawaii* is one of the most valuable assets for a woman, and one of her most powerful tools in social relationships. Thus, unlike some other misconceptions about women, *kawaii* is a stereotype that has a positive connotation. For instance, Shoko made the following claim about *kawaii* in excerpt (57).

(57)   *Nakute anoo son o suru koto no hoo ga ooi to omou node, yappari attara toku o surun jyanai ka to omou.*
'Well, if you don't have (cuteness), you'll suffer a greater loss, so I think if you have it, you will benefit.'

Shoko in her utterance suggests that being *kawaii* is beneficial to a woman, while absence of this feature is disadvantageous. She uses the adverb *yappari* 'as expected' to stress that she has noticed this issue and thought about it before. She further expands on her strategic use of *kawaii*, suggesting that she deliberately employs a childish way of speaking when she wants to be forgiven or receive a kinder attitude from her parents, friends, or romantic partner. For instance, she claims that in these circumstances she would incorporate such lexical elements as the sentence-final particle *mon* 'because,' (which is associated with a child's register) in order to make her fault seem more forgivable. When giving an example of this kind of behavior, she uttered *datte au to yuttotta mon* 'because as I told you I would meet.' As seen in Fig. 3.11, in tandem with her falling intonation, Shoko also shifted her gaze downward and away from her friend Eri's gaze—as if asking meekly for forgiveness.

By consciously performing a *kawaii* persona, Shoko aims to awaken feelings of kindness and strength in her fictive male interlocutor, imploring him for lenience and understanding.

The sisters Saya and Mana express a similar hope of receiving lenience through the use of *kawaii* behaviors. Mana defines a *kawaii* woman as a

Fig. 3.11 Expression of *kawaii*. Left to right: Eri, Shoko

person who is able to secure the liking and affection of other people skill-fully (*umaku hito ni sukareru*). She then identifies specific instances in which this quality proves useful and valuable, indicating a high degree of awareness of the importance of being *kawaii* in everyday life. An excerpt from her discourse is presented in (58) below.

> (58)　*Tatoeba kaisha demo shinnyuushain tte saisho haittara, shigoto toka dekinai kedo kawaisa, nanka umaku "oshiete kudasai" toka, chotto tanoshiku kaiwa dekitari toka de, kawaigatte moraeru yoo na tokoro tte iu no wa sugoi daiji dakara (0.1) jyosei toshite. Josei toshite? tte iu ka, ma, kawaisa wa sugoi daiji kana.*
> 'For instance, even at a workplace, when a new person enters a company, she can't do work, but cuteness (helps), by saying things like "Please teach me," or by being able to converse in a fun way. The ability to get liked is really important. For a woman. For a woman? Yeah, well, I think cuteness is very important.'

Mana here reflects on the practical utility of having a *kawaii* personal-ity. She shifts footing in order to animate the hypothetical situation of a new female employee who lacks work-related knowledge and must ask a superior for help. She initially looks downward meekly, as shown in the

Fig. 3.12   A new employee's obsequious cuteness. Left to right: Saya, Mana

first panel of Fig. 3.12, but then shifts her gaze upward and starts smiling (toward the hypothetical male superior) in the second panel, as she says *oshiete kudasai* 'Please teach me.'

The ascending gaze suggests the hierarchical relationship between the employee and her superior, underlining the supervisor's higher position. As noted above, this sort of a pleasing smile is a crucial part of appearing *kawaii*. In the survey data reported at the beginning of this section, more than 70 percent of the female respondents indicated that frequent smiling is a necessary component of the *kawaii* woman's persona. Mana also raises her vocal pitch considerably when animating the new employee's cute speech, while stretching the final syllable *sa* in *kudasai* 'please.' All of these features combine to facilitate the creation of an effective *kawaii* image. At the conclusion of her utterance, Mana affirms that this kind of behavior is strategically important for a woman. For a second, she seems to express mild doubt regarding the validity of her claim, by repeating *josei toshite* 'for a woman' with a rising intonation—but ultimately confirms her initial intuition by reiterating that cuteness is indeed very important.

As revealed in the excerpts above, the interviewees' stances toward the constellation of features associated with the *kawaii* persona is complex. On the one hand, women are expected to be *kawaii* in Japanese society and they are treated much better when they bring their words, actions, and appearances in line with these expectations. On the other hand, the requirement that cuteness must be spontaneous and natural forces women who are not "innately *kawaii*" to work to feign or cultivate these qualities. If, however, she is suspected of insincerity or 'acting', a woman risks being labeled *burikko*, which places her in an even more vulnerable category than before. As Sako states, *genki kawaii wa ii kedo, burikko kawaii wa iran* 'I like cheerful cute, but I don't need *burikko* cute.' For many women, however, the value of attaining *kawaii* cuteness outweighs the potential risks. As noted above, the threat of the *burikko* woman is really twofold—she not only indecently exposes her personal insincerity and manipulating nature but correlatively reveals the constructed nature of the whole system of gendered social relations codified in *kawaii*.

3.3.2   The Feminine Virtue of Kindness

Kindness was another feature deemed highly important by the female participants. In response to the question "What kind of a woman is ideal for you?" 16 of the 24 interviewed women (67 percent) referenced the quality of kindness in some form. In addition, in actual conversations, each of the women without exception brought up the topic of kindness when addressing the qualities of idealized femininity that she personally hoped to acquire. Unlike the quality of *kawaii* cuteness (which as previously discussed must come spontaneously 'from the heart'), *yasashisa* 'kindness' was framed by the interviewees as a consciously cultivated quality. The female participants emphasized that women need to actively work on themselves in order to develop greater kindness toward others. The distinctive features of the *yasashisa* quality also involve constant awareness of and attention to the needs and feelings of other people. According to the interviewees, the ideal woman would never disturb others or interfere with their goals, but would always remain attentive, kind, grateful, and considerate. When discussing kindness, women used such phrases as *kikubari ga dekiru* 'can consider others' feelings', *omoiyari ga aru* 'be very caring,' *ki ga kiku* 'be thoughtful of others,' and *jibun no naka ni yoyuu ga aru* 'have enough room inside oneself to think of others.'

Kindness is tied to "emphasized femininity" (Connell, 1987), an ideological construct that is viewed by scholars as an accommodating, subordinate complement to hegemonic masculinity (Charlebois, 2014). The force and scope of this type of femininity can be explicitly seen in the conversations of the female interviewees as they elaborated on the nature of kindness. For example, Rika and Natsu formulate their discourse in the following manner (excerpt 59).

(59)   1 RIK: *Ki no kiku jyosei wa risouteki da na to iu fuu ni wa omoimasu.*

      2   *Nanka patto ugokeru yoona jyosei wa ii na to omoimasu ne.*
'I think that a woman who is thoughtful of others is ideal. A woman who can
react fast is great, I think.

    3 NAT: *Soo desu ne. Tatoeba nomikai toka de* (0.1) *nan to iuka* (0.1)
'Yeah. For example, at a company get-together, how should I say-'

    4 RIK: *Sarada o tori wakeru toka* hhh
'Like divides and serves the salad for everyone.'

    5 NAT: *A, soo desu ne.*
'Oh yes, right!'

In excerpt (59), Natsu and Rika co-construct a narrative on ideal feminine behavior at a company *nomikai* 'get-together.' In lines 1 and 2, Rika suggests that she sees thoughtfulness about the needs of others as a necessary component for a woman, one explicitly linked to her rapid and efficient reactions in response to changing situations. Natsu expresses agreement with Rika's stance and chooses to elaborate further on it by bringing up a specific context—a company after-work get-together. As Natsu is struggling to give a concrete example of efficient, thoughtful behavior, Rika again takes the floor and offers a potential context (dividing and serving a salad for everyone) in which women's ability to react quickly and adaptively would be especially appreciated. Serving food to male colleagues has traditionally been considered good etiquette for Japanese women (Lebra, 1984), while currently it is seen as a representative feature of *jyoshiryoku* 'female power' (Ogawa, 2014). In line 5 of the conversation above, Natsu accepts Rika's example and laughs, confirming their shared knowledge on this issue.

Similarly, in her discourse Mana suggests that an ideal woman is able to skillfully take care of the people around her by being very attentive to their needs. In the following excerpt (60), she elaborates on an ideal woman's kind behavior in the context of group dining.

(60)   *Risoo no jyosee tte nanka tatoeba minna de gohan toka shitetemo, koo minna no jyookyoo o mitete, nanka hanashitenai hito ga itara umaku wadai futte agetari toka, nanka chotto hito no hanashi o kiite agetari toka demo jibun mo hanasetari toka, ato wa ne guai warusoo dattara guai warui no kizuitari toka, nanka chotto.* (0.1) *Kizukai ga dekiru to sugoi hyouka ga takai.*

'An ideal woman is for example when everyone is having a meal, she monitors everyone's state and if there is someone who is not talking, she skillfully brings the conversation topic to him, listens to other people, but is also able to speak up. Also, if someone looks like he is not feeling well, she notices it and (helps). If you are able to be mindful of others, you are highly praised.'

As seen in the excerpt, the ideal woman is constantly aware of the emotional and physical states of other people. She needs to keep track of those who are participating in the conversation and those who are left out, and must occasionally intervene constructively to maintain a balance in which everyone has an enjoyable experience. This constant monitoring may appear distracting for a woman, but it is further compounded by the requirement that she also participate in the conversation by expressing (tasteful and appropriate) opinions. In addition to observing others' engagement at the party and contributing selectively, Mana's ideal woman must also attend to physical and emotional conditions indicated by non-linguistic cues, and help to alleviate any discomfort or distress. After Mana gives a series of specific examples, she generalizes her stance by saying that in Japan a woman's value is elevated if she is able to be thoughtful and mindful of others.

Thus, according to the female interviewees, in addition to being *kawaii*, women also must be respectful and mindful of their colleagues, honing the ability to guess their moods and desires. Despite the fact that contemporary Japanese women engage actively in work and pursue career advancement, they are still expected to play the traditional role of a supportive homemaker at workplaces and after-work get-togethers. The respondents claimed that Japanese society praises and encourages women who are able to bring their 'feminine' nature into professional settings. Such gendered expectations did not appear unjust to the respondents, who rather aspired to develop these skills in order to raise their value at the workplace and improve professional relationships. Some respondents explicitly articulated the idea that women need to remember their biological sex and act accordingly, evoking traditional stereotypes and beliefs about the role of women in society. For instance, when discussing the attributes of an ideal woman, Mari (a graduate student) explained that she sought to master the art of acting femininely, especially by showing weakness and respect toward men. The interaction between Mari and her friend Mina is presented in excerpt (61) below.

(61)   1 MAR: *Jyosei rashisa o wasurenai tokoro ga-*
                'It's (important) not to forget your feminine side-'

      2 MIN: *Soo desu ne. Jibun ga onna tte iu koto o wasurenai yoo ni.*
                'Yes. So that you don't forget that you are a woman.'

      3 MAR: *Soo. Nanka jyosei toshite nanka koo dansei o tatetari toka-*
                'Yeah, and as a woman to honor a man, for example.'

      4 MIN: *A, SOO nan da!*
                'Oh is that so?'

      5 MAR: *Ma, sore wa kachikan no chigai kamoshirenai*
                'Well, it could be a difference in our values.'

As seen from the interaction above, Mari and Mina initially express agreement, co-constructing the dialog in lines 1 and 2. Mina shows solidarity with Mari's stance on the importance of remembering womanliness, promptly rephrasing Mari's statement in a more straightforward fashion. Whereas Mari had used the lexical item *jyoseirashisa* 'femininity,' Mina utilizes a more direct phrase *onna tte iu koto* 'the fact that you're a woman' emphasizing that women should not forget their gender. In line 3, however, Mari expresses a more overtly traditional notion—that women must honor men—using a phraseological expression *dansei o tateru* 'to treat man with due respect,' and suggests that an ideal woman

Fig. 3.13 Honoring a man. Left to right: Mina, Mari

should be able to make a man feel good about himself. To convey her stance, Mari supplements her language gesturally, raising her hand in order to dramatize the elevation of male self-esteem, as shown in the first panel of Fig. 3.13. When she completes her turn, Mina uses a change-of-state token *a* 'oh,' indicating that she was not aware of Mari's stance. In addition, she raises the volume of her voice, suggesting that this new information is unexpected and surprising to her. Mina's body movement also emphasizes the startling nature of Mari's statement, as shown in the second panel of Fig. 3.13. Prior to line 4 of the excerpt, she had been looking downward (as in first panel of Fig. 3.13), participating in the dialogue mainly through co-construction with Mari and expressing aligned stances. It takes Mina approximately three seconds to hear and process the new information regarding her friend's traditionalist stance toward men, after which she turns her head toward Mari and looks directly at her with an expression of bewilderment. She no longer speaks to the researcher, but instead directs her words to her friend, highlighting their difference in opinion. Her interjection in line 4 "Oh, is that so?" conveys her divergent stance, which Mari interprets as indicative of a difference in attitudes regarding the appropriate behavior of women toward men. In line 5, she attributes these differences to an underlying dissimilarity in their values.

Mari goes on to claim that the best women (*josei no toppu*) can skillfully honor men, and affirms that she personally views this ability as laudable and useful. Mina gradually defers to her friend, shifting her stance to one of partial agreement, and finally states that she would also like to cultivate this ability, if possible. However, in a later (private) conversation with the researcher Mina explained that she was shocked to learn of her friend's old-fashioned, patriarchal beliefs. The interaction between Mari and Mina draws attention to the heterogeneity of opinions amongst young Japanese women regarding gender and femininity. While many no longer support traditional gender ideology, it is still pervasive within the culture and maintains an important role in the value systems of some individuals. Most interviewees also conveyed ambivalent views, expressing positive stances toward female autonomy while simultaneously criticizing women who become too authoritative.

For example, Sako conveys a negative stance toward women gaining strength and power in relationships. First, she expresses discontent at the fact that men sometimes feel obligated to carry women's belongings, such as a purse. Her belief that this behavior is a capitulation to the whims of unreasonable girlfriends or spouses (rather than a man's autonomous choice or gender-based obligation) can be observed through her use of a causative verbal form *motaseru* 'make carry.' Through this form, she not only indicates that women compel male partners to carry their bags, but also positions men as victims. She then continues her discourse by providing other examples of emasculating male subjugation to women. In Sako's opinion, a man who stands in the train with a baby-carrier while his wife is comfortably seated is a victim of female oppression. An excerpt from her interaction with the researcher is presented in excerpt (62) below.

(62)   1 SAK: *Danna san ga koo mae kake o shite yatteru no wa iya.*
                 'I don't like when a husband carries a front baby carrier.'

       2   *Nanka josei tsuyoku natte kita tte kanji ga suru.*
                 'It feels like women became strong.'

       3 RES: *Iwakan ga-.*
                 'Do you have a sense of discomfort?'

       4 SAK: *Iwakan ga aru.*
                 'I do.'

       (5 liness omitted)
       10 SAK: *Mae kake mitaina no o tsukete aruiteru no o mite,*

11   *de okusan ga tonari de meccha kaimono o shitete,*
12   *danna san ga kou yatte kaimono o shiteru sugata o miteiru*
      no o mitara,
13   *°waa° onna no hito tte*
14   *nanka jyosei rashiku wa nai to omou.*

'When I see a husband carrying a baby in the front baby carrier and the wife who is shopping a lot next to him, while he watches her do that, I think to myself, "Wow, and that's a woman!" I think it is unfeminine.'

As seen from the interaction (excerpt 62), Sako's sympathy clearly lies with husbands who are made to carry babies because of their wives' strong positions in the household. This change in gender roles presents a source of discomfort for Sako, which she voices in her criticism of women as unfeminine for their deviance from traditional femininity. Sako's negative stance toward the growing strength of women in family and household relationships is expressed through both linguistic and non-linguistic cues. When she begins speaking about men carrying babies for their wives, she animates both the hypothetical, victimized man holding his baby and her own reaction. As seen from the first panel of Fig. 3.14, she lifts her arms upward toward her chest to demonstrate the way the man is holding the baby; through her facial expression of unpleasant surprise, she then conveys how this scene makes her feel.

As Sako terminates the nominalized structure (*Danna san ga koo mae kake o shite yatteru no* 'a husband carries a front baby carrier') with the

Fig. 3.14 Feeling discomfort at the sight of a man carrying a baby. Left to right: Yume, Sako

straightforward assessment *iya* 'unpleasant,' 'detestable,' she simultaneously moves her hands slowly downward and leans back. These gestures animate a figurative withdrawal from the enacted scene, and serve to accentuate her disagreement with such a social arrangement in which a woman appears stronger than a man. Her facial expression also undergoes a pronounced alteration just as she shifts footing to her past self during the encounter with the baby-carrying father. In addition to surprise and bewilderment, her facial features also communicate a feeling of unpleasantness and revulsion.

In line 2 of excerpt (62) above, Sako observes that women have gained strength in Japanese society, a phenomenon that makes her feel odd and uncomfortable, as confirmed by her response to the researcher's question in line 4. Sako's friend Yume then shows partial alignment by stating that she also dislikes it when a man uses a baby carrier. She adds that while she does not mind when a man pushes a stroller and a woman carries a baby, the opposite combination is appalling to her. After further elaboration, Sako provides another context in which it is displeasing to see a man carrying a baby: when a woman is doing a lot of shopping. Sako uses the adverbial intensifier *meccha* 'a lot' in line 11, emphasizing the unreasonable nature of a wife thoroughly engrossed in shopping. She depicts vividly a self-absorbed, negligent woman who exploits her husband's kindness to avoid direct motherly responsibilities. Sako conveys a critical stance toward the woman in the scene, but a sympathizing stance toward the man—who has been victimized by his strong wife. Sako paints a dramatic portrait of a man patiently holding the baby and watching passively as his wife buys multiple commodities, presumably for herself. As she describes the man obediently following his wife with the baby, Sako elevates her hands and produces a baby-rocking motion, as shown in the second panel of Fig. 3.14. Her facial expression in the image reveals the unpleasantness that she endures merely from considering such a situation. When conveying her feelings about the scene, she shifts footing and says, *waa onna no hito tte* 'Wow, and that's a woman.' By prefacing this utterance with a prolonged interjection *waa* 'wow' in a lowered voice, Sako emphasizes the disgust she feels toward the woman and her negligence of womanly duties. In line 14, she summarizes the reason why she disapproves of the woman shopping in a store, calling this type of behavior unfeminine.

Through the examples of the two female-led couples, Sako communicates her stance of repugnance toward modern, strong women, whom she sees as *jyosei rashiku wa nai* 'unfeminine'. Apart from compelling their husbands to carry babies, the women in her examples do not engage in activities traditionally considered unwomanly. The first woman merely sits comfortably on the train, while the second woman shops. Thus, their principal unfeminine fault lies in the subversion of male power and the domination of their husbands. Furthermore, despite Sako's radical disapproval of strong women, her manner of speaking does not conform to the artificial speech norms of Japan's ideal woman (metaphorically called *yamato nadeshiko* (lit. Japan's carnation) 'a woman who displays the feminine virtues of old Japan'). Though she and the researcher had never met before, Sako exclusively utilizes plain, informal structures, avoiding the more formal style (e.g. using politeness suffixes *masu/desu*) that would normally be considered appropriate in a research interview setting. Furthermore, she does not employ many mitigating structures or other linguistic devices aiming to convey indirectness, but rather produces concise and straightforward utterances. These atypical linguistic features might be attributed to the fact that she is speaking with a foreign researcher from an American institution. However, her style of speech does not alter markedly based on the presence or absence of the researcher. Instead, Sako's linguistic and non-linguistic behavior suggests that this 'upfront' mode of speaking merely reflects her typical lexical preferences. Later in the dialogue, Sako confides that in the presence of her professor, she can even say the swearword *kuso* 'shit' when offering an assessment. For instance, she used this lexical item to convey a critical stance toward the food she ate with her professor, which she considered unpalatable. Thus, despite the gender non-conforming behavior seen in certain aspects of her daily life, Sako still maintains rigid perceptions of what constitutes 'feminine' and 'unfeminine' modes of speech and action, and vigorously applies these judgments in relation to other women.

3.3.3 An (Im)Balanced Autonomy and the Heterosexual Male Gaze

According to the interviewees' responses, the desire to be cute, kind, and attentive to others is frequently in tension with the women's aspirations for strength and autonomy. Several women noted, for example, that men might not like women who are extremely independent; others suggested that while autonomy is crucial prior to marriage, it quickly becomes unnecessary afterward. Most women opined that it is critical to maintain a 'balanced autonomy' and to adjust it depending on the situation. In reflecting on their ideal selves, the vast majority of the interviewees included independence and self-sufficiency as necessary qualities, but at the same time, they were acutely sensitive to men's preferences on these issues. Thus, just as women's desire to be *kawaii* 'cute' and *yasashii* 'kind' were shaped by the perceptions and valuations of male colleagues, superiors, and romantic partners, so too their aspirations for autonomy and independence were conditional upon male approval. For example, Eri and Shoko discuss their ideals in the following manner in excerpt (63).

(63) 1 ERI: *Otoko no hito mo tabun jiritsu sita jyosei wa kirai dewanai kedo, yappari-*
'I think that Japanese men don't hate independent women, but expectedly-'

2 SHO: *[Amaetai toka-*
'They want to receive kindness.'

3 ERI: *[Tayoraretai toka aru daroo na to iu*
'They want to get relied upon'

4 SHO: *Demo tayori sugiru to omoi toka iwareru kara-*
'But if you rely too much, then they say, it's heavy, so-'

5 ERI: *Soko no - choosei o dekiru reberu de jiritsu sitai na*
'So that- I want to be able to be independent at the level when I can make adjustments.'

In line 1 of excerpt (63), Eri implies that men might not be entirely comfortable with a woman who exhibits excessive autonomy. To mitigate the harshness of the projected male stance, she uses a negative construction *kirai de wa nai kedo* 'not hate, but' implying that although men would not *hate* an independent woman, they also would not be especially pleased by her. At the end of Eri's utterance, she uses the adverbial item *yappari* 'expectedly,' suggesting that the issue is commonplace and part of the collective awareness of Japanese women in navigating romantic relationships. Shoko cooperatively interjects during Eri's turn and provides an example of a male preference (*amaetai* 'want to be treated kindly') that might potentially be in tension with female autonomy, while Eri simultaneously provides another preferential pattern of male behavior (*tayoraretai* 'want to be relied upon'). In this way, Shoko and Eri co-create the image of a man who has different needs at different times, and whom it is a woman's responsibility to satisfy skillfully. In line 4, Shoko suggests that over-reliance on men is also not desirable, because a man would feel burdened by the partner's constant needs. In response to this statement, Eri concludes that a balanced autonomy is ideal, in which a woman can control and adjust her behavior depending on the situation, but ultimately in conformity with men's feedback. Thus, a woman should not seek complete autonomy, but a partial autonomy that can be regulated by male desire, enhanced and subverted easily in the service of male needs and demands. When Eri conveys her stance toward female autonomy in line 5, she supplements it with an iconic hand gesture, as shown in Fig. 3.15. Eri first creates a circle in front of her body using her arms, and then moves them spherically, as if manipulating the volume of a space that represents the malleable breadth of female autonomy. By this gesture, she demonstrates how an ideal woman dilates and contracts her independence through occasional adjustments and maneuvers.

Eri thus desires to be autonomous to the extent that she is able to tune that quality to male wishes and needs. She does not aim to surrender her independence completely in the presence of men; rather she makes it less visible, obtrusive, and threatening in certain contexts, while in other circumstances she must bring it back in full fortitude. Throughout these transformations, her autonomy is always present and never completely erased, because it is in her possession and under her control. In a similar

Fig. 3.15 Adjusting female autonomy. Left to right: Eri, Shoko

vein, the desire to achieve a well-balanced autonomy was expressed in Kari's discourse in excerpt (64) below.

(64) 1 KAR: *Nanka ma, sonoo, dansei ga ita toshite,*
2   *Sono dansei ni sono monosugoku izon suru wake ga nakute,*
3   *Otagai chanto tamochi tsutsu kyooryoku shite iku mitaina.*
4   *Beta beta tayoru yori wa chotto jiritsu sita hoo ga ii kana to omoimasu.*

'Well, imagine that you have a man. You should not depend greatly on him.
You should support each other, work together. It is better to be a little
autonomous than rely on him clingingly.'

(3 lines omitted)

8 KAR: *Ii guai no baransu, tekido ga ichiban ii yo ne.*
'A good amount of balance, moderation is the best, right?'

When talking about her ideal self, Kari laughingly affirms that independence is a quality she desires, though she undermines the importance of her contribution by prefacing it with the mitigating construction *amari kankei nai to omou kedo* 'I don't think it's relevant, but.' When asked by the researcher to elaborate on her perceptions of autonomy, she situates her thoughts on independence by introducing a hypothetical male partner (*dansei ga ita toshite* 'Imagine you have a man'). In line 2, Kari suggests that a woman should not depend excessively on her male partner, using the intensifier *monosugoku* 'greatly' in order to distinguish between reasonable and unreasonable forms of dependence. While reasonable dependence is seen as acceptable or even salutary, unacceptable or burdensome dependence is not preferable. In line 3, she describes the functioning of an ideal relationship between a man and a woman, emphasizing the mutual support and collaboration of their partnership. Kari then returns to her main point on female autonomy, communicating the belief that independence is preferable to excessive reliance on a man. She employs multiple softening and mitigating expressions, and structures her utterances in a comparative way ('It is better to be a little autonomous, than rely on him clingingly'). By doing so, she implies that female autonomy may not always be optimal, but certainly presents a better alternative than burdensome dependence. Moreover, she uses an intensifying mimetic expression *betabeta* 'clingingly' to describe an undesirable type of female dependence on men, suggesting that a milder version of dependence may be acceptable. In addition, she quantifies autonomy by using the adverb *chotto* 'a little,' conveying the impression that only a small amount autonomy would truly be helpful. In response, Hanami expresses her agreement with Kari, indicating that while extreme dependence on a man is disadvantageous, a woman should still do what she can on her own. Hanami tries to formulate a more cohesive or holistic explanation of female autonomy and turns to Kari for help; her friend then summarizes her previous stance on female independence in line 8, claiming that moderation is key. Without autonomy, a woman would be clingy and burdensome, while excessive independence challenges the male-centered nature of Japanese romantic collaboration. As seen in Fig. 3.16, Kari supplements her verbal expression in line 8 with non-verbal signals. She raises her arms and gesturally depicts a sphere, while saying *ii guai no baransu* 'a good amount of balance.' Similarly to Eri, Kari also creates a symbolic space to represent the extent and limitations of normatively

Fig. 3.16 Proper balance of dependence and autonomy. Left to right: Kari, Hanami

acceptable female autonomy, using gestures to depict the manipulations by which she balances her autonomy in different contexts.

Kari concludes her utterance with an interactional sentence-final particle *yone* addressed at Hanami, who immediately aligns with her. In summary, Kari believes that a woman should possess a limited amount of autonomy, in order to be self-sufficient and so as not to burden a man. Indirectly, she conveys a critical stance toward women who engage in clingy, dependent behavior with their partners. When talking about independence, the interviewees generally tended to frame their assertions in relation to male partners (hypothetical or actual), suggesting that independence is revealed through those interactions. Furthermore, the Japanese interviewees claimed that the ability to limit their autonomy in certain contexts is essential for successful romantic relationships.

Some interviewees intimated that they would restrain their autonomy after getting married, explaining that after that point independence is no longer relevant or socially necessary. For instance, Ana explicitly stated that she would like to quit her job after marriage and devote herself to the family. Before marriage, however, she expressed a strong desire to become and remain self-sufficient. When her friend Satoko described the ideal woman as humble, modest, (*okuyukashii*) and passive (*ukemi taisei*), Ana suggested that she would try to cultivate these qualities only *after* getting married, while presently preferring independence and activity. Her brief statement is transcribed in excerpt (65).

(65)   *Kekkon shitara soo nari tai kedo, kekkon suru made wa chanto shigoto shite jiritsu shitai.*
'When I get married I would like to be like that (passive and modest), but until then I want to work hard and be autonomous.'

Thus, some Japanese women clearly view autonomy and marriage as mutually exclusive alternatives, expressing the opinion that one must choose one over the other (or at least eventually transition from one to the other). Despite the idealistic laws and policies employed by the government to promote gender equality in the workplace, the real-world economic and social pressures with which women are confronted still force many to quit their jobs after marriage or childbirth (Charlebois, 2014). Foreseeing this conflict, Ana decides that she would prefer to embrace family over career (*kekkon shitara soo naritai kedo* 'When I get married I would like to be like that'). The demonstrative term *soo* 'that' in her utterance refers to Satoko's previous description of the ideal woman as passive, modest, and traditional. In this way, Ana suggests that non-autonomous, subordinate existence will be an inescapable and necessary aspect of married life. In the limited window of young adulthood, however, she would like to enjoy activity and autonomy while she can.

As noted above, the concept of a balanced or limited autonomy was evoked by many Japanese interviewees and was framed consistently: as a valuable quality that must be regulated and adjusted in relationships with men. Despite the fact that autonomy (unlike other feminine qualities such as cuteness, kindness, and attentiveness) is supposedly a self-centered feature, some Japanese women still view it through the prism of other-centeredness. A heterosexual male gaze (Mulvey, 1999) is present in these women's discussions of autonomy, shaping their behaviors (real and hypothetical) in a way that amplifies or decreases their autonomy to suit (presumed) male preferences.

3.3.4   Ideal Japanese 'Women's Language'

Prior to the interview, participants were asked in written form: 'What are some features of an ideal woman's speech, in your opinion?' The responses addressed such components as vocal properties, speed of speech, vocabulary, utterance structure, and overall behavior during a conversation. Of the 24 participants, 11 indicated that a woman's speech must be slow-paced (*yukkuri*). Politeness, along with correct usage of *keigo* 'honorific speech,' was considered essential by eight respondents, while the same number of respondents considered calmness (*ochitsuki ga aru*) to be important. The ability to communicate in an easy-to-understand fashion (*wakari yasui*) was mentioned by six respondents, whereas four respondents stated that women should not raise their voices (*koe o araragenai*) but instead speak softly, ending their utterances with such sentence-final particles as *yone* (isn't it?) and *desho* (probably). Three respondents claimed that women should avoid using inappropriate lexical items, such as *wakamono kotoba* 'slang' (lit. 'young people's words') and *otoko kotoba* 'male language,' and should speak in a slightly lower tone. The use of *aizuchi* 'backchannel feedback' at appropriate moments, structuring a dialog so that it does not end abruptly, listening carefully to the interlocutor, and expressing one's own opinion were also deemed important by several respondents. Other points mentioned by the respondents included completing sentences, avoiding sound lengthening, laughing elegantly, using few interjections, and refraining from saying unnecessary things (*yokeina koto o hanasanai*).

In the subsequent interviews, participants emphasized the importance of producing a soft and calm impression while speaking slowly, clearly, and politely. For example, Sako indicates that the overall composure of one's posture, gestures, and speech is crucial to creating the desired image of a soft, pleasing woman. An excerpt from her discourse is presented in (66) below.

(66)   *Shabette te mo, nanka hyoojyoo ga yawarakai toka, hanashi shitete mo*
       "un un un" toka
       jyanakute, "Uun" mitaina. (3 lines omitted). *Hyoojyoo mo yuk-*
       kuri ugoite, me toka mo

nanka yukkuri ugoite, kuchoo mo nanka wakariyasukute, kokoro ni shimiru kanji.   Hanashikata wa sonna jyosei ga suteki dana to omoimasu.

'Even when she speaks, her facial expression is soft, and when she talks, she doesn't say things like, 'yeah, yeah, yeah', but something like 'hmmm'. Her facial expression changes slowly, gaze moves slowly, her speech is also easy to understand, and it goes straight to heart. I think a woman who talks like that is great.'

Sako stresses that softness must be present in both facial and verbal expression. A woman should not move from one emotional state to another hastily, but rather gradually and calmly. She portrays an image of womanly wisdom that is not fickle or hyper-sensitive but speaks thoughtfully and deliberately. Sako's ideal woman is attentive and considerate in speech, providing caring responses; her every word is full of deep meaning, yet also easily accessible for quick comprehension.

As evident from the similarity of the participants' views on womanly speech, Japanese women have a clear understanding about how an ideal woman should communicate—ranging from low-level details concerning the use from the specific phrases, vocal volume, and speed of speech to more complex communicative strategies, such as maintaining conversional flow, laughing appropriately, and incorporating complementary gestures. For instance, Tomoko in excerpt (67) suggests that the way a woman speaks is important primarily because it reveals her level of education and refinement.

(67)   *Tatoeba, kaiwa o shiteite, anoo, nanka shiranai koto iwareta toki ni, "wakaranai desu" tte iu n jyanakute, chanto sore nari ni wakaranakattara, chanto kiki kaeseru da toka, "sore nitsuite kuwashiku oshiete itadakemasuka" toka, ato "fubenkyoo de wakaranai desu keredomo donna hon yomeba ii desu ka" toka. Soo iu fuuna chotto koo anoo kaiwa owarasenai yoo na kaeshi ga dekiru to sugoku sono hito kashikoi n daroo na to omoimasu.*

'For example, when having a conversation and you are told something that you don't know, you don't say, "I don't know." Instead, if you do not know, you respond to the best of your abilities, like "Could you explain to me about this in detail?" or "I don't know because of lacking studies (in the area), what kind of books should I read?" If a person can give these kind of responses that don't end the conversation, I think she is very wise.'

In her discourse, Tomoko suggests that confessing deficiency of knowledge in a sophisticated manner is important in order to be perceived as intelligent and well-bred. Her ideal woman is someone who shows a high degree of culture and education in all respects. Tomoko suggested earlier that in some circumstances a woman must behave cutely, feigning ignorance in a conversation with a male superior in order to flatter his knowledge and/or competence (see excerpt 53). At other times, however, when her ignorance is real and unfeigned, she must nevertheless show sustained interest, ask politely for help and recommendations, and avoid terminating a conversation abruptly with a simple confession such as 'I don't know.' Thus, in Tomoko's opinion, a woman can appear wise even without substantive knowledge, if only she is able to confess her inadequacy and seek tutelage in a skillful manner. The first example of proper etiquette that she provides (*Sore nitsuite kuwashiku oshiete itadakemasuka* 'Could you explain to me about this in detail?') demonstrates an ideal woman's ability to give the floor to the interlocutor. It is no longer her responsibility to speak, while the male interlocutor would likely enjoy talking in further detail about his area of specialization. Another potential response that Tomoko finds appropriate is *Fubenkyoo de wakaranai desu keredomo donna hon yomeba ii desu ka*. 'I do not know because of lacking studies (in the area), what kind of books should I read?' This utterance confesses the woman's lack of knowledge in a humble manner and requests advice on further self-improvement. It again transfers the turn to the interlocutor, both framing him as an expert and simultaneously conveying respect for his authority. Thus, for Tomoko, a woman's education is not measured by or reflected in the depth or breadth of her actual knowledge—her education and refinement consist in the skills she has learned to manipulate conversations to sustain an interlocutor's enjoyment, interest, and appreciation.

In addition, though the interviewees claimed that their ideal selves would avoid swearwords and vulgar language in all interactions, they nevertheless admitted that in close circles of friends those expressions are sometimes acceptable. Examples of vulgar language mentioned by the respondents can be classified into three categories: (1) traditionally male vocabulary (e.g. sentence-final particles *zo/ze*, changing the adjectival *ai*-ending to the extended *e*-ending: *kitanai* 'dirty'- *kitanee* 'dirty'), (2) slang (e.g. *yabai* 'terrific', 'awful'), and (3) swearwords (e.g. *kuso* 'shit'). Many of the participants added that these words were especially undesirable for women, and if used could result in negative social sanction. The discrepancy between ideal and actual linguistic behavior became obvious when all 24 interviewees confessed that they had used the above-mentioned vulgarisms. According to the interviewees, the main utility of this type of vocabulary was in conveying a stance of close friendship, especially with male friends. For example, Shoko explained that in the company of male friends she used the sentence-final particle *ze*, whereas she avoided it zealously with female friends. Her argument is presented in excerpt (68) below.

(68)	1 SHO:	*Watashi wa amari onna no ko no tomodachi ni wa "ikoo ze" toka iwanai desu*
	2	*kedo, otoko no tomachi yattara gyaku ni meme shii kanji o-*
	3	*[dashitakunakute*

'I don't really say, 'Let's go ZE' to my female friends, but to my male friends
on the other hand (I say it), because I don't want to give out an effeminate feel.'

	4 ERI:	*[Wakaru wakaru*

'I know, I know!'

	5 SHO:	*Furanku ni tsukiatte hoshikute*
	6	*dakara gambaroo ze mitaina kanji de yuttari shimasu*

'I want them to be frank around me, so that's why I say things like 'Let's try
hard ZE' and such'

7 ERI: *Jyoshikan mo denai yoo ni*
          'So that the feminine feel doesn't come out'
8 SHO: *Soo, soo.*
          'Yes, yes.'

Shoko suggests that she uses male vocabulary strategically around men in order to be included in the group sincerely as a friend, rather than treated differently (i.e. as a woman) because of her gender. By using the sentence-final particle *ze*, she is able to discount her female gender in social interactions. She later confessed that this strategy has a negative impact as well, because once her gender has been de-emphasized, men often enjoy her company but no longer consider her as a potential romantic partner. Her friend Eri confirmed Shoko's concerns, stating that her boyfriend was deeply upset when she casually called him *omee* 'you' (male language), and asked her pointedly to stop.

Furthermore, women's use of male language is much more frequent in computer- and mobile-mediated communication than in spoken interactions. Some respondents confessed they frequently utilize the sentence-final particle *ze* in blogs and text messaging applications, even though they avoid it in face-to-face exchanges. This discrepancy supports Iwasaki's multiple grammar model (2015), which contends that the same linguistic feature can function differently in different modalities of communication. Respondents who claimed to employ male language in virtual and written modes of interaction explained that their messages are directed toward either a large audience (e.g. multiple blog readers) or their close friends. Thus, when the speaker is not physically visible, a woman is less restricted in her language use than in face-to-face communication, and no longer feels compelled to convey a feminine persona. Women's appropriation of male language in spoken and written discourse will be discussed in further detail in Chap. 4.

3.4   Summary

Just as Russian women aspire to appear as pleasing to men as possible, Japanese women also prioritize heterosexual male gaze and view themselves indirectly through the prism of male attention. The primary difference lies in the nature of the images and behaviors that are considered feminine in the two societies.

Overall, the qualities that were highly prized by the Japanese interviewees can be classified into three groups: (1) characteristics associated with *kawaii*, (2) qualities that emphasize traditional values and the female image *yamato nadeshiko* 'a woman who displays the feminine virtues of old Japan,' and (3) features linked with psychological strength, independence, and autonomy. The 24 Japanese interviewees considered an ability to be *kawaii* in appearance, movements, behavior, and speech highly valuable; the emphasis was frequently placed on innateness and effortlessness, while fake cuteness was criticized. This double-edged sword puts women in a complicated situation: they either take the risk of behaving too cutely and are potentially accused of being *burikko* 'women who counterfeit cuteness' or do not act *kawaii* and do not receive the associated benefits. The interviewees tended to enjoy the image of an innocent, childish cutie portrayed in televised commercials, while also claiming to emulate such a *kawaii* persona in moderation when talking to superiors, male colleagues, and in other interactions.

Japanese women also considered traditionally feminine characteristics to be of fundamental importance, especially such social virtues as kindness and attentiveness to others. They suggested that women should always strive to have 'room in their hearts' for others while simultaneously refraining from burdening others with their own problems. Taken together, their words and deeds should help everyone around them to feel comfortable and at ease. This stance reflects an element of emphasized femininity that seeks, above all, to accommodate men's needs and desires (Connell, 1987). Some interviewees even spoke of a woman's duty in Japanese society to honor and elevate men, while others blamed women who reversed traditional gender roles in their families. Autonomy and independence were also frequently mentioned by the interviewees, especially as part of the broader objective of achieving and sustaining financial and emotional self-sufficiency before marriage. In romantic relationships, however, they suggested that maintaining a balanced independence must be prioritized, adjusting their autonomy based upon context to respond flexibly to male partners' needs and preferences.

Japanese women seemed to have a particularly developed and rigid perception of how an ideal woman should speak, including details regarding appropriate sentence structures, speed, volume, and tone of communication. They claimed to occasionally appropriate men's language, particularly in computer- and mobile-mediated communication and in interactions with their male friends (in order to be treated equally, without respect to gender). This view differs from the interviewed Russian women's preference to restrict the use of swearwords to interactions with female friends and avoid them in mixed-gender conversations. The next chapter will further address Japanese and Russian women's appropriation of 'male' speech and discuss the possible motivations behind this phenomenon.

While expressing an awareness that women's social status is changing, the interviewees did not explicitly discuss gender as a social construction. Their discourse was replete with instances in which ideal gendered personas were performed (or ought to have been performed) for the benefit of others (especially men), but the interviewees did not reflect upon the historically contingent nature of these norms and obligations. All of the romantic relationships discussed by the participants involved heterosexual couples, with no acknowledgment of the gender identities of LGBTQ+ individuals. These features suggest that gender ideologies have a powerful impact on the ideals and values regarding gender developed by young women in Japan, but they also point to the need for further research on broader and more inclusive populations.

This chapter has helped to clarify how women think and speak about their ideals and values regarding gender and feminine beauty in both Japan and Russia. It is evident that gender ideologies, such as those promulgated by the media-circulated messages analyzed in Chap. 2, significantly permeate the discourses of the women interviewees in the present study. While exerting some measure of (sometimes covert) autonomy both in the construction of feminine beauty and in their engagements with the heterosexual male gaze (Mulvey, 1999), most of the interviewees also expressed the opinion that women should strongly differentiate their conduct from that of men. Women should not, ideally, appropriate typically 'male' behavior and language. In the next chapter (Chap. 4), I shall use spoken and blog corpora to assess in greater detail and depth the extent to which women nevertheless *do* appropriate and transform historically 'male' linguistic forms.

References

Asano, C. (1996). *Onna wa naze yaseyoo to suru no ka: Sesshoku shoogai to gendaa* [Why do women try to lose weight? Eating disorders and gender]. Tokyo: Keiso.

Asano-Cavanagh, Y. (2014). Linguistic manifestation of gender reinforcement through the use of the Japanese term *kawaii*. *Gender and Language, 8*(3), 341–359.

Baba, J. (1999). *Interlanguage pragmatics: Compliment responses by learners of Japanese and English as a second language.* Munich and Newcastle: Lincom Europa.

Burdelski, M., & Mitsuhashi, K. (2010). 'She thinks you're *Kawaii*': Socializing affect, gender, and relationships in a Japanese preschool. *Language in Society, 39*(1), 65–93.

Charlebois, J. (2014). *Japanese femininities.* New York: Routledge.

Connell, R. (1987). *Gender and power: Society, the person, and sexual politics.* Stanford, CA: Stanford University Press.

Gulevich, O., Osin, E., Isaenko, N., & Brainis, L. (2016). Attitudes to homosexuals in Russia: Content, structure, and predictors. *Journal of the Higher School of Economics, 13*(1), 79–110.

Gulevich, O., Osin, E., Isaenko, N., & Brainis, L. (2018). Scrutinizing homophobia: A model of perception of homosexuals in Russia. *Journal of Homosexuality, 65*(13), 1838–1866.

Ide, S. (1990). How and why do women speak more politely in Japanese? In S. Ide & N. H. McGloin (Eds.), *Aspects of Japanese women's language* (pp. 63–79). Tokyo: Kurosio.

Iwasaki, S. (2015). A multiple-grammar model of speaker's linguistic knowledge. *Cognitive linguistics, 26*(2): 161–210.

Jespersen, O. (1922). *Language: Its nature, development and origin.* London: G. Allen & Unwin.

Johnson, E. (2007). *Dreaming of a mail-order husband: Russian-American internet romance.* Durham: Duke University Press.

Kang, M. E. (1997). The portrayal of women's images in magazine advertisements: Goffman's gender analysis revisited. *Sex Roles, 37*, 979–997.

Kay, R. (1997). Images of an ideal woman: Perceptions of Russian womanhood through the media, education and women's own eyes. In M. Buckley (Ed.), *Post-Soviet women: From the Baltic to Central Asia* (pp. 77–98). Cambridge: Cambridge University Press.

Kinsella, S. (1995). Cuties in Japan. In L. Skov & B. Moeran (Eds.), *Women, media and consumption in Japan* (pp. 220–255). Honolulu: University of Hawai'i Press.

Lebra, T. (1984). *Japanese women: Constraint and fulfillment.* Honolulu: University of Hawaii Press.

Lipovskaja, O. (1997). Women's groups in Russia. In M. Buckley (Ed.), *Post-Soviet women: From the Baltic to Central Asia* (pp. 186–200). Cambridge: Cambridge University Press.

Lyon, T. (2007). Housewife fantasies, family realities in the New Russia. In J. Johnson & J. Robinson (Eds.), *Living gender after communism* (pp. 25–39). Bloomington: Indiana University Press.

Miller, L. (2004). You are doing *burikko*! In S. Okamoto & J. S. Shibamoto Smith (Eds.), *Japanese language, gender, and ideology: Cultural models and real people* (pp. 148–165). New York: Oxford University Press.

Mulvey, L. (1999). Visual pleasure and narrative cinema. In L. Braudy & M. Cohen (Eds.), *Film theory and criticism: Introductory readings* (pp. 833–844). New York: Oxford University Press.

Ogawa, K. (2014). *Shiesu wa joshiryoku de kimaru* [The quality of customer service is decided by female power]. Tokyo: Seisanseishuppan.

Okazaki, M., & Johnson, G. (2013). *Kawaii!: Japan's culture of cute.* Munich: Prestel.

Richie, D., & Garner, R. (2003). *The image factory: Fads and fashions in Japan.* London: Reaktion.

4

Russian and Japanese Women's Real Language Practices

The previous two chapters have sought to elucidate (1) the role of media-circulated messages in constituting and promulgating gender and beauty ideologies, and (2) the ways that women negotiate the space between their own ideals of womanh'ood and feminine beauty and the gendered expectations prevalent in Japanese and Russian cultures. In this chapter, I shall turn my attention fully to women's actual, spontaneous use of language, through the use of large spoken and written corpora. Through a corpus analysis of these materials, tensions will be identified between women's ideals and their practice, and notions of feminine beauty and conduct in Japanese and Russian cultures will be further problematized.

4.1   Overview of the Russian 'Male Language'[1]

Russian spoken language contains a variety of swearwords that function as highly emphatic markers. These emphatic markers help the speakers to convey their stances of strong determination, demonstrating their

---

[1] In this chapter I use the term 'male language' to refer to 'language which is ideologically associated with masculinity.'

© The Author(s) 2020
N. Konstantinovskaia, *The Language of Feminine Beauty in Russian and Japanese Societies*, Palgrave Studies in Language, Gender and Sexuality,
https://doi.org/10.1007/978-3-030-41433-7_4

resolution to perform a certain action (or lack of it). In addition, they alter the emotional tone of discourse, often with the effect of making speech highly expressive. According to Zemskaja et al. (1993), these types of words are especially characteristic of Russian men's speech: men often utilize derogatory forms for emphatic purposes, while women select hyperbolically emotional vocabulary to convey emphatic stances, avoiding swearwords (p. 131). It is argued that younger women, however, may utilize the vocabulary traditionally associated with male speech when among close female friends, while refraining from its use with men. Zemskaja calls this phenomenon "speech intimatization," suggesting that both men and women may use swearwords and vocabulary of a low register in order to signal closeness with the interlocutor (p. 122). For instance, a woman requesting an object from her female friend may use the low register lexical item *hrenovinka* "thing (general) (lit. horseradish)" to mark their close relationship (p. 122). Zemskaja argued that this 'speech intimatization' is not utilized in mixed-gender conversations and is abandoned if the conversation is joined by a representative of a different gender.

In the data presented in this chapter, the 20 Russian interviewees insisted that this type of vocabulary should be avoided by all genders, yet asserted that swearing was more permissible for male speakers. In spite of recognizing and affirming the prohibition on the use of swearwords, women admitted that they also use this type of vocabulary to some extent, blaming themselves for foul language use. Their answers revealed the disparity between gender language ideologies and real language practices.

4.2   Language Use in Assimilation and Transformation

The data analyzed in this chapter is comprised of conversations from the National Corpus of Spoken Russian (2004). This is the largest corpus of contemporary spoken Russian language containing more than five million words. It allows searching for a specific lexical element and provides speakers' demographic information and overall context. Specifically, I investigated the sub-corpus of spontaneous conversations, which includes male-to-male, female-to-female, and mixed-gender conversations. In total, there are 675,203 words in 705 conversations that include at least one male speaker, and 1,113,214 words in 1260 conversations that include at least one female speaker. Scripted conversations from movies and televised shows were intentionally excluded in order to analyze women's real use of language.

I analyzed the following five words, representing vulgar, coarse, and derogatory items that differ in intensity, arranged in ascending order from relatively lesser coarseness and to extreme coarseness: (1) *čjort* 'devil, deuce,' (2) *blin* 'damn,' (3) *blja* 'damn,' (4) *bljad'* 'damn (lit. slut),' (5) *pizdets* 'fuck' ('lit. 'vagina'). The first, fourth, and fifth items (*čjort*, *bljad'*, *pizdets*) can be used in their literal meaning as an insult, but these instances were excluded from the sample, given that the goal of the research was to observe the use of the swearwords in their emphatic function rather than in their literal meaning. Each of the five words can be used flexibly in almost any position within an utterance as an emphatic stance marker. The first lexical item *čjort* 'devil' is a relatively mild vulgarism, often used to mark frustration. The second item *blin* 'damn' is a common vulgar colloquialism, also relatively mild on the scale of vulgarity. The third item *blja* 'damn' is considerably stronger in its coarseness, representing a contracted version of the fourth item *bljad'* 'damn (lit. slut).' The lexical item *bljad'* (due to its literal meaning) is a relatively strong swearword inappropriate for polite contexts. As a contraction of *bljad'*, *blja* inherits significant coarseness and is also a harsh emphatic marker. Its contracted form, however, makes it less vulgar that the complete version *bljad'*. Finally, *pizdets* 'fuck' is morphologically formed by the addition of the suffix *ets* to the root word *pizda* 'vagina (vulgar).' This swearword is used as a strong emphatic marker to convey a variety of distinct emotions; in most of these instances, its original meaning is subordinate if not entirely absent.

Despite the common perception that men would be the primary users of all the five aforementioned lexical items, analysis based on the National Corpus of Spoken Russian reveals very different results. The findings are summarized in Table 4.1, indicating the number of conversations in which female and male speakers used the lexical items and the percentage

Table 4.1 Distribution of Russian vulgar emphatic terms between genders

Lexical item	Female speaker (No. of conversations; %)		Male speaker (No. of conversations; %)		Statistical results
čjort 'devil, deuce'	58	4.60	30	4.30	$\chi^2(1) = 0.359$, $p = 0.549$
blin 'damn'	217	17.20	83	11.80	$\chi^2(1) = 12.567$, $p = 0.00039$
blja 'damn'	28	2.20	17	2.40	$\chi^2(1) < 0.001$, $p > 0.99$
bljad' 'damn (lit. slut)'	21	1.70	19	2.70	$\chi^2(1) = 1.229$, $p = 0.268$
pizdets 'Fuck'	17	1.30	12	1.70	$\chi^2(1) = 0.0446$, $p = 0.833$
Total number of conversations	1260	100	705	100	

of these conversations out of the total number of conversations involving (respectively) female and male speakers. Instead of computing the overall number of tokens, I counted the number of conversations in which the swearwords were used. This avoids the possibility that outlier conversations with a large number of swearwords would bias the results. Overall, there are more conversations in the National Corpus of Spoken Russian with at least one female speaker than conversations with at least one male speaker. For this reason, it is important to consider the relative percentage of conversations using the target lexical items separately for each gender, and to conduct proportional tests.

As seen from Table 4.1, both Russian female and male speakers utilize vulgar expressions in their speech with a relative frequency depending on the lexical item. Statistical tests demonstrate that only the term *blin* 'damn' differed significantly between the two groups, showing a higher proportion among female speakers than male ($\chi^2(1)$ = 12.567, p = 0.00039). *Čjort* 'deuce,' *blja* 'damn,' *bljad'* 'damn,' and *pizdets* 'fuck' did not differ significantly in the proportion of conversations involving male and female speakers. This finding contradicts the notion that swearwords belong to the domain of male language. Thus, the present analysis suggests that in contemporary Russian it is no longer uncommon for women to use swearwords as emphatic markers in their speech. As the data shows, swearwords can be used to convey both negative and positive stances, depending on the contexts, as well as to index the level of closeness between the speakers.

4.3   Women's Appropriation of 'Male Language' in Russian

The analyzed swearwords frequently conveyed negative stances of frustration, disturbance, and disappointment. If they were utilized at the beginning or in the middle of an utterance, these terms often marked the introduction of an undesirable event. If utilized at the end of an utterance, they frequently summarized the speaker's negative feelings about the topic of conversation. For example, in the following conversation (excerpt 78), two women, Dasha (20 years old) and Alla (22 years old), are discussing the new building in which they are going to study.

(78)   *A kompa tam net, na Tsvetnom, net! Čjort! No zato inet est', vsjo ok!*
       and computer there no on Tsevnom no devil no rather internet be all okay

       'But they don't have a computer there, no! Deuce! But at least the internet is there, everything is okay!'

By utilizing the derogatory expression *čjort* in an emphatic capacity, the speaker conveys her critical stance toward the infrastructure of the building where she will have to teach. In addition, Dasha uses an array of contracted forms, such as *komp* instead of *kompjuter* 'computer' and *inet* instead of *internet* 'internet,' which are considered slang expressions. The swearwords, colloquialisms, and slang expressions, alongside the emphatic nature of her speech, combine to convey an interpersonal stance, marking Dasha's relationship with Alla as a close friendship.

Stronger than *čjort* 'deuce' in its vulgarity, the swearword *bljad'* 'damn (lit. slut)' also serves as an emphatic device to convey the speaker's acute negative emotion toward a certain event or person. Its usage by female speakers is common in situations of complaint. The conversation in excerpt (79) between two female speakers, Lita (19 years old) and Panika (18 years old), presents a typical example.

(79) 1 LIT   *V električke smotrju, vot sčitaj gde-to   metrov sto prošla, da.*
             In   train   see   here count somewhere meters hundred walked yes

      2   *Smotrju vse džinsy vot tak vot! Vse v grjazi.*
             look   all jeans here that here all in dirt

             'I notice in the train, you know, by then I had walked around
             100 meters already. I see my jeans are all terrible! All in dirt. '

      3 PAN *Ty ne odna takaja.*
             you not one such

             'You are not the only one like that.'

      4 LIT→ *Dumaju, bljad' čjo takoje? Možet, u menja   pohodka ne tak. Znaesh,*
             think   damn what such maybe by I:GEN walking not so know

      5   *vot   tak vot... Prjam po   jažki. Užasno!*
             here that here really until thigh terrible

        → 'I think to myself, damn what happened? Maybe, I walk wrong.
          You know, I can't believe it... Up to my thighs. Horrible!'

In lines 1 and 2, Lita provides factual information about an incident in which her jeans were stained. In line 3, her friend Panika expresses alignment with Lita by conveying solidarity (*Ty ne odna takaja.* 'You are not the only one like that'), suggesting that she has been in a similar situation. Lita is thus encouraged to continue her story in line 4, this time adding her affective stance toward the situation by using the swearword *bljad'* 'damn' in the reported thought ('I think to myself, damn what happened?'). In doing so, she is able to convey the frustration she experienced when she noticed dirt on her jeans, thereby adding immediacy to her utterance. In this excerpt, Lita communicates a traditionally feminine concern about her appearance through the use of 'male' language, employing a swearword in order to emphasize her strong emotions. Furthermore, in line 5 Lita uses a lexical item of low register *ljažki* 'thighs' instead of the more neutral equivalent. Her final lexical item in line 5 *užasno* 'horrible' summarizes the way she felt on the train. By utilizing language that underlines the informality of the setting, Lita accomplishes two goals simultaneously: she directly conveys a negative stance toward the accident that happened to her while indirectly marking her relationship with Panika as close.

The analyzed swearwords are also frequently used to introduce an unavoidable, disadvantageous side of an object or event that otherwise possessed positive characteristics. In excerpt (80), Manja (female, 22 years old), who is a gymnastics instructor for children, is telling Ksenia (female, 23 years old) about her new group of students. After she mentions that enrollment for this year is especially high, she begins sharing her concerns about the associated consequences, commencing her utterance with the coarse item *blin* 'damn.'

(80)   *U menja poslednee vremja   što-to   stol'ko narodu. Ja vrode radovat'sja dolžna.*
         by I:GEN recent time something so people I perhaps rejoice must

   → *Blin,   oni   tam   ne   umeščajutsja, im   tam   tesno.*
      damn   they   there   not   fit   they   there   tight

      'Recently, I have so many people. I should be glad, I suppose.
   → Damn, they don't fit there. It's too tight there.'

By utilizing the swearword *blin* 'damn,' the speaker conveys her stance of dissatisfaction with some of the negative consequences of high enrollment, even though she regards this as a positive development overall. Besides the emphatic marker *blin*, she does not use any other coarse or vulgar expressions. Without this swearword, her utterance might fail to express Manja's attitude toward the insufficient classroom space, merely presenting it neutrally as an issue, with which she needs to deal. The use of *blin* thus allows her to communicate to Ksenia her concern and emotional investment.

Similarly, in excerpt (81), Masha (female, 25 years old) uses the coarse emphatic item *blin* to express her frustration about a defect in an article of clothing she has purchased. Masha describes the beauty of the skirt, but stresses her strong discontent that it is exceedingly short.

(81) *Ya pravda poslednij raz jubku na vypusknoj odevala, v smysle to platje bylo, no*
I   really   last   time skirt on graduation wore   in meaning that dress was but

→*v principe odin hren... blin,   no ona pravda takaja koroten'kaja no s drugoj*
in principle one horseradish damn but she really   so   short:DIM
but from other

storony mne   že   ne poltinnik! Ja poka molodaja, simpatičnaja   vrode.
side I:DAT EMPH   not fifty   I still young pretty seems

'To be honest, last time I wore a skirt, it was for the graduation, I mean that was a dress,
→but in principle same shit. Damn, but it is actually really short, but on the other hand, I am not 50 yet! I am still young, pretty, it seems.'

Masha utilizes a mixture of lexical devices that are traditionally linked to male and female language, as she adopts both coarse (male) vocabulary and diminutive suffixes associated with feminine speech (Zemskaja, 1993, p. 124). She first justifies her recent purchase by stating that she has not worn a skirt for a long time and thus needs to do so. Then she uses the swearword *blin* to convey her concern about the skirt, which she suggests is potentially indecent because of its length. In addition to the swearword *blin*, she also uses the vulgar expression *odin hren* 'same shit (lit. same horseradish).' By using the emphatic marker *blin* and the vulgar expression *odin hren*, Masha communicates that her stance toward the new acquisition is dubious, while also marking her relationship with her friend as intimate. In these ways, she clearly draws upon linguistic elements traditionally associated with male speech. When describing the skirt itself, however, she uses the adjective *koroten'kaja* 'short' with a diminutive suffix -*en'k*, which softens her speech and further emphasizes the small size of the skirt. Masha then extends her trope, adding further rationalization for her purchase of the skirt by arguing that a short skirt is still appropriate at her relatively young age. She uses the colloquialism *poltinnik* 'fifty,' which in informal speech may refer either to 50 rubles or to 50 years of age (depending on the context). Taken as a whole, Masha's utterance shows how Russian women utilize a variety of linguistic devices, both coarse and mild, depending on their attitude toward the subject of the narration and the relationship they wish to cultivate with the interlocutor.

The swearwords examined in this corpus analysis can serve not only as markers of negative affective stances such as frustration or doubt but also as positive markers of excitement, joy, and delight. For instance, after using *blin* 'damn' to communicate her frustration with the shortcomings of her skirt, Masha later utilized *blin* to convey a positive stance toward the very same item, recalling her delight when she first saw it at the store. Her utterance is presented in excerpt (82):

(82) *A ja včera kupila sebe takuju prikol'nuju jubočku, koroten'kuju, ot talii*
and I yesterday bought self:DAT such cool kirt (dim.) short (dim.) from waist

do podola gde-to santimetrov 35, sama ot sebja ne ožidala, oranževgo tsveta,
to hem somewhere centimeters 35 myself from self not expect orange color

→ *očen'stil'nuju modnen'kuju. Blin, ja kak ejo uvidela, srazu vljubilas'.*
very stylish fashionable (dim.) damn I once her saw immediately fell in love

'And yesterday I bought such a cool skirt for myself. It's short, from waist to hem around 35 centimeters. I didn't expect that from myself. Orange color, very stylish,
→ fashionable. Damn, when I saw it, I fell in love at once.'

As seen in excerpt (82), Masha again combines gentle and coarse linguistic elements. She begins with a detailed description of the skirt, appending a variety of diminutive suffixes such as *-en'k* and *-čk* to the nouns and adjectives pertaining to it in order to convey her fascination. Instead of the dictionary form *jubka* 'skirt,' she uses the diminutive version *jubočka*, communicating her fondness for the new acquisition. Similarly, instead of the standard form *modnaja* 'fashionable,' Masha uses its diminutive version *modnen'kaja*, thereby emphasizing the positive characteristics of the skirt. Masha then employs the swearword *blin* 'damn' as a stance-marking device, confessing that she fell in love with the skirt at first sight. Here *blin* introduces and intensifies the speaker's feeling of admiration for the skirt, emphasizing the overall emotionality of her statement. Excerpts (81) and (82) also demonstrate that women employ tradition-ally 'male' vocabulary even in discussions of conventionally 'feminine' subjects.

Furthermore, the corpus analysis contradicts the notion that women stop using swearwords with mixed-gender interlocutors, or when initially female-to-female conversations are joined by males (Zemskaja, 1993). For instance, in the following conversation (excerpt 83) between Dmitriy (male, 19 years old) and Marina (female, 20 years old), the female speaker uses a swearword as an emphatic marker when they suddenly meet at the university.

(83) 1 Dmi: *Privet, Marin!*
　　　　　　　hi   Marina:VOC
　　　　　　　'Hi Marina!'

→   2 Mar: *Oj, blja Dim napugal- to oj!*
　　　　　　　oh   damn   Dima:VOC scare:PAST PP INJ
　　　　　　　'Oh damn, Dima you scared me oh!'

　　　　3 Dmi: *Ja ž tebe skazal Privet, Marin" i vsjo!*
　　　　　　　I   INJ you:DAT say:PAST hi   Marina:VOC and all
　　　　　　　'I just said to you, "Hi Marina" and that's all.'

Coarse vocabulary thus does not seem to be limited to single-gender (female-only or male-only) interactions but occurs in mixed-gender con-versations as well when speakers aim to communicate emphatic stances. The relationship between Marina and Dmitriy is unclear, but based on the contextual information, it can be deduced that they are close university friends. In line 2 of this excerpt (83), Marina expresses her surprise with the swearword *blja*, as well as the interjection *oj* 'oh' in both the initial and final positions. In so doing, she dramatizes her change of state at Dmitriy's unexpected approach. Here, Marina does not convey a negative stance toward Dmitriy himself, but toward the unexpected situation that caused her discomfort. Furthermore, prior to meeting Dmitriy, Marina had been talking to her female friend Katya (20), with whom she also used the swearword *blja* emphatically in a similar context. Thus, the defining factor in the use of coarse language does not seem to be the gender of the interlocutor, but rather the relationship that exists between the speakers. The use of swearwords does not conform to normative expectations that coarse language ought to be restricted to male speakers, but instead shifts to suit the stance that a speaker desires to convey toward her interlocutor, in conjunction with her overall persona.

Some women even utilized several swearwords consecutively in order to communicate highly emphatic stances. For example, in the following dialogue (excerpt 84), Tatyana (23 years old) is helping Anastasia (19 years old) to find an appropriate jacket, but Anastasia is not pleased with the store's selection. In response to Anastasia's hesitation, Tatyana uses two swearwords sequentially in order to show her impatience with her female friend:

(84) 1 ANA: *Ja ne nadenu.*
I NEG wear
'I won't wear it.'

→ 2 TAT: *Pizdets, bljad' Klava. Nu   koroče,   ja ne   znaju, dumaj esli čego.*
fuck damn Klava well fast:COMP I NEG know think:IMP if what:GEN
'Damn fuck woman. Okay, faster, I don't know, think about it'

3 ANA: *Oj, slušaj, v   njom... V njyom   žarko!*
Oh listen:IMP in he:PREP in he:PREP hot
'Oh listen, in it... In it,   it's hot!'

In line 1, Anastasia expresses her dislike of the jacket and her refusal to wear it. Her friend Tatyana conveys a divergent stance in line 2, highlighting her annoyance by using two swearwords consecutively. Both *pizdets* 'fuck' and *bljad'* 'damn' are strong swearwords, so when used together the message conveyed is extremely emphatic. Furthermore, Tatyana uses the proper noun Klava immediately after the sequence of swearwords. Because Klava is not her friend's name, it can be inferred that it is used as slang vocabulary to refer to all women, thereby encompassing female stereotypes. Anastasia's slow shopping and hesitant behavior prompts Tatyana to call her a derogatory name. By using two swearwords consecutively and employing an offensive indexical term, she expresses a high level of frustration and impatience toward her friend's behavior. Her next utterance *nu koroče* 'okay faster' then compels Anastasia to decide on her shopping preferences more efficiently. In order to distance herself from the female stereotypes of indecisiveness and irrationality, Anastasia tries to provide a reason for her hesitation and after a short pause, she states that the jacket is excessively warm for her. Thus, through the use of the consecutive swearwords *pizdets* and *bljad,* Tatyana conveys a strong negative stance toward her indecisive friend, pushing her to make a choice more quickly.

4.4 Overview of the Japanese 'Male Language'

In the sections that follow, I will analyze women's use of the two sentence-final particles *zo* and *ze*, which are traditionally classified as characteristic elements of the "male language" (Sturtz Sreetharan, 2004, p. 280). Examples (69) and (70) represent the way *zo* and *ze* are typically used by male speakers:

(69) *Ashita   gakkoo   yasumi   da   ze*
Tomorrow school closed COP *ZE*
"The school is closed tomorrow, you know." (rough sounding) (Iwasaki, 2013, p. 303)

(70) *Yoshi*   *zen'in*   *de*   *iku*   *zo!*
     Okay   altogether   INS   go   ZO
     "Alright, let's continue altogether!" (Nakamura, 2013, p. 25)

The particle *zo* is conventionally described as a pragmatic particle used to code a strong assertion, or to indicate a speaker's power and high rank, while *ze* is understood as encoding strong appeal or emphasizing masculinity (e.g. Iwasaki, 2013, p. 303; Sadanobu, 2014). Sturtz Sreetharan (2004) defines *zo* as a particle that "emphatically states an opinion, insistence, and authority," while *ze* is used "among intimates," expresses "friendly insistence," and "marks asymmetrical status" (p. 89). Even in the exceptional instances in which *zo/ze* are used by a female speaker, it has been argued that the male gender is still indirectly indexed through the coarseness conveyed, with the suggestion that in such cases women are merely taking a man's perspective (Cook, 1989, p. 118). Ochs (1992) claims that the gendered particles index stances directly, while indirectly indexing gender. According to Ochs' theory of indexicality, *ze* indexes coarse intensity that in turn is associated with the male 'voice.'

However, Shibuya (2004) has questioned Ochs' attempt to explain the use of the male particle using the theory of indexicality, saying that it was "not attestable with the case of Japanese gendered particles" that are sex-exclusive language forms (p. 40). According to Bodine (1975), sex-exclusive forms are used restrictedly by one gender, while sex-preferential forms are utilized by one gender more frequently than by the other. Bodine claims that European languages most frequently have sex-preferential differentiation, while such languages as Thai and Japanese have various sex-exclusive features, such as particles and pronouns (1975, p. 138). Making use of Bodine's theory, Shibuya (2004) states that the Japanese sentence-final particle *ze* has a direct connection with gender and, therefore, is sex-exclusive (p. 52). She argues that the particle *ze* seems to convey coarse intensity (a claim made by Ochs (1992)) precisely because native speakers know that this is a male particle, and men are stereotypically believed to have coarseness in their character intrinsically. As a result, it is natural for Japanese speakers to connect the male particle *ze* with the expression of masculinity and roughness. In general, Shibuya questions the validity of primarily linking Japanese sentence-final particles with stances of delicate/coarse intensity, arguing that these linguistic elements began to be connected with certain well-defined stances because of their straightforward association with a particular gender. She thus claims that the direction of indexicality proposed by Ochs should be reversed for Japanese gendered particles—they directly index the speaker's gender, while indirectly conveying various stances (2004).

Indeed, there is much evidence in support of a direct linkage between *zo/ze* and masculinity. Japanese grammar textbooks of the pre-war and war period (1918–1945) refer explicitly to *zo* and *ze* as "male" speech elements, expressing strong language ideologies that instructed Japanese women how they must and must not speak (Nakamura, 2014, p. 180). Even today, in many modern textbooks for Japanese learners the particles *ze* and *zo* are introduced as key elements of "strongly masculine" speech and presented as essential for male students to master (Miura & McGloin, 2008, p. 34). I argue, however, that the directionality of indexicality is fluid, with the operative contextual frame defining what content is being indexed directly and indirectly. I propose to subdivide "interactional frames" (as described by Fillmore, 1985) into three types: conventional, subcultural, and discursive. Depending on which type of frame is activated in a specific context, gender may or may not be indexed.

The conventional frame encompasses the general cultural norms and values that are known to the vast majority of native speakers in a given society. Therefore, the meanings created within this frame can be understood by almost anyone familiar with the language and culture. For instance, all Japanese speakers are familiar with the fact that the sentence-final particles *zo/ze* are elements of male language. Because of this shared understanding, the particles *zo* and *ze* can be strategically used in advertising in order to create a recognizable male character. For example, in a recent Japanese cell phone commercial a female protagonist receives and peruses a long series of text messages, one of which says *matteru ze* 'I am waiting ze.' In this minimal context, in which no information is known about the woman or the man or their relationship, the viewer's interpretation naturally falls back on the conventional interactional frame: the use of *ze* signals that the message is from an assertive man (Sturtz Sreetharan, 2004, p. 91).

At a second, intermediate level, the subcultural contextual frame refers to the set of more specific features that characterize a delimited community of speakers in certain contexts (e.g. graduate students, carpenters)—features that may not be known to Japanese society as a whole. Close friends or family may be especially inclined to use various linguistic forms unconventionally or even to create their own words, thereby producing a strong sense of belonging to a particular group or community. For instance, Japanese lesbians frequently appropriate male language in conversations with one another, including sentence-final particles *zo/ze*, in order to foster intimate relationships and create a feeling of inclusiveness (Abe, 2004, p. 218). Example 71 presents an interaction between two lesbian women in a bar, as they try to remove a stain from a toy:

(71)   Employee: *Kosutte mo torenee n da.*
        'We can't get rid of it even by rubbing.'
        Customer: *Nanika iro ga chigau zo.*
        → "Hey, the color is somehow different ZO." (Abe, 2004, p. 217)

Not all Japanese people are aware that lesbians use a variety of traditionally masculine language features in conversations with one another. A Japanese person unfamiliar with this subcultural practice, on hearing lesbians utilize *zo/ze*, might think that they are trying to self-identify as 'men' or to emphasize masculine traits of character. In fact, Japanese lesbians both deliberately avoid using feminine language and incorporate conventionally male speech in order to articulate independent identities and express powerfulness (Abe, 2004, p. 218). Thus, *zo/ze* in the subcultural contextual frame can be used to create powerful female identities that are unrelated to many aspects of male gender manifestation. In addition, sentence-final particles serve as a tool to treat an interlocutor as an in-group member and convey female solidarity.

Finally, the lower-level or 'discursive frame' comprises the stances chosen by speakers in a given interaction. In such cases, knowledge of the whole conversation as well as participants' relationships are both essential for the correct decoding of the meaning in linguistic forms. At this level, using Kiesling's terminology (2009), interior indexicality is operative, as speakers engage in stance-taking activities that construct their persona for a particular conversation. For example, in a private email correspondence, a Japanese female writer produced the following sentence, using the sentence-final particle *ze*: *mata kondo sukaipu shiyoo ze* "Let's skype again ZE!" (Iwasaki, 2013, p. 329). *Ze* here was employed not to mark masculinity or to convey powerfulness, but rather to create a nonchalant, relaxed tone in a personal letter, and to emphasize the closeness of the relationship (Iwasaki, 2013, p. 329).

Distinct grammatical and lexical features within interactional frames are uniquely suitable for specific genres or modalities of communication (i.e. blogs versus spoken conversation) (Matsumoto, 2015, p. 290). I argue that as a result of the interaction between the three frames (conventional, subcultural, and discursive) and defined genres associated with particular grammatical and lexical features, women are able to convey a diversity of stances, construct nuanced personae, and build relationships with readers, all while avoiding the creation of male 'voice' in their discourses.

4.5 Women's Appropriation of 'Male Language' in Japanese

4.5.1 'Male Language' in Japanese Spoken Interactions

In the televised commercials analyzed in Chap. 2, women occasionally utilized several linguistic forms that are traditionally associated with masculine language, but predominantly conform to the ideals of traditional femininity and cuteness. No tokens of *zo/ze* were detected.

In the twelve hours of recorded, face-to-face communication analyzed in Chap. 3.3, Rika (21) was the only individual who used the particle *zo*, and she employed it only once. It occurred during a discussion of the third commercial viewed by the participants, which featured a young woman turning into a cat after having received *neko meiku* 'cat make-up.' Both Rika and Natsu, expressed their discomfort at the sight of the thick, grotesque eyeliner, finding such strong make-up inappropriate for the woman's delicate facial features. In discussing the commercial, Rika conveyed her critical stance toward the woman's appearance, saying *Sore wa kowai zo mitaina* 'Is was like that's scary *ZO*.' Here *zo* is embedded into the headless, utterance-final pronominal construction. The pronominal form *mitai-na* "be-like" without a head noun is used in informal interaction to invoke emotional subjectivity, quote interpretive thoughts, and constructed speech (Fujii, 2006). Here, it serves as a mitigating expression, somewhat alleviating the strong stance conveyed through the use of *zo*. By marking her utterance with the particle *zo*, Rika emphasized the shock that she felt in the moment in the past when she first saw the woman's revised appearance. Being scared is a quality strongly dissociated with masculinity, and even incompatible with ideal notions of courageous manhood. Thus, in light of the stance-mitigating strategy used, as well as the contextual information surrounding Rika's utterance, it is evident that Rika does not appropriate the particle *zo* in order to sound manly. Instead, she does so to communicate her emphatic stance toward the woman with the 'cat make-up,' while also marking the closeness of the relationship she shares with her friend. The conventional meaning of the particle is irrelevant in Rika's utterance, while its meaning is being shaped within the discursive frame.

During a subsequent interview with the researcher, when Rika was explicitly asked if she ever added *zo* or *ze* to utterances in her daily life, she claimed *Tsukenai desu ka ne. Tabun tsuketa koto nai n janai kana* 'I think I don't add (these particles). I don't think I have ever added them.' Even though she had used the particle *zo* only ten minutes ago, she did not seem to recollect ever having done so. Her response thus illustrates that speakers frequently employ certain linguistic elements unconsciously and may not always be able to give accurate self-reports (Trudgill, 1972). Rika later remembered, however, that she frequently used *zo/ze* when text messaging with her close friend, claiming that to her *zo* and *ze* were features of the male language in oral, but not electronic communication. Her friend Natsu suggested that in electronic communication (such as texting) she needs a device that would emphasize her assertions (*shuchoo*) without eliciting confirmation from the interlocutor. For this purpose, she finds the particle *zo* especially useful.

All 24 Japanese interviewees claimed that they tried to avoid using male language in their speech because it would paint them in a negative light before the eyes of society. Out of the 24 interviewees, however, 20 women admitted that they sometimes used the sentence-final particle *zo*, while ten women confessed that in addition to *zo*, they also use *ze* mostly in their conversations with close male friends and especially in electronic messaging applications and blogs. Most women were able to identify at least one close friend (or relative) with whom they sometimes used *zo* and *ze* when texting for emphatic purposes. For example, Natsu (22) suggested (in excerpt 72) that she uses these particles when texting with her brother in order to convey closeness.

(72)   *Koredake kudaketa kotobazukai ga dekiru otooto mitaina kanji no ishiki ga*
moshikashitara aru kamoshirenai.
'I think that maybe I have an awareness that this is my younger brother, with whom I can use such a strongly casual style.'

Thus, Natsu used traditionally male language in electronic communication with her brother in order to convey an interpersonal stance of close friendship, showing that with him she does not need to follow the societal norms of etiquette. With the help of the sentence-final particles *zo/ze*, she was able to communicate in an open, nonchalant manner. Thus, women's use of traditionally male language is seen as more suitable within the genre of electronic communication, while spoken discourse is not a hospitable environment for such linguistic appropriation. This divergence in the use of male language across modalities might perhaps be attributed to the paramount significance of social norms of conduct in Japanese society—norms that sometimes lessen in stringency with more informal modes of interaction.

4.5.2 'Male Language' in Japanese Blog Corpora

Since the beginning of the twenty-first century, blogs and electronic diaries have gained tremendously in popularity, exhibiting informal features that make them compatible with the appropriation of traditionally 'male' linguistic elements *zo/ze* by women. This communicative modality is especially intriguing from the standpoint of sociolinguistic analysis of sentence-final particles, because these lexical features are usually thought to be used for interactional purposes and to be exclusively restricted to dialogic speech. In contrast, written texts are generally held to lack them (Iwasaki, 2015, p. 163). Blogs thus present a unique environment for sentence-final particles: a hybrid genre combining features of both written and spoken registers, making private information instantly available online for public readers.

The image of womanhood that emerges from blogs produced by female writers differs markedly from the artificial, scripted representations of women developed by advertisers. By examining the occurrences of traditionally masculine linguistic features in women's blogs, I will demonstrate the underlying differences between the actual language that women choose for self-expression and both (a) the idealized women's language depicted in media and (b) women's perceptions of normative language use. I argue that the "male" particles are not used to index masculinity, as previously suggested (Cook, 1989; Ochs, 1992), but instead employed to convey strong emphatic stances, and create a sense of solidarity, community, and a special "bond." Despite the tight linkage of *zo/ze* and normative masculinity within the conventional frame, in the environment of online blogs other social meanings become apparent, while conversely the traditional meaning of masculinity fades in prominence.

These processes may be facilitated by the distinct interactional contexts in which blog writers operate. In contrast to female participants in spoken discourse, female bloggers have less of an imperative to consider the possible interpretations of their utterances by interlocutors, or to follow social norms and conventions generally. For example, in spoken conversation, female speakers may be expected to moderate strong assertions, to solicit confirmation, or to defer to the judgment of superiors. In blogs, women have a higher degree of control, presenting what is effectively a sustained monologue to interested readers. Moreover, female bloggers may have a very different set of perceptions and concerns with respect to their audience. In conversation, women may have to speak to one or more specific interlocutors simultaneously and may need to calibrate their utterances or their stances precisely based upon their antecedent relationships. In writing a blog, the authors effectively construct their own audiences (interestingly, much as media representations construct their viewership) and the reader is invited to participate in a one-sided dialogue on the authors' terms. Such considerations may explain why blog writers feel at greater liberty to impinge upon social norms that they might habitually respect in speech.

Because conventional social restrictions are lifted for blog writers, they are able to express their sentiments more vividly than in conversations. The contextual meaning of *zo/ze* in blogs primarily removes their gendered aspect while maintaining their function of strong emphasis; this allows female writers to convey stances of confidence and certainty through the appropriation of traditionally 'male' particles. In spoken conversation, a woman utilizing these particles might convey meanings that would be interpreted very differently by her interlocutors. The ambiguity of subversive or alternative usage of *zo/ze* may thus bear undesirable consequences for a female speaker. In blogs, however, they are shielded from such criticism.

The present study includes analysis of 200 recent blogs written in 2015 from the online collection of internet blogs *Goo Burogu*. The entries used for analysis were sampled randomly from the total *Goo Burogu* corpus, with the only inclusion criterion being the presence of *zo/ze*. The gender of the blog writers was inferred based on the user's profile information. If gender information was lacking in a profile, then the associated blog was excluded from analysis. Naturally, there is no method for checking the validity of the blogger's claims regarding their gender. However, the primary goal of the analysis is to assess general trends associated with gender and the use of *zo/ze*, rather than assess the gendered features of any one blogger's communications. As such, in the absence of compelling reasons to think that users are systematically misrepresenting their gender in the

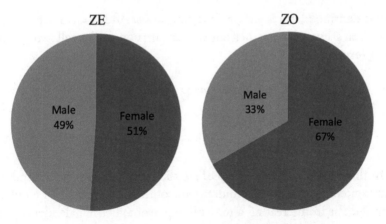

ZE   ZO

Fig. 4.1   Gender distribution in usage of *zo* and *ze* between blogs

Goo Burogu corpus, it seems reasonable to treat the reported gender as accurate. Prior to conducting any comparisons between male and female bloggers, it is necessary to determine the base rates of female and male participation in the blogs collated by *Goo Burogu*. In order to do so, 100 blogs were randomly sampled from the corpus as a baseline group. In this sample, 51 bloggers identified as female and 49 identified as male. This suggests that the number of female and male bloggers in general population of *Goo Burogu* blogs does not differ substantially.

Analysis of the sampled blogs utilizing *zo/ze* reveals that, contrary to conventional expectation, women outnumber men in usages of *zo* and are roughly equivalent in usages of *ze*. (see Fig. 4.1).

Analysis of the specific usages of *zo* and *ze* in these discourses suggests that female writers do not deploy these sentence-final particles in order to convey masculinity. These findings are in conflict with previous theorizing (Cook, 1989, p. 118), according to which *zo/ze* effect the creation of a male persona on the level of indirect indexicality. Many female writers in the analyzed blogs used *zo* and *ze* to articulate stances pertaining to their desires, intentions, accomplishments, setbacks, and successes. By using *zo* and *ze*, female speakers were able to communicate confidence, emphatically expressing their decisions to perform various actions. For instance, one woman's blog frequently summarized her children's daily activities using pictures and short descriptions. After a vivid depiction of New Year's Eve, this mother ended her entry with the following statement (excerpt 73):

(73)   *Ashita   mo tanoshii koto ga   matte iru   zo.*
       Tomorrow   also   fun   thing   NOM   wait:TE-
       ASP:NONPAST ZO
       'Tomorrow fun things are also waiting ZO.'

In this excerpt, with the help of *zo*, the writer conveys her confidence and excitement about the children's upcoming schedule in an emphatic manner. Far from creating a masculine persona, her female identity as a mother is strongly conveyed. In this way, the particle *zo* contributes to the articulation of a protective motherly persona, who is actively involved in the upbringing of her children.

In the analyzed blogs, *zo/ze* frequently co-occur with evaluative adjectives (such as *omoshiroi* 'interesting,' *warui* 'bad,' *ii* 'good,') that project the speaker's stance to a certain object, action, event, or behavior. In the following example, a woman writes about her private life, complaining about her partner and expressing an urgent desire to leave him. However, she understands that he will experience great suffering if she acts upon this desire. Her contemplations are presented in excerpt (74).

(74)   *Watashi ga   sonzai o   kesu? Demo sore o   shite shimattara, kare*
       I   NOM   existence ACC   erase but   that   ACC   do:TE-
       MOD:COND he

       wa mi o   kirareru omoi ni   naru   no   wa
       TOP   self ACC   cut-POT   thoughts DAT   become
       NML   TOP

       wakatte   iru   kara   watashi   ni   wa
       sonna   zankokuna
       understand:TE-ASP:NONPAST   because   I   DAT
       TOP   this kind   cruel

→   *koto, dekinai.   Yasashi sugiru   ZO, watashi.*
       thing do-POT:NEG   kind   excess   ZO   I

'To disappear? But if I do that, I understand that he will have agonizing thoughts, so I
→   cannot do such a cruel thing to him. I am too kind *ZO.*'

The particle *zo* here is self-evaluative, reflecting the author's conclusion
that she cannot pursue a desired course of action because of her excessively kind personality. In this case, *zo* does not stress masculinity at all,
in spite of its meaning within the conventional frame. In fact, the writer
here emphasizes her kindness, a traditionally feminine characteristic.
Thus, it appears that in electronic communication through blogs there is
no mandatory link between *zo/ze* and masculinity. Female bloggers do
not index male identity by using *zo/ze*, nor are they trying to speak like a
man—rather, they appropriate male language in order to convey powerful emphatic stances toward oneself. In such cases, the discursive frame
(involving the context of communication between the speaker/writer and
her audience, and her specific intentions in a given communicative act) is
brought forward, while the conventional meaning is rendered practically
irrelevant. Thus, different functions of a linguistic form are highlighted
depending on the interactional frame, in which it appears (Iwasaki, 2015;
Taylor, 2010).

Within specific discursive frames, *zo/ze* may also convey the writer's
strong intention or wish to perform a specific action. In these contexts,
zo/ze often help to articulate the author's inner voice, aimed at urging
herself to undertake a challenging task. In the text preceding the next
excerpt, a female writer talks at length about her interest in golf. After
describing her last visit to the golf course, she makes the following statement (excerpt 75), emphasizing her determination to play golf next time.

(75)   *Ashita   mo iku zo.*
         Tomorrow also go zo
         'I will go again tomorrow ZO.'

In excerpt 75, the female blogger does not project herself as a male
speaker or adopt a masculine persona by adding *zo* to her utterance, but
rather conveys her strong determination to play golf again as soon as

possible. *Zo* in blogs is frequently addressed to oneself rather than other readers and has a self-motivational function. The examples presented above show that it is essential to analyze *zo/ze* in blogs within the discursive frame, remaining sensitive to the particular meanings a writer conveys to her online audience as she explores the freedoms brought by computer-mediated communication. This kind of assertive self-expression may not be deemed appropriate for women in face-to-face conversations, but blogs are a welcoming platform for various forms of disclosure.

Furthermore, some women utilized features of male language to an even greater degree, incorporating them in hashtags that label their posts. This explicit annotation strongly suggests that *zo* and *ze* are essential components of their writing style, and that these particles are deployed deliberately, rather than incidentally. For example, a woman named Chako concludes a blog post with the hashtag *da ze*. The copula *da* is considered a moderately masculine feature and the sentence-final particle *ze* is characterized as strongly masculine (Miura & McGloin, 2008, p. 34). In comparison to *zo* that is self-evaluative and self-motivational, *ze* is more other-oriented, creating an impression that the writer is talking to a reader.

In one of Chako's blogs using this hashtag, she narrates her emotional response to the family situation surrounding the approach of her daughter's university entrance exams. After informing the reader that examination admission cards have arrived, she turns her attention to her personal feelings, as seen in excerpt (76), in which she utilizes *ze* at the conclusion of each statement.

(76) → *Tooi ze. Jyuken kaijyo wa   erabenai   shi, shikata ga   nai ze. Gambaru*

far   ze   exam   place   TOP   choose:POT:NEG   an
d   way   NOM   be:NEG ze   Try hard

shika nai   ze. Demo haha   wa   nanimo shite   yarenai ze. Hagayui ze.

only   be:NEG   ze   but   mother   TOP   nothing   do:TE
do:POT:NEG ze impatient ze

→ 'It's far ZE. But you can't choose an exam location, so nothing to be done ZE. You can
only do your best ZE. But a mother can't do anything ZE. I am so impatient ZE.'

By adding the sentence-final particle *ze*, Chako emphasizes her impatience and vexation in every sentence. Whereas *tooi* without a subsequent particle would merely communicate the fact that the test location is far, *tooi ze* underlines that the distance is onerous and expresses the mother's feelings of annoyance at the situation. The reader can easily sense her feelings of dissatisfaction in the next sentence as she admits that nothing can be done to change the situation. Chako continues to convey her critical stance toward the entrance test procedures by repeatedly completing her utterances with the particle *ze*. In the last sentence, she summarizes her feelings (*Hagayui ze*. 'I am so impatient ZE'), a fact which has been thoroughly communicated to the reader throughout her blog entry—in large part because of the repetitive particle use. As in the previous excerpts, the use of the particle *ze* does not portray Chako as having a manly character, suggest that she is speaking in a manly fashion, or imply that she is expressing a man's perspective. In fact, she is worried about her child, displaying concerned and nurturing behaviors that are conventionally associated with femininity and feminine social roles. Thus, the conventional meaning of *ze* in this blog is almost completely suppressed, while the discursive frame predominates and informs the readers of the writer's stance.

Unlike Chako, many blog writers avoided profligate or repetitive use of masculine particles but employed them judiciously in strategic places in order to highlight their feelings and associated stances. For example, Haru utilizes *ze* only in the title of a blog entry, which announces, *Yatto kesa todoita ze*. 'Finally, it arrived in the morning today *ze*.' Haru is keenly interested in music, and frequently writes about her experiences at concerts and live performances. By appending *ze* to her blog entry's title, she conveys the intensity of her affective stance so that the readers can understand the importance of the parcel that has just arrived. Later, in the body of the blog, the readers find out that the long-awaited item is a CD that she ordered online and that is now ready for a pick-up from a convenience store. Through the title, the readers are able to infer immediately that Haru has been looking forward to receiving this item and is now excited about its arrival. The particle *ze* makes the title more emphatic and significant by conveying the writer's feeling of anticipation, while simultaneously signaling the close relationship between Haru and her readers. Again, the conventional frame of interpretation for masculine particles is not activated in the minds of the readers, while the discursive frame is prioritized.

In segments of blog entries with reported speech, however, the conventional meaning of *zo/ze* remains prominent, especially in attributing to a male third person's speech or thought. For instance, a female high school student describes her father's utterance in the following manner in excerpt 77.

(77)   *Tekitoo ni   rokuga shita bangumi wo   mite-itara   chichioya*
       Random   DAT   record   do-PAST   program   ACC
       watch:TE-ASP:COND   father

→   *kara hiruhan iku zo to iu   denwa   ga   kakatte kita node   iku*
    from lunch   go ZO QT say   phone call NOM ring:TE
    come:PAST because   go

koto   ni   shimashita.
NML DAT do-PAST

'I was watching some show that I recorded when my father called, saying 'I am going
→   to lunch *ZO*', so I decided to go (with him).'

By using *zo* in direct speech, the female writer makes it easy for the readers to distinguish her utterances from her father's words. Further, by adding *zo* to her father's words, the student conveys a stance that is instantaneously linked to authoritative masculinity. *Zo* projects a stance appropriate for her father, thereby enabling the readers to visualize his personality. Thus, the conventional frame dominates the construction of meaning in such instances, and signals that the utterance belongs to a confident male speaker.

4.6 Summary

The analysis of Russian conversations from the National Corpus of Spoken Russian has provided evidence that both female and male speakers utilize coarse and vulgar vocabulary. Swearwords are no longer a gender-preferential feature that is mostly used by male speakers, as was suggested earlier (Zemskaja, Kitajgorodskaja, & Rjazanova, 1993). Emphatic usage of swearwords allows speakers of *both* genders to communicate positive and negative stances, while indirectly conveying interpersonal relationships (Ochs, 1992). Moreover, swearwords are merely one of the many resources that women utilize to express their feelings and opinions. Depending on the stances they desired to convey, women combined conventionally 'male' and 'female' modes of speech, incorporating both emphatic, coarse vocabulary and softening expressions. By doing so, they were able to add emotionality to their narration, explicitly communicate their feelings, as well as create individual styles and identities. Though the actual conversations of Russian women evidence a wide range of emphatic, stance-marking devices, the examination of televised commercials in Chap. 2 did not reflect such variability. Instead, in advertising materials, women's speech was universally portrayed as soft, unassertive, and lacking confidence.

The analysis thus far has shown that both *zo* and *ze* appear frequently in blogs created by women, a phenomenon that does not conform to the notion of idealized *kawaii* femininity presented in advertisements. Women in blogs use traditionally masculine linguistic features in order to convey various positive and negative stances, emphasizing their strong will and conviction. Based on the written and spoken discourses analyzed above, the conventional frame of interpretation for these particles does not always dictate their meaning. In computer-mediated communication, as well as in some conversations, women are able to appropriate 'male' language forms to convey stances unrelated to masculinity. This research demonstrates that the sentence-final particles *zo* and *ze* have lost their strong linkage to the male gender in informal computer-mediated communication, such as blogs. When *zo* and *ze* are utilized in quotations as a part of reported speech, however, they mark the third person's speech as male, while conveying the writer's attitude toward or about him. Thus, women's use of these sentence-final particles is a compelling example of the widening gap between women's linguistic representation in media and their real language choices in discourse.

Both Russian and Japanese female respondents in Chap. 3 expressed an acute awareness that 'male' language should be avoided by women. This perception, however, was rejected or ignored in women's real discourses. Thus, there are wide and important differences between societal norms, women's perceptions of ideal femininity and feminine language, and their actual linguistic practices. In the final, concluding chapter of this book, I will elaborate further on the discrepancies and tensions between representations, ideals, and realities, and discuss implications for the changing gender representations in Japan and Russia.

References

Abe, H. (2004). Lesbian bar talk in Shinjuku, Tokyo. In S. Okamoto & J. S. Shibamoto Smith (Eds.), *Japanese language, gender, and ideology: Cultural models and real people* (pp. 205–221). New York: Oxford University Press.

Bodine, A. (1975). Sex differentiation in language. In B. Thorne & N. Henley (Eds.), *Language and sex: Difference and dominance* (pp. 130–151). Rowley, MA: Newbury House.

Cook, H. M. (1989). Sentential particles in Japanese conversation: A study of indexicality. *Dissertation Abstracts International, 50*, 5.

Fillmore, C. J. (1985). Frames and the semantics of understanding. *Quaderni di Semantica, 6*, 222–254.

Fujii, S. (2006). Quoted thought and speech using the *mitai-na* 'be-like' noun modifying construction. In S. Suzuki (Ed.), *Emotive communication in Japanese* (pp. 53–96). Philadelphia, PA: John Benjamins Publishing Company.

Iwasaki, S. (2013). *Japanese*. Amsterdam: Johns Benjamins Publishing Company.

Iwasaki, S. (2015). A multiple-grammar model of speaker's linguistic knowledge. *Cognitive linguistics, 26*(2), 161–210.

Kiesling, S. F. (2009). Style as stance. In A. Jaffe (Ed.), *Stance: Sociolinguistic perspectives* (pp. 171–194). Oxford: Oxford University Press.

Matsumoto, Y. (2015). Partnership between grammatical construction and interactional frame: The stand-alone noun-modifying construction in invocatory discourse. *Constructions and Frames, 7*(2), 289–314.

Miura, A., & McGloin, N. H. (2008). *An integrated approach to intermediate Japanese.* Tokyo: Japan Times.

Nakamura, M. (2013). *Hon'yaku ga tsukuru Nihongo: Hiroin wa "onnakotoba" o hanashitsuzukeru.* [Japanese language created by translation: Heroines continue speaking "women's language"]. Tokyo: Hakutakusha.

Nakamura, M. (2014). *Gender, language and ideology: A genealogy of Japanese women's language.* Amsterdam: John Benjamins Publishing Company.

National Corpus of Spoken Russian. (2003–2014). Retrieved from http://www.ruscorpora.ru/en/

Ochs, E. (1992). Indexing gender. In A. Duranti & C. Goodwin (Eds.), *Rethinking context: Language as an interactive phenomenon* (pp. 335–358). Cambridge: Cambridge University Press.

Sadanobu, T. (2014). *Shojo no "zo" nitsuite* [About the "zo" of the young female characters]. Retrieved from http://dictionary.sanseido-publ.co.jp/wp/

Shibuya, R. (2004). *A synchronic and diachronic study on sex exclusive differences in modern Japanese language.* Doctoral dissertation, University of California, Los Angeles.

Sturtz Sreetharan, C. (2004). Japanese men's linguistic stereotypes and realities: Conversations from Kansai and Kanto regions. In S. Okamoto & J. S. Shibamoto Smith (Eds.), *Japanese language, gender, and ideology: Cultural models and real people* (pp. 275–290). New York: Oxford University Press.

Taylor, Y. (2010). Approximative –tari in Japanese: Focus on interaction and information. *Japanese/Korean linguistics, 17,* 533–546.

Trudgill, P. (1972). Sex, covert prestige and linguistic change in the urban British English of Norwich. *Language in Society, 1,* 179–195.

Zemskaja, E. A., Kitajgorodskaja, M. V., & Rjazanova, N. N. (1993). Osobennosti mužskoj i ženskoj reči [Features of feminine and masculine speech']. In E. A. Zemskaja & D. N. Shmelev (Eds.), *Russkij jazyk v ego funktsionirovanii* (pp. 90–136). Moscow: Nauka.

5

Conclusion

In the previous chapters, I have undertaken to analyze the reciprocal con-
nections between ideology and identity as they pertain to feminine beauty
in Japan and in Russia. In this cross-cultural investigation, I have focused
on media representations in beauty advertisements, women's perceptions
of femininity and feminine beauty, and women's real language practices.
The confluences and divergences between the different forces shaping the
expression of gender and beauty ideals in language have become increasingly apparent. On the one hand, gender ideologies continue to have a
normative influence, promulgated through beauty advertisements and
instilled in women from an early age. On the other hand, women's growing autonomy increasingly allows them to appropriate language for their
own purposes in the construction of beauty—accommodating, evading,
or even straightforwardly rejecting traditional expectations regarding
gendered language in the service of their own self-expression and stance-
taking. In between these forces lies the still-contested ground of collective
and personal ideals. In the consonance and clash of ideology and

© The Author(s) 2020
N. Konstantinovskaia, *The Language of Feminine Beauty in Russian and Japanese
Societies*, Palgrave Studies in Language, Gender and Sexuality,
https://doi.org/10.1007/978-3-030-41433-7_5

autonomy, women form their ideals in distinct ways, with diverse implications for their use of language and their response to other people's language use.

Traversing this three-level analysis of language (in societal ideologies regarding gender and beauty, in the ideals of individual women, and in the practices of discourse participants) is the important potential of intercultural comparisons. Only by directly posing the similarities and differences between gendered language in multiple linguistic contexts as an object of study are we able to appreciate the generalities and continuities in linguistic behavior, as well as to correctly assess the unique opportunities and hindrances for women posed by specific historical and social circumstances. The study of gender and language cannot be conducted on the assumption that the processes operative in any one language or cultural context will hold equally in others. On the other hand, we should also not assume that linguistic and cultural contexts are absolutely distinct and hermetically isolated. Rather, as globalism brings into contact (and sometimes into conflict) different traditions, ideologies, and attitudes regarding gender and beauty, commonalities and differences in perception and action will need to be negotiated. Increasingly, if it is to comprise the diverse experiences and perceptions of women, the study of gender and language must be posed as an international and intercultural project.

In this concluding chapter, I will summarize the main findings and contributions of this book to the field of gender linguistics, highlighting the importance of comparisons both intra-culturally (across levels of ideologies, ideals, and practices) and interculturally (between languages and forms of social organizations). I wish to emphasize the contributions that accrue from comparing different types of linguistic evidence regarding the encoding and expression of ideas concerning feminine beauty in language, from widely circulated media messages to personal opinions shared relatively 'locally' through social media. I hope also to reiterate the necessity and value of an international approach to the study of gender and beauty, and the linguistic acts that express and constitute these categories.

5.1 Televised Advertisements in Russian and Japanese Societies

Advertisements of both Japanese and Russian 'beauty products' prioritized the heterosexual male gaze (Mulvey, 1999) as the ultimate arbiter of a woman's success and the final measure of her worthiness. Although the presence of the heterosexual male gaze in commercials has frequently been debated by feminist linguists (e.g. Lazar, 2002), the present study illustrates how its characteristics, roles, and representations differ cross-culturally. In Russian advertising heterosexual men are portrayed as the covert, passive appreciators of women's good looks—they are the final audience, for which beauty is constructed and maintained, but do not create or even necessarily understand it. By contrast, in Japanese advertising men are frequently the sole creators and explicit connoisseurs of women's beauty. Women are not mysterious creatures in the ideological language of Japanese media, creating and manipulating their special beauty in order to please or manipulate male evaluators. Instead, they are passive objects that male experts shape to their own purposes. In brief, the male involvement in the analyzed Japanese televised commercials is much more salient than in Russian commercials, resulting in the creation of dissimilar idealized femininities.

Russian advertising of beauty products deploys something of a 'boomerang' representation of both women's autonomy and the heterosexual male gaze. Women create their appearances primarily with the goal of flattering men's esteem and satisfying men's preferences. Happiness and satisfaction redound upon women as a result of their effect upon men, rather than emerging directly from their creation of beauty. Men, for their part, do not merely observe feminine beauty that appears on its own terms and at its own instigation. Their appreciation and evaluation are the ultimate cause of beauty, impelling it forward on its course; they are also the final point of return, or distal objective, of beauty-making processes.

The importance of the heterosexual male gaze (Mulvey, 1999) in visual culture has long been noted, as eloquently and succinctly summarized by Berger (1972): "Men look at women. Women watch themselves being watched at. This determines not only most relations between men and women but also the relation of women to themselves. The surveyor of woman in herself is male: the surveyed female. Thus she turns herself into an object- and most particularly an object of vision: a sight" (p. 47). This theory of seeing is applicable to representations of women in Russian advertisements, which portray women constantly monitoring their looks, examining themselves through the male prism of objectification and sexualization. Of special importance, however, are the specific forms in which power relationships are embedded within the structure of the 'boomerang' effect. It is women who must labor and cultivate their beauty—and they are encouraged to identify with the process of the production of beauty even when they are not the primary or direct beneficiaries. Men merely gaze. Their gaze conjures up forms commensurate with its ideals and priorities. This process involves a double deception on the part of both men and women: it conceals from women the subordinate and derivative nature of their autonomy in the construction of feminine beauty, and it conceals from men their causative (and potentially oppressive) force in dictating norms of beauty to women.

Despite the fact that "feminism" as a term is highly unpopular in Russian society (Johnson, 2007, p. 29), women's real status as essential wage earners necessitates that advertisers create images portraying working, self-sufficient, "modern" women. To do so, without jeopardizing consistency with patriarchal norms, advertisers strategically incorporate and subvert elements of (post)feminist discourse—often in simplistic ways and in minimal doses. 'Beauty ads' targeted at Russian women manipulate representations of female confidence and autonomy by linking beauty with guaranteed success in romantic relationships, more steadfast friendships, and greater overall appreciation by others. These putative linkages are impressed upon the audience through various linguistic and non-linguistic cues, which simultaneously highlight women's skills and construe their utility solely in terms of their effectiveness at seducing and charming (heterosexual) men. Self-oriented concerns are de-emphasized and displaced, as women are depicted enjoying attention and positive assessments from men and (more rarely) children and friends. Meanwhile, traditional feminine ideals are reiterated through ubiquitous presentations of women "as devoted and nurturing, as emotional and instinctual, and as indecisive and unpredictable" (Lazar, 2014, p. 206). In Russian advertisements, women feature prominently in the roles of mothers, homemakers, wives, and objects of male sexual desire. These depictions prioritize other-centeredness insofar as women realize their potential and achieve self-fulfillment only derivatively through pleasing people around them (predominantly men) (Lazar, 2002). Women are urged to take responsibility in order to create beauty and encouraged to take charge of their looks in order to acquire and sustain the male gaze. This ideological directive constitutes a form of "double-entanglement" (McRobbie, 2004), which simultaneously pretends to empower women by lauding the supremacy of their beauty while necessitating that they subordinate their own ends and concerns. Undergirding this entanglement is an appeal to women's 'innate feminine self,' which invariably refracts their gaze away from self-oriented aspirations and bends it onto the ultimate objective of the preferences of others. This process results in an oxymoronic 'self-oriented other-centeredness' in which the cultivation of the self is itself a service to others. Women are tasked with being their own, most stringent monitors and regulators: they must conform in thought, word, and deed to the selves they are expected to be in relation to men.

Russian advertisers struggle to accommodate themselves to the reality that women are often economically and financially independent (e.g. through sporadic infusions of subverted post-feminist ideals) while also promulgating traditional values. Similarly, Japanese advertisements seek to integrate conventional gender norms with contemporary social developments, but the specific forms and mechanisms by which this combination occurs are different. The Japanese advertisements analyzed in this book integrate three major components: *kawaii* cultivation, traditional feminine ideology, and microscopic injections of postfeminist thought. *Kawaii* cultivation is the most prominent and most often reiterated trope in the media representation analyzed above—women are consistently portrayed as innocent, naïve, pure, and child-like. Japanese 'beauty ads' ascribe immaturity and infantilism to women as innate qualities, implying that these attributes are natural, desirable, and inescapable. Because the femininity of *kawaii* is based largely on childlike behaviors and attitudes, women in the Japanese commercials are not as overtly sexualized as women in Russian commercials. They are, however, reduced in their perceptions and intellect to the capacities and aptitudes of children, lacking understanding of basic phenomena and bereft of the ability to perform even simple tasks adequately (e.g. washing hair or applying makeup). In place of their vacant cognitive faculties, an entrepreneurial male figure must be inserted in order to reveal their potential and actuate their full feminine beauty. Men in advertising act, while women appear (Berger, 1972, p. 47). Men speak and pass judgment, while women remain silent and receptive. These representations reinforce traditional notions of female submissiveness, dependency, and weakness, reproducing and recycling portrayals of women's innate difference from (and inferiority to) men (Nakamura, 2004, p. 136). In addition to the contemporary ideology of *kawaii* and the rhetoric of traditional femininity (which complement and inform each other), postfeminist ideals are dispersed in the commercials in strict moderation and frequently under male supervision. These subverted, postfeminist sensibilities are layered on almost as an after-thought, and seem either patently insincere or transparently ingratiating. Women may be presented as female robots, armed with immense power in fantastic surroundings but stripped of any emotion. Alternatively, female protagonists may claim that they have 'graduated' from *kawaii* while still exhibiting *kawaii* behavior (and being rewarded for doing so). What women may not do is present themselves as authentic, powerful, and beautiful in themselves. In all cases, women's voices are infrequently heard, while male voices dominate. The desperate attempt to fashion a modern woman who is at once strong, *kawaii*, and traditionally feminine results invariably in failure. The tensions between these disparate characteristics tear the meaning of the narrative apart at its ideological seams.

The comparative analysis of televised commercials in Japanese and Russian contexts has revealed that gender is indexed differently in different cultures, creating images of femininity that are uniquely relevant and appropriate. These observations contest the existence of any unitary or universal theory of gender and language, arguing instead that language can both construct and deconstruct gender. In the case of advertising, language plays a crucial role in constructing varied and culturally specific depictions of idealized femininity. Often, the same or similar linguistic devices are manipulated very differently in Japanese and Russian contexts to create normatively appropriate femininities. Both Japanese and Russian advertisers clearly perceive language as an essential tool to construct pleasing femininities that satisfy social norms and stimulate economic consumption.

However, as noted above, language can also be used to deconstruct or reformulate conceptions of gender. While advertisers possess vast resources, and often use them to saturate social spaces with their ideologically grounded appeals, they cannot monopolize all spheres of linguistic production. In women's language use in articulating their own ideals of femininity, and even more so in their appropriation of male language in actual discourse, the meaning of gender can be contested and renegotiated.

5.2   Japanese and Russian Women's Discourses on Ideal Femininity

The prevalence of the heterosexual male gaze in Russian advertising recurs in the discourse of Russian women as they articulate their ideals about femininity. Russian interviewees insisted that women must possess a dual persona: an 'onsite' identity in the presence of a man and an 'offsite' real identity in his absence. This concept is similar to the Japanese concepts of *ura* 'private face' and *omote* 'public face,' a duality representing the division between the inner true self and a persona created in public. *Ura* and *omote*, however, are not gendered concepts and are less specific than the dual persona described by the Russian interviewees. The onsite and offsite persona reiterated by the Russian women is applicable exclusively in interactions with men. The interviewees asserted that such an arrangement serves the purpose of making a man feel masculine, which is conceptualized as a woman's duty; for this reason, the pretense of weakness and the adoption of overtly 'feminine' behaviors were not only perceived as normative but also as strategically smart. By shifting between these two personas flexibly, Russian women believe they are able to manipulate their feminine power to achieve success in romantic relationships. The deceptive or artificial source of this power and control in relationships was further justified through the conviction that women's innate wisdom and emotional strength are superior to men's.

With respect to power in relationships, Russian women (and arguably men) again seem to be caught within a form of "double-entanglement" (McRobbie, 2004). Precluded from overtly contesting for power, Russian women believe that they are able to wield authority anyway by manipulating men's desires for autonomy, masculinity, and sufficiency in the role of breadwinner or provider. In so doing, however, they must take overt or covert action to flatter men's sense of power, and may be unable to adjudicate disagreements candidly. At the same time, they perpetuate stereotypes about women that have deleterious effects in relationships as well as more broadly within society. Lastly, they are burdened with the effortful task of balancing incongruent self-identities, without either revealing manipulativeness or allowing their 'authentic' self-image to be corrupted by the pretense of powerlessness.

Overall, Russian women tend to believe that gender involves both innate and constructed components. On the one hand, they argued that women are innately different from men in possessing characteristics such as kindness, the desire to tend the family hearth, and an inalienable beauty, inside and out, that brightens and decorates every environment. On the other hand, Russian women explicitly argued that femininity is created in the presence of men in order to satisfy male ego and maintain a nourishing relationship. Thus, their views are in some respects reminiscent of certain perspectives in cultural feminist theory that emphasize the difference between men and women (Gilligan, 1993; Tannen, 1991), at times claiming women's superiority over men (Holmes, 1993).

However, an essential component of feminism—the struggle for equality—is absent in Russian women's discourses. The interviewees claimed that independence and autonomy were necessary for women, but also asserted that the importance of these values to women should be concealed from men. A strong woman challenges a man's sense of superiority, his confidence that he is the head of the household, and his faith in his ability to function as a provider. Because these components of traditional masculinity are so crucial for Russian men, challenging them by asserting strength and autonomy can make a woman less attractive. The small demonstrations of powerlessness that women described (e.g. waiting for a man to open the door, allowing a man to carry her bags of groceries) were symbolic rather than real. None of the Russian participants indicated that they wanted to quit their jobs or become financially dependent upon men; they insisted rather that it was important to maintain the appearance of gender-normative behavior. The results of the present research thus echo Lyon's argument (2007) that Russian women have a rigid perception of gender roles, yet do not practice them consistently in their daily lives. Present results also indicate that Russian women value the symbolic representation of gender identities, and try to preserve gendered rituals even when their roles in society are far from traditional.

The pronounced difference in self-perceptions in the presence versus the absence of men extended to women's notions about language use as well. The Russian interviewees considered swearwords permissible under certain conditions in same-gender (all-male or all-female) groups, but unacceptable in mixed-gender conversations with men. The interviewees felt that the use of swearwords would diminish their feminine beauty and the corresponding value in the eyes of men. Insofar as they deploy conscious strategies to adjust their behavior in same-gender versus mixed-gender company, Russian women exhibit a consciousness that (certain aspects of) gender and gendered behavior are constructed rather than innate.

In contrast to the Russian interviewees, Japanese interviewees did not explicitly claim that womanliness could be fabricated in order to satisfy the male gaze. Instead, they emphasized that true femininity is innate and spontaneous. The characteristics that they deemed important for a woman included the ideals of *kawaii* and traditional ladylikeness, in addition to modern attributes such as independence and autonomy. Despite the fact that true *kawaii* can only be instinctive and intrinsic, the interviewees provided numerous examples of instances in which they sought to actively create an image of innocence and naivety (e.g. by downplaying their knowledge or expertise). This intentional conformity to *kawaii* suggests that Japanese interviewees, much like their Russian counterparts, believe (on some level) that women "perform femininity" (Coates, 2004). In comparison to Russian women, who are quite conscious of their attempts to utilize a pretense of powerlessness for strategic aims, Japanese women face a more complicated task. They must maintain an appearance of cuteness and femininity not only to others but also to themselves. The normative structure of the ideology of *kawaii* places a harsh judgment on those who are perceived to cultivate artificial or unnatural cuteness (Miller, 2004). To the extent that women internalize these ideals, they must pursue *kawaii* cuteness while simultaneously deflecting their own consciousness from the process of this pursuit. In other words, they must maintain an intentional blindness at the core of their concept of femininity. As argued in Chap. 3, the purpose of this blindness is to conceal from Japanese women and men the coercive force of gender ideology, and instead to invest the processes of conformity with a feeling of naturalness and inevitability.

Furthermore, the Japanese interviewees asserted that gender-normative behavior must extend beyond heterosexual romantic relationships to encompass many male-female interactions, such as those at workplaces and in universities. Some women even suggested that it is a woman's duty to 'elevate' men generally, making them feel honored and respected. Several women expressed a desire to quit their current or future jobs after getting married in order to become stay-at-home wives and mothers. Moreover, the language deployed in these responses implies that the need to elevate men is not a voluntary lifestyle choice, but a normative expectation which the interviewees would apply to other women as well. The interviewees repeatedly lauded extreme, almost telepathic thoughtfulness (especially in the service of male interests) as a central and indispensable virtue for Japanese women. This type of accommodating femininity could in part result from women's subordinate position at the workplace and the lack of equal promotion opportunities there (Charlebois, 2014, p. 35); in highly masculinized workplaces, the ability to cultivate the esteem and favor of male colleagues may be essential (Nemoto, 2012). According to "dominance" theory, male privilege and power do not primarily consist in the exploitation of individual women by individual men, but in the operation of a system of regular oppression in which everyone is involved, regardless of intentionality or desire (Bucholtz, 2014, p. 30). Significantly, more Japanese women than men are employed through "part-time" contracts that receive reduced benefits (39% of women in contrast to 13% of men), while women's opportunity to rise to leadership positions is scarce (Global Gender Gap Report of the Economic World Forum, 2018, p. 21).

The Japanese interviewees exhibited strong convictions about how an ideal woman should talk, including her intonation, pitch, volume, register, and overall manner of speech. They insisted that women should avoid using swearwords and male language, while admitting its permissibility among close friends. With close friends, they use male language in order to mark in-group belonging and remove certain connotations of their female gender. Poststructuralist feminist scholar Judith Butler asks, "If I am a certain gender, will I still be regarded as a part of a human?" (Butler, 2004, p. 2). In Japanese society, however, the female gender is often constructed as atypical and may even be seen as an inferior or defective type of human being. Because emphasizing fully human qualities and traditionally feminine traits conjointly may pose difficulties (Nemoto, 2008), women employ alternative communicative strategies when they desire to remove connotations of gender from certain interactions. The Japanese interviewees claimed that in circumstances in which they wanted to be treated as friends, rather than women, they employed traditionally male vocabulary, while it would be unacceptable to do so in contexts in which gender cannot be erased (such as their romantic relationships with men). Thus, although male language in Japanese is not a neutral default, it is nevertheless used as a resource for some women to engage in conversations with close friends without emphasizing womanhood or femininity. In informal conversations, neutral linguistic forms (such as *watashi* "I") are considered feminine (Miura & McGloin, 2008, p. 34), and would thus not afford a woman a means of distancing herself from the societal connotations of her gender. Therefore, women resort to traditional men's language not with the intention of projecting themselves as men, but with the aim of sounding more neutral and less feminine. In so doing, they are effectively 'masculinizing' their speech in order to be treated apart from traditional gender norms. Because of the overbearing influence of gender norms in Japanese society, this privilege is possible only with very close friends or relatives and inconceivable in most other situations.

As previously discussed, remarks reflecting pervasive stereotypes about gender were ubiquitous in the media coverage of Haruko Obokata's putative discovery of STAP cells (which was later uncovered as a fabrication). Even in the political arena, sexist remarks are commonplace. For example, in a 2014 meeting of the Tokyo Metropolitan assembly, assemblywoman Ayaka Shiomura became a victim of sexist remarks from male congressmen after arguing for better government support for pregnant women. Their comments included *Hayaku kekkon shita hou ga ii n jyanai ka* 'Shouldn't you get married?' and *Umenai no ka* 'Can't you bear a child?' According to a 2016 Kyodo News survey, 60 percent of assemblywomen admitted that they have been harassed by their male colleagues. Thus, because gender in Japan is frequently emphasized and scrutinized even in situations that presume its irrelevance (Ogasawara, 1998), women may strive to eliminate or attenuate the connotations of gender by using male language in contexts where it is feasible (such as in communication with close friends). In other cases, however, this language strategy is deemed highly inappropriate and can potentially result in negative social judgments.

5.3　Japanese and Russian Women's Actual Linguistic Practices

Both Japanese and Russian women were hesitant to appropriate male language in spoken discourse, and did so only those limited circumstances in which criticism or penalties were unlikely. In addition, women in both cultures endorsed the sentiment that the use of male language is unfeminine and should be strictly avoided in most mixed-gender conversations. However, both Japanese and Russian women utilized characteristically male lexical items and constructions frequently in their real linguistic practices.

As revealed in the analysis of blog data in Chap. 4, Japanese women incorporate male vocabulary much more extensively in electronic communication, usually in order to emphasize strong emphatic stances. Here, the traditional association of the sentence-final particles *zo* and *ze* with masculinity is no longer relevant. In contrast to spoken conversations, in which women may use these linguistic features to 'de-gender' the interaction and adopt a more neutral tone, female bloggers appropriate traditionally male language in order to convey powerful emotions, such as the desire (or refusal) to perform a specific action. Because indirectness, modesty, and elegance are considered the hallmarks of lady-like or feminine speech, language regarded as suitable for Japanese women lacks robust and flexible linguistic resources that could be used for emphatic functions. In contrast, traditionally male speech is replete with lexical items and constructions equipped for straightforwardness and the expression of strong emotions (Lebra, 1984; Nakamura, 2014). Online, ordinary non-lexical mechanisms for communicating emotion (e.g. through prosody and gesture) are also lacking, so women must avail themselves of alternatives in order to convey the sincerity and intensity of their stances. Because male language is suited to emphatic expression, it proves especially useful for women in underlining the strength of their assertions. In online interaction, the pursuit of feminine beauty is thus subordinated to other (sometimes more utilitarian) ends, with the consequence that explicitly masculine language is tolerated.

In spoken conversation, a strong stigma adheres to a woman using male language, placing her at risk of being considered uneducated, uncultivated, rude, and ignorant (Miller, 2004). Apart from computer-mediated communication and interaction with close friends, "gender deviant behavior does not go unnoticed and may incur social sanctions" (Charlebois, 2014, p. 24). In blogs, however, a writer can construct her own readership, or write purely for herself, disregarding the complexity of human relations that have to be taken into account in spoken discourse. Social norms in blogs are de-emphasized and the author has the liberty to write with less concern for others' judgments. Thus, in electronic media such as blogs, women can choose to incorporate male language to convey their feelings in an emphatic manner and will not risk being socially condemned. Furthermore, blogs are highly self-oriented, focusing on topics that are of interest to the writer and often express the writer's personal attitudes, making the use of emphatically strong language elements essential.

Women exploit the unique potential of online environments, activating interactional frames encompassing lexical and grammatical features that would not be appropriate in spoken discourse. Through the use of these features, writers are able to mark their stances in a number of ways, crafting personas that communicate thoughts and feelings effectively— on terms that they themselves establish with their readers. Rather than indexing rough intensity indirectly by using *zo/ze* as suggested by Ochs (1992), Japanese women in blogs are able to index a range of emphatic stances using 'male' language, while not conveying inappropriate vulgarity or masculinity in the least. The conventional link between linguistic forms and masculinity in blogs is almost completely effaced, while new (feminine) meanings are possible in ways that are precluded in spoken conversation. In understanding the function of male language in blogs and online communication generally, it is the discourse frame that must be investigated. Only by understanding the stances that female writers aim to convey, and the relationships they create with their readers, will we be able to appreciate the ways in which 'male language' is indexed and the functions it serves.

Analysis of Russian conversations demonstrated that women also subvert and ignore the traditional norms of the women's language, but do so in ways that differ markedly from those of Japanese women due to their different cultural and linguistic contexts. In particular, women used swearwords in a variety of contexts, as revealed by corpus analysis, even though the usage of these lexical items contravenes both explicit gender norms in Russian society and Russian women's self-reported ideals. Despite female interviewees' perceptions that swearwords were especially unacceptable for use in discourse with male interlocutors, the analysis showed that this is not a restriction by which Russian women abide in practice. Furthermore, though Russian interviewees claimed that swearwords are particularly inappropriate for women in public places, corpus investigation provided no evidence that public settings discouraged their use. In fact, the analysis showed that Russian women and men do not differ significantly in their use of most swearwords, while the swearword *blin* 'damn' is used significantly more frequently by women than by men.

These dissonances between ideal and reality demonstrate that gender-based rules have a strong influence on Russian women's perception of 'correct' gendered behavior, even when most women knowingly deviate from the ideal. Like Japanese women—who utilize male language in blogs to convey emphatic stances—Russian women also use swearwords as strong emphatic markers. 'Female-friendly' emphatic markers that do not involve swearwords carry less evocative power and thus cannot satisfy a wide range of potential stance-taking demands, forcing women to resort to more powerful language resources. As construed by dominance language theory, forms that are traditionally perceived as "male language" represent expressions of high epistemicity and emphasis (Spender, 1990). Thus, if women desire to convey strong stances, they often must utilize linguistic elements associated with male language. They, however, do not frequently wish to convey masculinity, coarseness, or other un-feminine attributes. In fact, the similar frequency with which women and men currently utilize these features suggests that in reality swearwords are no longer male-gender preferential features. These emphatic markers, however, are still linked to 'male language' in people's minds due to prescriptive gender ideologies disseminated into the society through a variety of channels.

Of course, real behavior often diverges from our ideals, but it is instructive to consider the reasons why Russian women violate gender norms in their use of swearwords. Gendered ideals of language use in Russian society, as in Japanese, restrict the range of stances that women can express, and limit their ability to communicate their thoughts and feelings sincerely. Women are not allowed to express themselves vulgarly, emphatically, or assertively because they are not supposed to be vulgar, emphatic, or assertive creatures. In rejecting normative rules regarding language use, women therefore reject not merely a regulation of their lexicon, but also the underlying constraints upon the range of stances they are permitted to adopt and communicate.

5.4 Gender as a Social Construct in Japanese and Russian Societies

As Butler (2004) concludes, "Terms such as 'masculine' and 'feminine' are notoriously changeable; there are social histories for each term; their meanings change radically depending upon geopolitical boundaries and cultural constraints upon who is imagining whom and for what purpose. That the terms recur is interesting enough, but the recurrence does not index the sameness (…)" (p. 10). The performance of "feminine" (and "masculine") linguistic and non-linguistic behavior is a result of socialization processes that dictate how men and women should act in accordance with their gender (Coates & Pichler, 2011). The socialization processes, and the underlying ideologies of gender that they inculcate and enforce, are not invariable and universal but time-varying and culture-dynamic (Connell & Messerschmidt, 2005). This book corroborates the theory of social construction and performativity of gender (Connell, 1987; Messerschmidt, 2010), viewing "femininity" as a fluid and culturally sensitive construct (Schippers, 2007). The research presented above reveals clear dissimilarities between the idealized femininities created in the Russian and Japanese cultures by comparatively analyzing televised commercials, non-scripted interviews, and corpora of conversations and blogs. The discrepancies exposed in the idealized Japanese and Russian femininities highlight the fact that gender ideologies are deliberately constructed, enforced, and maintained.

In Chap. 2 on Japanese and Russian televised commercials, I delineated specific linguistic and non-linguistic mechanisms of gender construction by outlining how men's and women's scripted language in advertising produces and recycles stereotypes about women and feminine beauty. In Chap. 3, through the analysis of Russian and Japanese women's discourses, I explored women's perceptions of ideal femininities and demonstrated that they are frequently constructed on the foundation of socially preferred gender-normative behavior. Finally, examination of women's linguistic behavior in blogs and naturally occurring conversations in Chap. 4 revealed that gender stereotypes were frequently subverted by gender non-conforming language practices in women's actual discourses. Japanese women's continued avoidance of male language in spoken conversations suggests that normative expectations regarding language use still have a strong influence on women's speech. In blogs, however, where dialogical constraints are lifted, women can make an array of linguistic choices motivated by the stances that they aim to convey. Similarly, Russian women subvert gender norms in their spoken conversation by extensively utilizing swearwords that are considered exclusive to male language.

The present book has demonstrated that there is a considerable gap between socially imposed notions of gender and gender-normative behavior, on the one hand, and women's actual language use on the other, in both contemporary Russian and Japanese societies. Between the normative realm of ideology and the reality of women's actual self-expression, the spaces of women's collective and individual ideals are forged. Clearly, women's ideals are impacted by normative expectations, directly imposed by social approbation and promulgated unceasingly in media representations. However, the results of the present study also provide evidence for a reciprocal and continuing interaction between women's ideals and their evolving linguistic behavior. This finding suggests that in both Japanese and Russian cultures, notions and ideals of gender feminine beauty are undergoing transformations that may ultimately have far-reaching implications.

Thus, women in both countries are moving toward freer gender expression, and away from the socially imposed language canons. For example, the long-term ramifications of the use of traditionally male interactional particles in online discourse by women writers can be considerable. Online avenues of expression such as weblogs, social media outlets, and discussion forums simply did not exist for previous generations of Japanese women. However, present and future generations of women may grow up pervasively using traditionally male linguistic features to express themselves. Even if social prohibitions against spoken use of male language remain strong for some time, Japanese women writers will grow accustomed to expressing strong stances straightforwardly in ways that were not previously permissible. It would be wrong to underestimate the potentially liberating effect that these modes of linguistic expression offer, and their resultant effects on the social construction of gender and beauty in Japan.

5.5   Gaps and Absences

The present study is qualified by several major limitations, each of which ought to be carefully addressed in future research. First, at the ideological level of media-circulated messages, this book only investigated the patterns of women's representation in 'beauty ads.' Because they focus on female beautification and presume a wide audience, such advertisements are likely to emphasize features 'uncontroversially' associated with traditional femininity. For this reason, they are a useful domain from which to extract and examine elements of reigning gender ideologies concerned with appearance, feminine beauty, and sexuality. However, media representations encode normative expectations regarding gender in many ways and across disparate domains. In the future, it will be beneficial to analyze a broader sample of advertisements (and other media-circulated messages), including appeals targeted at both genders, in order to determine if and how women are portrayed differently in other contexts. It would also be useful to examine commercials oriented toward male audiences in order to facilitate explicit statistical comparisons of men's and women's scripted modes of speech and behavior.

Another important limitation concerns the limited age range of the interviewees recruited and analyzed in the current study (all of whom were between 20 and 30 years of age). This range represents a crucial, but quite limited, subset of the female population. Their perceptions and ideals regarding femininity do not necessarily represent the views of women in other age groups. In addition, the number of interviewees is limited to 20 Russian and 24 Japanese women due to time and resource constraints associated with intensive and detailed multi-modal analysis. In future work, however, a larger sample size will be crucial, and will enable comparison of views on ideal femininity across different age cohorts. I also aim to improve the study of Japanese blogs by increasing the sample size and investigating additional elements of traditionally male language, in addition to sentence-final particles. In a similar vein, I hope to examine other linguistic elements associated with male language in Russian, expanding the analysis beyond the domain of emphatic markers.

As noted in the introduction (Chap. 1), the present study is limited also by the presumed homogeneity of race/ethnicity, gender identity, and sexuality in contemporary Japanese and Russian advertising and the lack of diversity of the participants along these same dimensions. As much as the interviewees in the present study question, challenge, and negotiate the shifting meanings of traditional concepts and categories related to gender, beauty, and feminine language, their experiences and their reflections are largely circumscribed by heteronormative assumptions regarding sexuality, binary assumptions regarding gender, and marginalizing attitudes toward the contribution of racial diversity toward feminine beauty. These lacunae do not allow the diverse experiences of racial/ethnic minorities and LGBTQ+ individuals regarding gender and beauty to be properly heard, and must be remedied in future cross-cultural, international work on gendered language and beauty.

Finally, this book considers only Japanese and Russian cultural contexts, but future work can profitably incorporate multi-modal, comparative analysis of other languages and cultures. In this way, valuable culture-specific as well as cross-linguistic inferences can be made, contributing to the study of gender, language, and media by exploring how gender is manifested and transformed across differing times, geographies, and communities.

5.6   Contributions

Rather than using a single framework, the present book explored various feminist theories and models of gendered language regarding feminine beauty, investigating their cross-cultural applicability. In conclusion, a social constructionist approach for viewing gender and its manifestation in women's speech seems most appropriate and useful. Nevertheless, previously established 'dominance,' 'difference,' and 'deficiency' models—as well as stance and indexicality frameworks—also informed the research with insights on perceptions and interpretations of gendered language. The unique contribution of this book to the literature on gender linguistics derives from its cross-cultural, three-layered data analysis: comprised of televised commercials, interviews with women, and conversation and blog corpora (i.e. at the level of ideology, ideals, and practices). Analysis of commercials targeted for Japanese and Russian audiences revealed gender stereotypes and ideologies circulating in the two societies, while the latter investigation of women's perceptions and actual language choices exposed the ways women position themselves in relation to the dominant gender ideologies. The book's findings add to our understanding of the constructed nature of femininity, its components, and its significance in both Japanese and Russian societies. The findings also highlight the culture-sensitive, nuanced construction of gender, and reveal the cultural inhomogeneity of its manifestations.

The book also contributes to the study of feminist linguistic theories, gender, language, and media. The fact that both Japanese and Russian women utilize 'male' vocabulary in contexts of (relatively) free expression suggests a similar cross-cultural pattern. Women's appropriation of male vocabulary can be indicative of both the loosening of gender norms and women's desire to move toward modalities of speech that do not constantly highlight their femininity. Only examining and contrasting language use at multiple levels (ideological, ideal, and practice) allows us to appreciate the ways in which different channels of linguistic expression evolve in tandem and mutually inform one another. Focusing on self-reported ideals alone, or on media representations, would clearly miss intriguing emergent phenomena in women's actual language use; conversely, neglecting the importance of normative representations of language use would fail to appreciate the power these expressions exert on women and their behavior.

A cross-cultural, international approach is equally essential, in that it allows for a nuanced understanding that avoids potential pitfalls and over-generalizations. In the absence of cultural comparisons, it would be impossible to determine which aspects of gendered representations and language use (if any) are likely to remain invariant and which are most likely to develop in response to historical and social change. Moreover, within a single cultural context, it is difficult to disambiguate the correlated effects of economic, political, and social transformations in order to properly trace the causal relationships underlying alterations in language use. It is important to acknowledge that the type of femininity that is idealized in Russian and Japanese televised commercials differ, as well as women's perceptions of what constitutes 'feminine' and 'unfeminine' behavior. Furthermore, Japanese women utilize 'male' vocabulary predominantly in computer-mediated communication, rather than in spoken conversations, whereas Russian women appropriate 'male' speech primarily in conversations. These differences uniquely shape the development of gendered language in ways that would be difficult to understand through the lens of any one linguistic culture, however intriguing and fertile. For these reasons, cross-linguistic and international research is valuable in its ability to produce results that are of appropriate generality and specificity.

References

Berger, J. (1972). *Ways of seeing*. London: British Broadcasting Corp.

Bucholtz, M. (2014). The feminist foundations of language, gender, and sexuality research. In S. Ehrlich, M. Meyerhoff, & J. Holmes (Eds.), *The handbook of language, gender, and sexuality* (pp. 23–48). Chichester, West Sussex: Wiley-Blackwell.

Butler, J. (2004). *Undoing gender*. New York: Routledge.

Charlebois, J. (2014). *Japanese femininities*. New York: Routledge.

Coates, J. (2004). *Women, men, and language: A sociolinguistic account of gender differences in language*. Harlow: Pearson Longman.

Coates, J., & Pichler, P. (2011). *Language and gender: A reader*. Chichester, West Sussex: Wiley-Blackwell.

Connell, R. (1987). *Gender and power: Society, the person, and sexual politics*. Stanford, CA: Stanford University Press.

Connell, R., & Messerschmidt, J. (2005). Hegemonic masculinity: Rethinking the concept. *Gender & Society, 19*(6), 829–859.

Gilligan, C. (1993). *In a different voice: Psychological theory and women's development*. Cambridge, MA: Harvard University Press.

Global Gender Gap Report of the Economic World Forum. (2018). Retrieved from http://reports.weforum.org/global-gender-gap-report-2018/

Holmes, J. (1993). New Zealand women are good to talk to: An analysis of politeness strategies in interaction. *Journal of Pragmatics, 20*(2), 91–116.

Johnson, E. (2007). *Dreaming of a mail-order husband: Russian-American internet romance*. Durham: Duke University Press.

Kyodo News survey. (2016). Retrieved from http://www.japantimes.co.jp/ news/2016/05/29/national/social-issues/survey-finds-60-assemblywomen-sexually-harassed-male-colleagues-voters/#.WU9NuevyvDd

Lazar, M. M. (2002). Consuming personal relationships: The achievement of feminine self-identity through other-centeredness. In L. Litosseliti & J. Sunderland (Eds.), *Gender identity and discourse analysis* (pp. 111–129). Philadelphia, PA: John Benjamins Publishing Company.

Lazar, M. M. (2014). Feminist critical discourse analysis: Relevance for current gender and language research. In S. Ehrlich, M. Meyerhoff, & J. Holmes (Eds.), *The handbook of language, gender, and sexuality* (pp. 180–199). Hoboken: Wiley-Blackwell.

Lebra, T. (1984). *Japanese women: Constraint and fulfillment.* Honolulu: University of Hawaii Press.

Lyon, T. (2007). Housewife fantasies, family realities in the New Russia. In J. Johnson & J. Robinson (Eds.), *Living gender after communism* (pp. 25–39). Bloomington: Indiana University Press.

McRobbie, A. (2004). Postfeminism and popular culture. *Feminist Media Studies, 4,* 255–264.

Messerschmidt, J. W. (2010). *Hegemonic masculinities and camouflaged politics: Unmasking the Bush dynasty and its war against Iraq.* Boulder, CO: Paradigm Publishers.

Miller, L. (2004). You are doing *burikko!* In S. Okamoto & J. S. Shibamoto Smith (Eds.), *Japanese language, gender, and ideology: Cultural models and real people* (pp. 148–165). New York: Oxford University Press.

Miura, A., & McGloin, N. H. (2008). *An integrated approach to intermediate Japanese.* Tokyo: Japan Times.

Mulvey, L. (1999). Visual pleasure and narrative cinema. In L. Braudy & M. Cohen (Eds.), *Film theory and criticism: Introductory readings* (pp. 833–844). New York: Oxford University Press.

Nakamura, M. (2004). "Let's dress a little girlishly!" or "Conquer short pants!" Constructing gendered communities in fashion magazine for young people. In S. Okamoto & J. S. Shibamoto Smith (Eds.), *Japanese language, gender, and ideology: Cultural models and real people* (pp. 131–148). New York: Oxford University Press.

Nakamura, M. (2014). *Gender, language and ideology: A genealogy of Japanese women's language.* Amsterdam: John Benjamins Publishing Company.

Nemoto, K. (2008). Postponed marriage: Exploring women's views of matrimony and work in Japan. *Gender & Society, 22*(2), 219–237.

Nemoto, K. (2012). Long-working hours and the corporate gender divide in Japan. *Gender, Work and Organization, 20*(5), 512–527.

Ochs, E. (1992). Indexing gender. In A. Duranti & C. Goodwin (Eds.), *Rethinking context: Language as an interactive phenomenon* (pp. 335–358). Cambridge: Cambridge University Press.

Ogasawara, Y. (1998). *Office ladies and salaried men: Power, gender, and work in Japanese companies*. Berkeley, CA: University of California Press.

Schippers, M. (2007). Recovering the feminine other: Masculinity, femininity, and gender hegemony. *Theory & society, 36*, 85–102.

Spender, D. (1990). *Man made language*. London: Pandora.

Tannen, D. (1991). *You just don't understand: Women and men in conversation*. New York: Ballantine.

Index

© The Author(s) 2020
N. Konstantinovskaia, *The Language of Feminine Beauty in Russian and Japanese
Societies*, Palgrave Studies in Language, Gender and Sexuality,
https://doi.org/10.1007/978-3-030-41433-7